D1467686

$3\frac{50}{K.}$

GARDEN DESIGN

GARDEN DESIGN

by

SYLVIA CROWE

LINE DRAWINGS BY
CAROL MØLLER

HEARTHSIDE PRESS • INC.
Publishers • New York

© *Sylvia Crowe* 1958

AMERICAN EDITION
Printed September 1959

CONTENTS

Key to Diagrams   *page* 9

Introduction   11

PART ONE—HISTORY

Chapter I.   The Oasis Garden   17

II.   The Sino-Japanese Garden   20

III.   The Hispano-Arabic Garden   24

IV.   The Italian Garden   31

V.   The French Tradition   38

VI.   The English Garden   44

VII.   The Contemporary Garden   73

PART TWO—PRINCIPLES OF DESIGN

VIII.   Principles of Design   81

PART THREE—MATERIALS OF DESIGN

IX.   Land-Form   101

X.   Plant Material   106

XI.   Water   131

XII.   Sculpture and Stone Work   137

XIII.   Garden Boundaries   145

XIV.   Ground Pattern   154

PART FOUR—SPECIALISED GARDENS

XV.   The Private Garden   165

XVI.   Parks   185

XVII.   Allotments   200

XVIII.   Communal and Flat Gardens   202

Chapter XIX. Wild Gardens   *page* 209
        XX. Rock Gardens   214
       XXI. Factory Gardens   217
      XXII. School Gardens   222
Conclusion   224
Bibliography   225
Index   227

ILLUSTRATIONS

PLATES

1. Court of Myrtles, Alhambra, Granada. *facing page* 15
2. The Italian Garden, Villa Garzoni, Collodi. 15
3. A garden plan by De Cerceaux. 17
4. Vaux-le-Vicomte. 17
5. One of Kip's views. 48
6. Montacute, Somerset. 48
7. The English lake. 49
8. Stowe Park. 49
9. The pool at Hidcote. 70
10. The main vista at Hidcote. 70
11. A Scandinavian garden. 71
12. A garden by Lawrence Halprin. 71
13. Another garden by Lawrence Halprin. 79
14. Memorial garden, Copenhagen. 81
15. Focal point of a small garden. 81
16. The lime walk, Sissinghurst Castle. 99
17. Gardens of the Tiefenbrunnen, Zurich. 99
18. Part of the garden, Sissinghurst Castle. 101
19. Receding wings of trees. 101
20. English landscape park. 112
21. An artificial hill at the Stockholm Crematorium. 112
22. Clear-cut basin to the fountain, Belvedere, Vienna. 113
23. The strong foliage pattern of Hosta. 113
24. Foliage contrast—Box and Banana. 116
25. Umbrella pine contrasted with Cypress. 116
26. Gardens of the Generaliffe, Spain. 117
27. Water at the Villa Lante, Italy. 117
28. Gardens of the Belvedere, Vienna. 124
29. Water in the Tivoli Gardens, Copenhagen. 124
30. The central fountain, Villa Lante. 125
125
132

33. Epstein's Dove with background of bamboo. *facing page* 132
34. Yuccas contrast with a statue by Barbara Hepworth. 132
35. Little lion at the Villa Marlia. 133
36. Steps may be narrow, steep and exciting. 133
37. Steps at the Villa D'Este, Tivoli. 140
38. Steps at Isola Bella. 140
39. Steps at Bramham Hall, Yorkshire. 141
40. Steps at the Villa Lante. 141
41. Free-soaring steps. 148
42. Drama of high walls, Villa Gamberaia. 149
43. Flats near Stockholm. 149
44. Hills beyond the terrace at Powerscourt. 156
45. Duke of Alba's garden, Seville. 156
46. Boundary between wood and garden, Villa Lante. 156
47. Corrugated shuttering gives interesting effects. 157
48. Use of wrought iron, Boboli gardens, Italy. 157
49. Abstract pattern by Eywin Langkilde. 160
50. Unifying pattern in Seville. 161
51. Diagonal pattern in the Alcazar, Seville. 161
52. Tree grids form part of a pattern, Gothenburg. 176
53. Pattern of setts, University College, Oxford. 176
54. Garden in Onslow Square, London. 177
55. Cedar in an asymmetrical garden. 196
56. Yews form a linking colonnade. 196
57. The classic façade of Tintinhull House. 197
58. Setting to flats, Gröndal. 204
59. Honey-comb pattern of brick paving. 204
60. Filling a narrow space with interest. 205
61. Small children's playground. 205

DIAGRAMS IN THE TEXT

1. Garden of the Shalimar Bagh, Lahore. *page* 18
2. Japanese hill garden. 22
3. The gardens of the Alhambra. 26
4. Garden of the Villa Lante. 36
5. Plan of Vaux-le-Vicomte. 42
6. The garden at Montacute. 47
7. Plan of Stowe Park. 56
8. Fastigiate trees and Scots pine. 58
9. Section of Stowe avenue. 59

ILLUSTRATIONS

10. The Great Avenue, Stowe.   *page* 62
11. Design by Gustav Ammann.   74
12. Garden by Lawrence Halprin.   75
13. Design by Burle Marx.   76
14. Trees forming a grouped composition.   89
15. At Holland Park.   90
16. Avenue of limes, Holland Park.   91
17. Chestnut avenue, Holland Park.   91
18. Gorse contrasted with thorn.   112
19. Poplar, willow and water.   112
20. Flowering cherry and pine.   113
21. Silver birch and Scots pine.   120
22. Hiding the concrete edge of a pool.   135
23. Combined bank and ha-ha.   148
24. Design for a car park, University College, Oxford.   162
25. Garden scooped out of encircling wind-shelter.   167
26. House set on a cross fall.   173
27. The Chaussee Garden by Eywin Langkilde.   178
28. The Little Garden by Jorn Palle Schmidt.   179
29. Garden plan, Tintinhull House.   183
30. Tivoli Gardens, Copenhagen.   190
31. Small public garden, Sutton-on-Sea.   193
32. Plan of Holland Park.   194
33. Protection for grass in a town square.   199
34. Rock, bamboo and azalea of a Japanese garden.   215
35. Temple, tree and shrub of the English park.   215

KEY TO DIAGRAMS

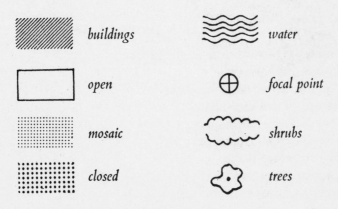

buildings   water

open   focal point

mosaic   shrubs

closed   trees

ACKNOWLEDGMENTS

The author gratefully acknowledges that in the preparation of diagrams use has been made of plans and data from the following sources:

Fig. 1. Gardens of the Great Moghuls—Mrs Villiers-Stuart
   2. Japanese Gardens by Jiro Harada—The Studio Ltd.
   3. The Gardens of the Alhambra—Prieto Moreno
   4. Gardens of the Italian Renaissance—Shepheard & Jellicoe
   5. Gardens of Vaux-le-Vicomte—Duprat
   6. Gardens of Montacute—*Country Life*
   11. *Werk*, article by W. Leder on plans by G. Ammann
   13. Modern Garden—Burle Marx
   27. The Chaussee Garden—E. Langkilde
   28. The Little Garden—J. P. Schmidt
   30. Tivoli Gardens—Aksel Andersen, in co-operation with G. N. Brandt
   32. Holland Park—L.C.C. Parks Department

The loan of photographs and permission to reproduce them is gratefully acknowledged to:—

Plate 2. A. du Gard Pasley
   3, 5. The British Museum
   4. Brenda Colvin
   6, 44, 20. *Country Life*
   7, 9, 10, 23, 54, 57. *Amateur Gardening*
   8. Aerofilms
   11, 49. E. Langkilde
   12, 13. L. Halprin
   14, 21, 61. Susan Jellicoe
   17. Walter Binden, Photographer; J. Schutz, Architect; H. Nuzbauer, Landscape Architect
   36. P. Porcinai
   41. G. Ammann
   43. M. Laurie

INTRODUCTION

GARDENS are the link between men and the world in which they live, for men in every age have felt the need to reconcile themselves with their surroundings, and have created gardens to satisfy their ideals and aspirations. The watered oasis in an arid land, the monastery garden walled off from the turmoil of the Dark Ages, and our own craving to grow plants as a counterpoise to technology, are all expressions of an ideal and of the need for compensation, and the more complex a civilization becomes, the more deeply this need is felt.

It is not therefore surprising that there is greater interest in gardens to-day than ever before, for to many they represent not only a peaceful refuge in a noisy world but the only opportunity for creative expression and close contact with nature. Yet few gardens to-day give that complete sense of peace which above all we are seeking. More often they are restless and leave their owners with a faint sense of dissatisfaction far removed from the rapturous contentment expressed in the inscription on the old Moghul gardens, 'If there is a heaven on earth it is here, it is here, it is here.'

A garden can give two separate pleasures—the pleasure of the growing plant with its individual beauty, and the pleasure of the garden as a whole, as a world to live in and to look at. To create and enjoy the first, a knowledge of horticulture and sensitivity to the colour and form of the plants suffices. But to make a garden which can give the second, and far rarer, pleasure entails the same understanding of the laws of harmony and composition that go to the making of any work of art. For garden design is an art, and just as a knowledge of painting and music is necessary not only for performance, but even for full enjoyment, so some understanding of landscape design not only opens up the possibilities in one's own garden, but adds to the pleasure of seeing others.

Even without knowing why, we are aware of the immense peace of certain gardens, while others give a sense of exhilaration, which draws one on to explore. It is worth studying certain of the great historic gardens which have these qualities to a marked degree, to discover whether they have any common characteristics which may still be applicable to-day.

Blind copying of another garden never succeeds, because gardens are a personal expression of desire made in response to a unique set of circumstances: the stress and aspirations of the age, set against the climate and the landscape of the country. No garden which grows up in response to these conditions will be worthless, however crude. But one transplanted bodily from another age or country lacks the basis of sincerity. This falseness can be sensed in the *jardins anglais* copied all over the world from the English landscape garden, and in Japanese gardens copied in England, without there being in either case an understanding of the principles underlying the designs, or the affinity which they had with the life and landscape of their native lands.

On the other hand, the gardens of Persia, adapted and re-designed to the conditions of India, produced the masterpiece of the Taj Mahal, while the classic gardens of Italy were transmuted and re-forged in seventeenth century France to evolve into the great tradition of Le Nôtre's Versailles. In the former cases there was uninspired imitation, in the latter the acceptance of a fertilizing idea to create a new form.

Underlying all the greatest gardens are certain principles of composition which remain unchanged because they are rooted in the natural laws of the universe, those same mysterious laws which are revealed in the mathematical relationship between the harmony of colour and of music. Since the dawn of civilization men have found their deepest satisfaction in discovering and expressing their own relationship to these laws. That was the basis of the classic theories of proportion and it is the basis of our pleasure in certain combinations of colours and juxtaposition of forms.

The quest for this relationship between our minds and the universe makes us first organize natural forms into easily grasped patterns and then re-arrange them into new compositions which please us by opening up fresh and less obvious fields of comprehension. New forms must continue to appear in every living art, but they satisfy us only as long as they are based on the unchangeable laws of proportion and rhythm.

The laws of composition are perhaps less evident in garden design than in any other art because, alone among the arts, it uses a living medium which left to itself develops a beauty of its own. Nevertheless, lack of these principles beneath the furnishing of flowers robs the great majority of our gardens of that serenity which we are seeking.

The small gardens set in unattractive surroundings which are the lot of the average British householder are not easy to recognize as the raw material for a work of art. But their very limitations make good design even more necessary than for the larger country gardens, where fine views and spaciousness may at least give some pleasant chance effects, whereas a small space bounded by fences relies entirely on its own resources. The most successful of these small gardens often deceive by the very simplicity which is part of their good design. They have a look of easy inevitability and it may be difficult to appreciate that the classic laws of proportion and balance lie behind the apparently haphazard arrangement of tree and sculpture or to realise that the laws of colour harmony are responsible for the self-same flowers giving us so much more pleasure in one garden than in another. Often a visiting gardener's reaction to a well-designed small garden is disbelief that the original site was no better than his own.

The boundaries concealed or made more interesting, the use of shadow and perspective to increase the apparent size, the restfulness which comes from good proportion, are all part of the technique of garden art. Their application is subject to infinite variation, but their principles apply to gardens of every size and type, and bring with them the serenity which comes when the eye is satisfied with what it sees and rests upon it in peace.

The lack of peace in the English gardens of to-day is intensified because, although throughout history garden traditions have fertilized each other, never before have there been so many cross-currents and so little oppor-tunity for the flood of ideas to evolve a tradition adapted to local conditions.

Only by understanding why certain forms were adopted by certain peoples shall we be able to select, eliminate, adapt and finally evolve for ourselves gardens which will express our ideas, our wants and the character of our surroundings in a form which will satisfy us as completely as the great gardens of the past satisfied their owners. If we succeed in this we shall create something which future generations will find as rewarding and as revealing of our age as we find the gardens of the past.

1. Court of Myrtles,
Alhambra, Granada. The
simplicity of water and
clipped myrtle contrasts
with the richness of the
architecture.

2. The Italian garden is a
sculptural composition of
towering cypresses,
flanking the cleft views,
solid bosquet, high
hedges, terraces and steps.
Villa Garzoni, Collodi.

PART ONE

HISTORY

THE OASIS GARDEN
THE SINO-JAPANESE GARDEN
THE HISPANO-ARABIC GARDEN
THE ITALIAN GARDEN
THE FRENCH TRADITION
THE ENGLISH GARDEN
THE CONTEMPORARY GARDEN

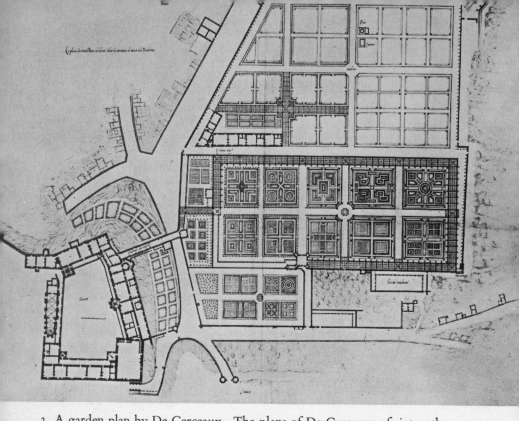

3. A garden plan by De Cerceaux. The plans of De Cerceaux of sixteenth-century gardens show the richness of garden design to which Le Nôtre was heir.

4. Vaux-le-Vicomte: The dark trees enclose the space as precisely as the walls of a room.

CHAPTER ONE

THE OASIS GARDEN

THE desire of men for a garden is as old as civilization and so deep-rooted that the first signs of it appear in the early history of peoples in all parts of the world. The earliest source of the garden tradition is religious, starting as an adjunct to the temple. Each of the ancient religions has its mythical garden—the Jewish garden of Eden, Eridu of the Assyrians, the Hindu Ida-Varsha. Parallel with the religious origin was the development of an enclosure for growing food, thus making the garden a link between the spiritual and physical needs of man. These earthly paradises, serving one or both sides of man's dual nature, are seen in the oasis garden of the desert, the fenced hunting parks of the Assyrians and the medieval monastery gardens with their herbs and fish ponds and flowers for the altar.

The idea behind all these early gardens is expressed in the Ispano-Arabic word *Glorietta*, the little private paradise. In every case they express the ideal of paradise as conceived by their creators.

The earliest recorded gardens are the Egyptian, and here, naturally enough, the idea of paradise centred on the fruitfulness of the oasis. Water, without which there could be neither fruit nor flowers nor the shade of trees, became the central motif of the garden, both by necessity and symbolically, as representing the river of life.

From this motif of water as the fount of fertility developed all the Asian gardens of irrigation, including the Arabian, the Persian and the Indian. Its influence reached far into the Western world, in classical times through Greek and Roman conquests, in medieval Europe through returning Crusaders, and finally, in a purer form, entering the portals of Spain with the Moorish invaders. The characteristics of its basic form are the logical result of its origin. It is enclosed, to shut out the surrounding desert, formal and level, because its central feature is a water canal or a rectangular tank. On each side of the water are the trees and flowers of the idealized oasis. This simple pattern evolved and changed as it passed to different countries, influenced by the land and often by the religion of its adopters. Cascades developed in the hills of Persia and the water channels became the four rivers of life in India. (See Fig. 1.)

With this tradition of the oasis there mingled in Asia another which derived from a very different terrain, that of the wooded hills of Assyria.

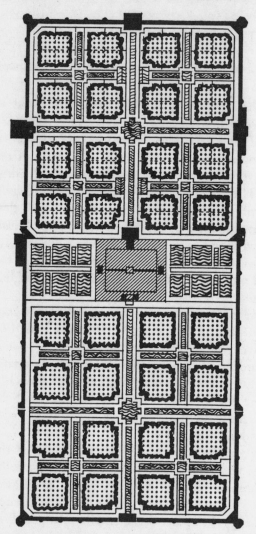

Fig. 1. Garden of the Shalimar Bagh (Lahore). Irrigation channels form the pattern of the garden (From a plan by Mrs Villiers-Stuart).

Here, the king's idea of paradise was a hunting forest, more beautiful and more richly stocked with game than any natural woodland. It was the true ancestor of the park, large in extent compared to the oasis garden—for there was no circumscribing desert—and informal in treatment, since it sprang from the natural fertility of the countryside instead of following the straight lines of irrigation. From these two sources—the irrigation of the desert and the idealization of the forest—came the Persian garden whose design was handed down to us through the pattern of the persian carpet. Here the pattern of irrigation takes the form of canals representing the four rivers of paradise and forming a cross in the centre. Often the garden was also surrounded by a border of water within the encompassing walls. In the four corners are the fruit and flowers of the oasis and sometimes, in addition, a token of the more extensive forest of the Assyrians.

The Arabs, those great masters of irrigation, adopted the same pattern and we meet it again in the garden of the Alhambra in southern Spain.

In Persia itself, these paradise gardens had a great flowering as late as the sixteenth century and it is possible, from the remains and records left, to appreciate the immense impression which they made on all who saw them. They were precious and jewel-like in conception. Often the water would flow over blue tiles and in the parterres between the intersecting canals were beds of carefully grouped flowers, or sometimes whole gardens of one kind of flower. There were fruit trees, and much use was made of the symbolic grouping of the eternal cypresses with the almond which renews its birth each spring.

The tradition re-appeared in India, brought by the Moghul conquerors of the early sixteenth century. Modified to suit the great heat of India they gradually evolved from the Persian pattern of many small rills to the great expanse of water of the Taj Mahal. Strongly influenced by the Mahomedan religion, these gardens are often divided into eight parterres representing the eight divisions of the Koran. In the centre of the largest tank a pavilion was placed to take advantage of the coolness of the water, and from this focal point flowed the four rivers of paradise. Round the walled enclosure an avenue of trees represented the vestigial remains of the Assyrian forest.

Mrs Villiers-Stuart, in *Gardens of the Great Moghuls*, gives a record of these gardens seen and studied at first hand which shows them to have ranked with the greatest gardens of the world, rooted in an older tradition, yet taking a new form and vitality from the character of the country of their adoption.

Long before the legacy of Persia came to India, India herself had influenced gardens in the Far East. Indian Buddhism travelled to China and thence, in the sixth century, to Japan, taking with it the idea of the Buddhist temple garden, with its hills, its lotus pools and trees; an informal composition, in complete contrast to the straight canals and oblong parterres of the garden of irrigation. These temple gardens added their influence to the remarkable tradition of the Sino-Japanese gardens.

CHAPTER TWO

THE SINO-JAPANESE GARDEN

A tradition far removed from the formal garden of the oasis evolved in China and was already established during the Han dynasty (140–87 B.C.). A distant breath of it was destined one day to cross-fertilize with the West and to influence not only the English landscape gardens and the *jardins chinois-anglais*, but also the modern gardens of northern Europe and America. Its more direct descendant was imported with so much else of Chinese culture into Japan in the eighth century. The basis of the Sino-Japanese garden is a veneration of nature which had its roots in Taoist nature-mysticism and was later reinforced by Zen-Buddhism, with its cult of the hill, the grove and the lotus pool, and its love of quiet meditation.

The Chinese garden is essentially a place in which to philosophise, to withdraw from worldly strife. Nothing in it can be hurried or sudden or blatant. The paths are not, as in the West, direct means of access from one point to another; but rather means of enjoying slowly and fully every view and mood of the scene which unfolds along their length. To this end they wind and even zig-zag, while the bridges, by their steep arcs or by a sudden change of direction, encourage a pause to admire the reflections.

The natural landscape which the Chinese most venerated was the sublime; great mountains, falling water, misty valleys and lakes. Their gardens were so much creations of the mind that a great landscape could be indicated by a few carefully placed rugged rocks; the rest of the picture was filled in by the imagination. In this it showed its affinity with Chinese landscape painting, in all its economy of evocative line and shadow. The connection was indeed very close, and the garden through which one slowly wandered was a creation in the round of the long scroll of the Chinese landscape painters.

When the Chinese garden travelled to Japan it went through many changes, but the underlying principles were never lost. It was drawn in firmer lines into a more clear-cut composition, losing perhaps in poetry what it gained in clarity. It was not until the sixteenth century that the tea ceremony was introduced, which to western minds is the essence of a Japanese garden. To the European, the careful setting for this ceremony may seem an over-emphasis on trivial etiquette, but to the Japanese it had a deep meaning; a deliberate drawing aside from the strife and ambition of the world and a recognition of the spiritual values of philosophy and aesthetics.

The Japanese garden is rooted in symbolism and tradition, but although religious and philosophic reasons may be given for the rules of design, they are in fact precepts of good composition. The prescribed grouping of 3, 5 and 7, the carefully related shapes and sizes of the hills, the half-veiling of the waterfall, the placing of the tall guardian stone in the foreground of the picture, all have their traditional significance, but also they are sound tenets of design. Two of the underlying principles of Japanese composition are the grouping together of the upright, the re-cumbent and the prostrate, and the contrast between passive and dynamic forms. Recognized shapes of rock are used to compose these groups, such as the statue stone, the arching stone and the recumbent ox stone. Rocks are also named for their specific place in the composition, to emphasize a view, a focal point or a mood. Such are the mist-enveloped, the clear-moon shadow, the guardian and the waiting stone.

Three main forms of garden finally crystallised, although later they were also all combined into a large 'stroll garden'. Each form might be carried out in a varying degree of finish, from the mere indication of a sketch design to the fully worked out picture in the round. The three types of garden were the flat garden, the dry garden, and the lake-and-island or hill-and-water garden.

The flat garden is often used in the smallest courtyard or even passage. The ground may be of sand, sometimes raked into a pattern. The com-position is given by the careful grouping of rock, ornament and plant. A lantern (the recumbent form), a bamboo (the vertical form), and a flat stone (the prostrate form) may be the whole picture.

In the dry garden there are hills, but water is only indicated by the placing of stones, rather as the mountains were in the Chinese gardens.

The hill-and-water garden is a complete landscape of grouped hills, a water course and an arrangement of foreground rocks, or of a lake set with islands. The finished view is infinitely varied, but the basis of the design follows definite rules. (See Fig. 2.)

Plants are an essential part of the Japanese garden and the shape and placing is as carefully controlled as that of the rocks. The tradition of artificially stunted trees is well known, and if a plant does eventually grow too large for its place it is replaced by a smaller one. The plant forms most used are the closely rounded recumbent ones, like the Japanese azalea and dwarf conifers; the gnarled tree, typified by the wind-riven pine, and the vertical bamboo. Some of the most lovely Japanese gardens are entirely carpeted with moss, a covering which accentuates the moulded formation of the ground and makes the perfect textural contrast to the rock. Texture plays a more important part in Japanese gardens than in any of the other historic traditions.

Fig. 2. The Japanese hill garden, although infinitely varied in detail, follows rigid principles of composition. A. Side mountain; B. Middle mountain; C. Distant mountain; D. Cascade; E. Guardian stone; F. Central island; G. Lake; H. Worshipping stone; J. Beach; K. Mountain spur; L. Near mountain; M. Lake outlet; N. Guests' island.

Although the Sino-Japanese garden is an idealization of nature, it has always been closely related to the buildings and it is only in relation to oriental architecture that the shapes of the lanterns and bridges can be appreciated. They show the same exuberance and dynamic form, which is yet firmly rooted to the ground by reason of its sense of equipoise. In their own setting they are part of a whole world in keeping with themselves, but strayed into western surroundings they can well look bizarre.

The influence which the Sino-Japanese garden has had on the West is not easy to assess. Garbled though the early accounts of the Chinese garden may have been, yet they certainly helped to fire the imagination of the English landscape school and, while the results were totally different, the ideas behind the two gardens had much in common. Both were an idealization of nature, both relied on balance and natural form instead of on symmetry, and both incorporated the traditional architecture of their respective civilizations. Above all, both were closely allied to the art of landscape painting. It is revealing but not surprising that the highest achievement of the English landscape garden resulted from translating an idea into the native language of the English countryside and philosophy. The less happy result of the *jardin anglo-chinois* came from a more direct copy of an original not fully understood. The serpentine paths on the plan of an old Chinese park are clearly recognizable as the ancestor of the winding walks of the *anglo-chinois* garden, but what the plan does not show are the hills and valleys, the rocks and ever-changing views which give reason for the windings. The map of a mountainous district shows the same twisting and turning of roads, meaningless without the contours.

The blind copying of Japanese gardens would give no happier result to-day, but we have much to learn from their unfailing sense of balance, the evocative shapes, the economy with which their landscape is sketched in and the quiet restraint of their composition.

CHAPTER THREE

THE HISPANO-ARABIC GARDEN

ISTORICALLY and geographically, Spain is the bridge between Europe and the Middle East, and in her gardens are reflected these two streams of civilization. One flowing up from the South, full of the powerful simplicity of a great nomadic people, while from the North comes the French tradition, with its complex sophistication and sense of order.

But Spain can do more than claim a place in garden history by reason of a geographical position. It may also claim to have produced one of the great garden traditions of the world, for while gardens throughout Spain are interesting, some of the Hispano-Arabic gardens, notably those of the Alhambra and Generaliffe, bear the unmistakable hall-mark of a genuine creation arising from a unique conjunction of place, climate and philosophy.

Prieto Moreno, in *Los Jardines de Granada*, traces clearly the background which was built up in this south-east corner of Spain by the forces of history, geography and culture. While from one side this bastion of the European mainland was the first to receive each wave of culture and invasion from the Mediterranean, on the other side the natural defences of its mountains ensured that it should be the last Islamic stronghold to be reconquered from the West.

For this reason the French influence is less evident than in other parts of Spain and, curiously, the stronger Western influence is in the remnants of the medieval tradition which the Arabs found already installed when they invaded the country in the eighth century. The patio is a descendant of the Roman atrium, via the medieval cloister. This enclosed garden, closely related to the dwelling yet asymmetric to it, is akin to the medieval gardens illustrated in the *Roman de la Rose*. Each one has its focal point, usually a fountain, and the design of the patio, the pattern of the paving, the placing and choice of plants are complementary to it. The walls, white or of a pale, cool colour, are a perfect foil to the dark green of jasmine or the more lustrous leaves of orange. Pot plants are carefully grouped as part of the design, the pots being sometimes painted to accord with a definite colour scheme. Colouring is cool and restful, except for occasional brilliant blossoms.

The patio is essentially an open-air room, and used as such throughout Spain. For this purpose the rigid symmetry of a renaissance parterre would be as inconvenient as an indoor room in which the furniture was arranged in a formal and immovable pattern. In fact, where a renaissance courtyard was laid out to conform with fashion after the reconquest of 1491, a second patio in the old style was often added to serve as a living room, and in some cases the new fashion was done away with in favour of the older and more functional arrangement.

The Alhambra and the Generaliffe are in effect a series of patios adapted and modified by the ideas of the Islamic settlers. Uniting them into one conception is the theme of the Paradise garden. (See Fig. 3.)

To a nomadic people, from the arid desert, the fertile slopes of the Sierra Nevada, above the watered valleys of Vega and Douro, was paradise indeed. From their desert life they brought with them a love of nature, of distant views, of the open air, and above all a veneration for water, which experience had taught them to regard as both the greatest need and the greatest luxury in life. Faced with the boundless opportunities of bringing water from the snow-capped Sierra Nevada, they constructed aqueducts which, for centuries after the reconquest, remained the only irrigation system in Spain.

In these new surroundings the tradition of the paradise garden, with its rigid and confined lines, opened up to take advantage of the wider area of fertility and the views over the countryside of orchards, olive groves and distant mountains. There is no greater contrast in character than between this love of open spaces by the Arabs and the passion for closing in, which was shown by the Kings of Spain after the reconquest. Apart from the one impermeable block of the palace of Carlos I, there is perhaps nowhere in the world a more complete inter-penetration of landscape and architecture than in the Alhambra. It is true that the Palladian mansion sits in perfect relation to its surrounding landscape, but the landscape and the mansion, though complementary, are separate. In the Alhambra there is such permeation between the two that one cannot always say whether one is inside or out. The views of the Sierra Nevada penetrate the open arcades of the buildings and give the sensation of being in a tent upon the mountains. Halls, porticos, arcades and patios lead one into another. The patios with their fountains, flowers and cypresses are rooms open to the air. The rooms with their wide arches open to the view, their plants in tubs and again their fountains are gardens roofed over.

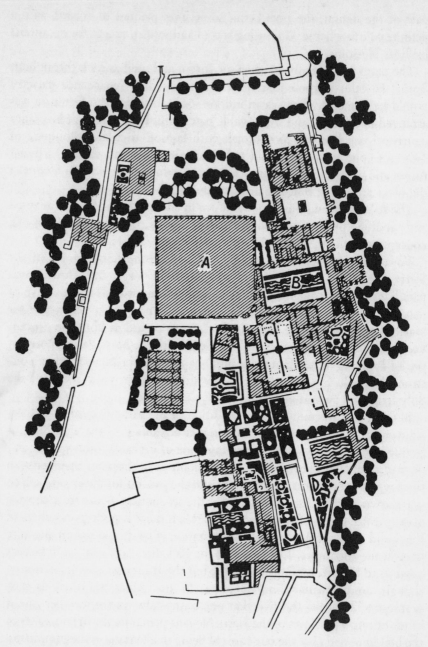

Fig. 3. The gardens of the Alhambra show a complete interpenetration of landscape and architecture. Through an interlocking system of patios runs the theme of the river of life. A. Charles V palace; B. Patio de Los Arrayanes; C. Patio de Los Leones.

The conception of the Alhambra is a metamorphosis into stone of the palm trees of the oasis, their slender trunks supporting a light canopy of branches. It shows in fact precisely what was in the minds of its creators—a nomadic encampment, with the tents turned to stone, watered with eternal springs and lapped about in the green of the oasis.

The nearest analogy to this flow between garden and dwelling is the most modern tendency of all—the house, all glass and windows opening on to the garden, and the interior invaded by the green of indoor plants. In time and in place, it is a far cry from the Alhambra to modern America. But there is a greater kinship between them than can be found in the centuries between, and indeed the link of history through the Spanish tradition in South America and California is clearly seen.

Even the light contributes to this liquid transition from inside to outside, the varying degrees of luminosity are like those encountered in a forest, giving an amazing depth and mystery to some parts, and focusing attention on objects in the open patios.

Nor is this the only respect in which the gardens of Grenada have spanned the centuries. The Moors had many ideas which are far more sympathetic to us than those which inspired the French garden tradition. They had a veneration for nature and a respect for the individual, which led them to use plants for their individual worth, rather than for mass effects. The carefully placed vine in the Duke of Alba's garden (See p. 156), the orange tree in the patio, might be taken from examples of the modern use of plants with architecture. They have nothing in common with the regimented and clipped plants of Versailles. There are, it is true, clipped hedges, either serving a strictly architectural role, like the myrtle hedges in the Patio de Los Arrayanes (Plate 1), or used as an outline to beds of free growing trees and flowers. This use of the free-planted bed contained in the box hedge is universal in Spanish gardens and is yet another link with our modern gardens, reminiscent of Hidcote and Sissinghurst.

In spite of the luxuriance of the planting, there is also restraint which recognizes that intricacy must be contrasted with plain surfaces. The rich incision of the arches at the end of the Patio de Los Arrayanes is contrasted with the severe simplicity of the myrtle hedge surrounding its reflection in the tank. On the other hand the exuberant flowers of the upper garden of the Generaliffe are seen against plain walls and simple architecture. 'The beauty of a rose reflected in the surface of the water must not be disturbed by over-rich carving on the marble surround' (Prieto Moreno).

This simplicity and restraint is another point of contrast with the renaissance gardens. Richly wrought fountains are the exception, that in the Court of the Lions, for instance, being placed in a position of great honour, with a dignified setting. The majority are either the plainest of runnells or circular basins, or they follow the two traditional types of the open lotus flower and the closed lotus bud. Often the water bubbles up from below the surface, to give the effect of a natural spring, another example of the love for the natural. In this respect it is interesting to compare the Generaliffe with the Villa D'Este at Tivoli. Both have as their theme a joy in the abundance of water. They play with it, draw patterns with the jets, and fill the air with its music. But at the Villa D'Este the jets come from strange beasts and fall into elaborate wrought basins, while great sheets of water are used to form set pieces. In the Generaliffe the walls are plain, the water comes from hidden sources, and the great water stairway is roughly formed, the channels in the balustrades looking as if they had been scooped out of wet clay. The richness of the Generaliffe is formed by the plants which at the Villa D'Este serve only as a frame and background.

But if the stonework of the Arab fountains is often plain, great ingenuity is shown in the manipulation of water, particularly in relation to light. A device in the shaping of the channel feeding the tank in the Patio de Los Arrayanes causes a pattern of waves, designed to reflect the light.

The two connecting themes which run through the Generaliffe and the Alhambra are the old Eastern motif of the irrigation channel and the new conception of the view over the countryside.

The channel appears in every possible guise, wandering far indeed from its Persian prototype. The nearest in appearance to the original is the impressive canal in the Patio di Ria, from the sides of which slender jets arch over to form an avenue of water (See p. 117).

While this is the only one whose size and proportion recalls the original, that in the Court of the Lions, though minute in size, is a vestigial remnant of the full pattern of the river of life, with its four branches. No garden or courtyard in the whole Alhambra-Generaliffe complex is without its water in one form or another, from the minute jets which give life to some of the small gloriettas, to the great tank which fills almost the whole of the Court of the Arrayanes. It was, after all, not only the most joyous element which the Arabs knew, but also necessary to their religious observances. The ritual washing of feet accounts for so many of the fountains being at ground level. The low plane of the water, brimming its containers, adds immensely to the sense of space and serenity. The ground level appearance had to be carefully considered, for the viewers were frequently seated on the ground, and the full effect of the reflections, in the Court of the Arrayanes, for instance, can be appreciated only from this position.

If the water is the internal connecting link, the view is the external one.

From every patio and garden, except where it has been blocked by later additions, the view forms an essential completion to the composition. It is seen over the side of the garden at the entrance to the Generaliffe and through the arches of the miradore at its end. It is this constant opening up of the world beyond, which prevents any feeling of restriction, in spite of the very small scale of some of the gardens. This small scale was another manifestation of the Islamic attitude to life: love of the individual and of contemplation. The meaning of 'glorietta' is a small private paradise, and the gardens abound in them. All have a sense of privacy, of secrecy and of being safely closed in within the encircling bower of plants; but in each there is still the glimpse of the bigger paradise without, and always the sight and sound of the glorietta's own spring of water.

With this love of solitude and meditation went the Islamic ideal of quiet, perpetual content, utterly unlike the ideal of Western man, who craves some great climax of exhilaration, even at the cost of preliminary hardship. Where the renaissance garden works up to climax, the Islamic garden proceeds quietly from one lovely retreat to the next, making it impossible to say which is the culminating point.

A love of colour was one of the legacies brought from the East, and while in other Hispano-Moorish gardens, such as the Alcazar at Seville, brilliant colours are provided by the green and blue glazed tiles, at the Alhambra there is a softer, riper range of colours. The walls merge through every shade of peach and apricot and honey, but the stronger colours and the greens are supplied by the plants. As important as the colours and the scents of daylight are those of the night, when the moon turns the walls to white and accentuates the darkness of the cypress and the warm night scents. In the short, cold nights of our northern summers, it is hard to realize the importance of the moonlit hours from sunset to midnight. De Falla's nocturne of the Generaliffe is the most evocative description of these magic hours.

In a climate where, in spite of irrigation, grass cannot be regarded as a normal ground cover, it is natural that a particular cult of paving should have developed. The beauty and intricacy of the patterns made by setting narrow black and white pebbles on edge is an endless delight throughout Granada, where they are used in market-places and gutters as well as patios. In gardens they are made to contribute a special pattern serving to link together the other elements. Yet these, too, are used with restraint, and in gardens full of flowers are more often replaced by plainer surfaces.

In those parts of Spain where the Moorish domination was more quickly ended, there is still an Eastern influence which gives them a distinct character of their own, particularly in their combination of informal, free-growing plants, within a hedge of clipped box, outlining a formal ground plan. Aranjuez is typical of the gardens showing a strong French influence, while still in its romance and profusion of flowers remaining essentially Spanish. Yet it is probably true to say that these Franco-Spanish gardens hold too much of the renaissance tradition to rank as an entirely new conception, and it must be left to the tradition of south-east Spain to make one of those unique contributions which place them as landmarks in the development of garden art.

CHAPTER FOUR

THE ITALIAN GARDEN

To understand why garden art flowered with such perfection in Central and Northern Italy during the fifteenth and sixteenth centuries would be to understand all the historic and emotional reasons which lay behind the phenomenon of genius which was the Italian renaissance. But even to trace, within the larger picture, the development of the Italian garden, one must turn back to find the roots of the Western conception of a garden in ancient Greece. Here, already, in the garden courts of the peristyle was the idea of an open-air extension of the living rooms and, in the public parks and the gardens of the philosophers, the conception of a garden as a place of recreation and meditation. For the first time, a garden is considered solely as serving the spirit of man, not necessarily based on the production of food, like the oasis garden, nor on the hunt, like the Syrian parks, nor on the service of the gods. In this, as in all else, Greece affirms the value of individual man. In form, the gardens of Greece borrowed extensively from earlier civilizations, particularly after the return of Alexander the Great from his conquests in Persia and India.

The Romans found inspiration for their villa gardens, as for so much else, in Greece, and the extent to which they copied and enlarged the Greek ideas may be seen in the remnants of Hadrian's villa near Tivoli. Here, a vast area was covered by a series of different gardens and buildings, only loosely related either to each other or to the palace. They reveal their Greek origin by names such as the Lyceum, the Academy and the valley of Tempe, and they show an amazing diversity of treatment, ranging from the strict formality of the long canal of Canopus to the natural garden of the valley of Tempe. Roman gardens may have been strongly derivative, yet because of their numbers and the scale and solidity of construction, they served to perpetuate forms which had evolved in other parts of the world and which were destined to be reborn in the great days of the fifteenth century. The development of the atrium, and even more of the open peristyle, was the forerunner of the idea of extending the house outward into the garden.

This has been a strong influence in western gardens ever since, and the idea took a great step forward in the terraces of the renaissance gardens, which virtually became a series of open air rooms. Equally, the open space of the Hippodrome with its apsidal ends, and surrounding trees, is not only the ancestor of the landscaped sports arenas, but in varying forms is the basic pattern of the open lawn contrasted with its background of massed planting. Fountains, canals, grottoes, sculpture and topiary were already there, but it is possible that if one were to see one of the larger Roman gardens to-day it might have the same undigested look with which we are familiar in late nineteenth century gardens, for the Romans, like ourselves, had borrowed too many elements from too many lands and had not yet found the secret of organizing them into a whole.

When their descendants, at the end of the fourteenth century, came out from the cloistered medieval gardens towards a new age of freedom and discovery, they looked back to the expansive days of the Roman empire to give them inspiration in their desire to express once again the limitless possibilities of the human mind. The elements were all there—the basic shapes, the breadth and scale, the union of art and nature represented by the classic statues and garden temples. They took them and began to re-create them into a whole as an artist organizes the subject of his picture. The parts took on a relationship to one another, and the whole a relationship both to the house and to the countryside in which it stood.

Symptomatic of this development was the importance given to terraces and steps. The terrace was an almost inevitable development in a hilly countryside which already provided a pattern in its terraced vineyards, but their value was now realized as a means of uniting the architecture of the house with the contours of the land; moreover steps, which in Roman gardens had either been omitted or treated purely as necessities, were now elaborated and stressed as the connecting elements between the vertical and horizontal planes which are the basis of these gardens carved out of the hillsides of Italy. For the Italian garden is essentially a sculptural composition; the towering cypresses, the bosche which flank the main vistas, the high hedges, the terrace walls and steps, all build up into a solid three-dimensional form accentuated with dramatic verticals forming clefts which frame the distant view (Plate 2). They are entirely different in feeling and proportion from the series of calm and wide tree-enclosed spaces which are the basis of the French garden (Plate 4).

This is a natural result of the combination of a hot sunny climate, which favours the pattern of deep clefts cut in surrounding shade, and of a steep terrain which led to the development of terraces. But it perhaps also reflects the fact that one of the spurs to the creation of the renaissance gardens was a delight in sculpture and a desire to give the classical statues a worthy setting. Never before, or since, have all the arts been so closely concerned in the creation of gardens. In this they are a reflection of their age, when the universal man saw life as a whole and not from the distorted angle of a specialist. The gardens themselves were the work of artists, sculptors and architects, one of the greatest of all being that by Raphael at the Villa Madama.

Their kinship with music may not be so self-evident, but cannot be doubted after a visit to the Villa D'Este at Tivoli. Here water forms the connecting link in the garden. It is not a garden to be seen as a whole, like a picture, but one through which to progress as if through the playing of a sonata, passing through the successive movements and variations of a theme. Unlike most Italian gardens, the interest of the individual terraces is even greater than that of the central vista, so that one is compelled to follow the moods of the water through all its movements, the repetitive theme of the hundred jets, the playful mood of the plopping fountains, the pattern of the intersecting jets and the gentle music of the rill through the bosche until the crashing chord of the great cascade is reached, beyond which there can be nothing but the quiet sostenuto of the placid tanks on the lowest parterre, where the water, like the emotions, comes to rest and takes breath.

In spite of the richness of its detail the Italian garden is essentially simple in plan. In the typical terraced garden there is usually a main vista stretching out from the house across successive terraces, with secondary vistas opening laterally along each terrace. While the main vista may be symmetrical, there is endless invention and variation in the treatment of the different terraces, their steps and terminal features, and an evocative placing of the occasional asymmetric group of trees. There is less rigidity than in the French plans. Thick bosche frame the view and contain the ends of the terraces.

One of the commonest causes of failure in imitations of Italian gardens is the omission of these supporting plantations. Their role is partly to give scale and solidity to the composition held within them, and a sense of mystery to the views along the terraces which disappear into their shade, but they also play an important part in linking the garden with its sur- roundings. For the essence of the Italian garden is that it is the meeting place of man's spirit with the countryside in which he lives. It takes the elements of the Italian landscape and transmutes them into the utmost possibilities of beauty. The vine terraces, following the contours of the hills, become the garden terraces richly wrought and varied and perfectly proportioned; often dramatic, but never contradicting the configuration

3

of the ground. The olive groves become the bosche which flank the terraced vista. The piled-up hill towns and vertical accents of church towers are reflected in the aspiring compositions of columns, statues and cypresses. The strong pattern and mosaic shadow of the vine leaves and the gnarled trunks of the olives are the parents of the carved and patterned stonework.

These sublimated elements of nature give a unity between the garden and the landscape. Because of this harmony there is a peculiar serenity about Italian gardens. Although they are an expression of man's spirit in ascendency over nature, it is an ascendency which transmutes her, rather than conquers. They have neither the ruthless mastery of the French garden nor the dependence on nature's moods and growth which characterizes the English. They rather form the natural meeting place of man and nature, stretching out from the house as an extension of living space and throwing out tentacles of architecture in the form of terraces and statues to enrich and civilize the landscape.

Just as they transmute the natural features of their countryside, so they make a virtue of their climate. It dictates the form of a garden carved out of the solid of shade trees, while the visual opportunities are seized to make full use of the black shadows as a foil to the patch of brilliant blue sky appearing as a window between the cypress tops or as a background to the gleaming white of a statue. Flowers can be used only sparingly as a touch of brilliant colour seen through the dark shadows, or as a vivid splash against a wall. Too great a use of colour in the composition of stone, dark evergreens, gleaming water and deep blue sky, is as unsatisfactory as the painting of a statue.

The great age of the Italian garden lasted only as long as the men who made them kept the spirit which inspired them.

By the seventeenth century, the joy and wonder in man's creativeness and in nature, which shines like silver through the gardens of Raphael, Vignola and Pirro Ligorio (architect of the Villa D'Este) had given place to a complacent pride in the cleverness of man. Many of the later Baroque gardens are marvels of composition and inventiveness, expressing the robust exuberance of the age in luscious curves and prancing statues, but they are gardens of display rather than gardens of contemplation, they are to be looked at rather than lived in.

The garden of the Villa Aldobrandini at Frascati is a magnificent piece of stage scenery, but it is little more than a backcloth to the villa. Instead of the seductive paths of the Villa D'Este, conducive to conversation and thought, only steep zig-zag paths or ladder-like steps lead up into the garden at the side of the spectacular cascade; it is as if the designer did not care for the garden as something in its own right, but only as an opportunity to arouse wonder when seen from the house.

THE VILLA LANTE

The simplicity and clarity of the garden plan of the Villa Lante (Fig. 4) make it a perfect illustration of the ideas behind the Italian garden. Designed by Vignola in 1564 at a time when Italian renaissance gardens had reached their zenith, it has the distinction of being one of the few gardens which takes precedence over the house, for the Villa Lante is divided into two pavilions in order that the central vista of the garden may pass uninterrupted between them.

The theme of the composition is the progression of a rill rising from a grotto in the wooded hillside and flowing down through a series of terraces, at each step growing in sophistication, until it opens out into a great water parterre at the lowest level. There are two parallel developments in the theme. One is the opening out from the thick woodland at the source to the open, spacious parterre at the foot. The other is the transition from the native woodland, where the water gushes out from the natural rock, and the columns of the pergola echo in stone the white trunks of the great plane trees (See p. 156), to the formality and architectural intricacy of the water parterre, which links the garden with the village beyond whose campanile seems but one more architectural feature of the garden.

The beginning is a sublimated woodland, the end a sublimated piazza. Between them the connecting link of the water changes its form on each successive terrace, always growing in volume and sophistication. From the almost natural source in the grotto it flows down a narrow stairway, whose stone is wrought in the form of water ripples (Plate 27). It re-appears on the next terrace gushing from the great carved figure of the Neptune fountain, and from here it steadies itself in the long tank whose formal shape is emphasized by the flanking bosche, hedged firmly round in contrast to the informally grouped trees of the source.

The line of the pavilions seems to mark the final demarcation between the influence of the natural landscape and the architectural domination of the town. Below them the water spreads out into the great tanks of the parterre and gushes from the star held in the upstretched hands of the three figures of the central fountain (Plate 30). Here is finality, the lowest level reached, the water at rest, the woods left behind, and architecture supreme over nature.

There is symmetry in the design and an absolute sureness of touch, yet

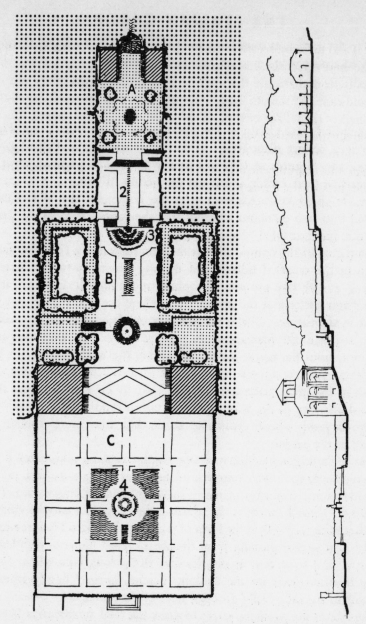

Fig. 4. *Garden of the Villa Lante shows a double theme of progression: From the closed wood to the open parterre* (C) *and from the woodland rill to the great star fountain* (4).

A. *Gardens emerging from wooded hill.*   1. *Colonnade leading to woods.*
B. *Central garden.*   2. *Rill.*
C. *Architectural water parterre.*   3. *Neptune fountain.*
                                            4. *Star fountain.*

36

there is also the most sensitive integration with surroundings. The flanking bosche here give the impression that the central garden has grown naturally from them and that they in their turn are a part of the surrounding landscape. At the other end, the parterre composes perfectly with the buildings of the village beyond, to which it is linked with a great gateway. Originally the garden was flanked by a park, which must have added even more to the flow of the garden into the countryside. There still remains the magnificent introduction of the great sea-horse fountain at the entrance to the garden (Plate 31).

CHAPTER FIVE

THE FRENCH TRADITION

AT the moment in history when the spirit of a nation is translated into a garden, a new and distinct garden style is born—a style which will be the perfect expression of its own place and age and which will never again be seen at its best in other lands or future times.

In France this moment came in the seventeenth century, and the genius who crystallized the spirit of his age into the setting of his country was André Le Nôtre.

France had already a long garden tradition, dating back to the days of Rome. From then, until the seventeenth century, the course of development ran roughly parallel to that in England, with France always slightly ahead both in extent and time. There were the same simple medieval gardens, enclosed against a hostile world; the same horticultural tradition handed down in the safe keeping of the monasteries. But in France the monk's fish ponds and the castle's defensive moats expanded during the fifteenth and sixteenth centuries into ornamental water allées on a scale which was seldom seen in England, even at a much later date; a development which was encouraged by the flatter terrain and high water table of much of Northern France, as well as by the greater power and wealth of the nobles.

The derivation from the large, still expanses of fish pond and moat, rather than from the narrow rill of the irrigation channel, bequeathed to the French gardens a use of water in their design quite distinct from that of the gardens of the South and East. Their other strong individual feature—the long allée cut through the wood—is a direct descendant of the rides through hunting forests. It was the background of these extensive forests which gave solidity to the design of radial avenues; a solidity which was lacking when the style was transplanted to the more open country of England and carried out in the emaciated form of avenues running across open parks or agricultural land (See p. 48). Both these features—the formal expanse of still water and the patterns cut in the forest—were clearly indigenous to France. So were the simple medieval gardens of rectangular beds and gothic fountains. But from the renaissance onwards there was a steady infiltration of Italian influence, particularly on the return of Charles VIII in 1494 from his campaigns in Italy, and during the sixteenth century there was a growing use of parterres, fountains and stone ornament.

A comparison between the gardens of the fifteenth century illustrated in the *Tres Riches Heurs de Duc de Berry* and the engravings of de Cerceaux in 1597 show the immense development of gardens during the intervening century. They not only increased in size and complexity, but took on a symmetrical relationship to the house, marking the transition from the turbulent times when the essential surround of a castle was defensive to the more peaceful time when its beauty and magnificence could be enjoyed. The pictures of Charleval and the Tuilleries show the richness of the garden tradition to which Le Nôtre was heir (Plate 3).

To appreciate why the classic French garden developed as it did, one must understand not only its past history, but the land in which it grew and the mentality and social life in which it blossomed. The birthplace of the Le Nôtre tradition was Northern France; temperate, more genial than England, less sun-baked than Italy; a climate whose light was clear rather than strong, and where a precise and steely picture would be reflected in a clear, still sheet of water; a land of wide forest, fertile soil and gently rolling terrain.

Against this background was a society ruled by a rich and powerful aristocracy, grouped round the magnet of the king and court. It was an age which glorified power; power of wealth, of intellect, and of man's ascendency over nature. When Le Nôtre said: '*Je ne pouvait souffrir les vues borneés*,' he was expressing not only one of his tenets of garden design, but also the spirit of his age; the age of discovery, of logic and of fearless thought which recognized no limits. But this freedom of intellect was encased in a rigid social structure; fear of nature and the unknown was replaced by fear of political enemies. Although the aristocracy had great estates, their interest was centred on the court and on political power rather than on the husbandry of their lands. A garden was required, not as a part of a gentleman's estate, nor as a quiet retreat for meditation, but as a stage for the display of magnificence and an open-air setting for the crowded life of court intrigue and amusement.

Such conditions might have led to monstrosities of design, but in spite of the ostentation, it was an age of cultivated taste and a genuine love of the arts. Moreover, it was at that robust and self-confident moment in a civilization's history which precedes decadence.

Nevertheless, it is difficult to say whether the age had inevitably to produce a Le Nôtre or whether it was only the happy accident of his genius which translated the moment into one of the great classics of garden art.

VAUX-LE-VICOMTE

Because Vaux-le-Vicomte is less grandiose than Versailles it is easier to comprehend as a unity. Moreover, it was conceived and carried out in a short space of time—from 1656 to 1661—by a Le Nôtre in his prime, finding for the first time an opportunity to express to the full his ideas of garden art. It has the imprint of a conception evolved through years of thought and experience, and then expressed with unfaltering execution. It is essentially a finite design as independent of time as a picture, and at the opposite pole from the English gardens which are organic growths. Nor has it the romance and lyric quality of the Villa D'Este, which unfolds itself gradually in space, to be read like a poem as one walks through it. Instead, it has the clear-sighted logic of a mathematical problem, beautiful in its inevitability. In it Le Nôtre expresses not only his own love of order, unity and logic, but the enduring qualities of French mentality.

Vaux shows very clearly its debt to history. The approach to the chateau with its *cour d'honneur* and the encircling moat are entirely traditional: so are the embosking woodlands. The clear-cut distinction between the dark mass of woodland and the light of the open central space is typically French, contrasting with the Italian pattern of light piercing through the dark, and the English pattern of misty tracery. These dark woodlands enclose the space as precisely as the walls of a room, while their height and over-hanging tops define the ceiling (Plate 4).

The scope of the operations at Vaux was typical of the ruthless magnificence of the age, a village and two hamlets being swept away to make room for the park.

Le Nôtre was too great an artist to ignore the topography of the site, but it is kept in its place as the servant of man. The north to south fall to the river valley and the rising ground beyond is brilliantly exploited as part of the design, but the east to west cross fall, which, if recognized, would destroy the classic axial design, is overcome by building up the lower side.

Le Nôtre's invariable principles are each illustrated in the clearest possible way. His first principle—to give space round the building—is achieved first by the flanking moat, then by the two parterres stretched out beyond. In front of the chateau the garden stretches out in perfect proportion and logical progression. His second theory, that of space division, was very simple; one strong main axis, with cross axes at right angles to it, and, within the angles thus formed, a series of panels, decorated with parterres, statues and fountains. There was perfect symmetry of balance on each side of the main axis, but infinite variety in the detail design.

Within the rigid symmetrical outlines there is a beautiful scheme of contrast and progression in the design of the compartments. First, the entrance to the chateau on the north side is austerely simple; then, passing through the *avant cour*, over the moat and through the *cour d'honneur*, there is a gradual heightening of interest as the chateau is approached. On the south side of the chateau the process is reversed and the greatest richness and intricacy is concentrated on the first terrace, with its closely patterned *parterres de broderies*, and from there each terrace increases in breadth of treatment, culminating in the huge magnificence of the great canal and cascades. Keeping pace with the progressive broadening of effect, each cross axis gives a deeper and more seductive penetration into the containing frame of woodlands, thus emphasizing the concentration of interest nearest the building. Interlocking with the progressively deeper penetration of the cross axes is a stepping in at each terrace of the green walls of the flanking trees, concentrating the central view as it recedes (See Fig. 5).

This opposition of two forces is met with again and again in garden design, the compelling force of a central interest played against the seduction of diversion. Without it a garden can be very dull, but it needs skill to carry it off without confusion or duality.

Le Nôtre's third principle—that the main axis shall have a grand climax, beyond which the eye may travel on to the horizon—is fulfilled by the culminating grotto and cascades, and beyond them the Farnese Bull on the hill which rises behind it to the far horizon.

The mathematical quality of the garden and the perfect clarity of Le Nôtre's conception is beautifully illustrated by its classic example of the science of optics. The levels are so arranged that from the upper terrace the waters of the canal are not seen; instead the cascades on their far side appear to be gushing into the raised square fountain on the second terrace. Looking back from the banks of the canal the entire façade of the chateau can be seen reflected in this same square pool. In that we have the epitome of the French tradition; clear-sighted, precise, rejoicing in the beauty of the intellect.

The beauty of Le Nôtre's gardens depends on the conviction which he brought to them, his perfect sense of proportion, and the genius which never allowed a rigid convention to stultify infinite invention. After Le Nôtre a gradual emasculation set in. It was inevitable that conviction

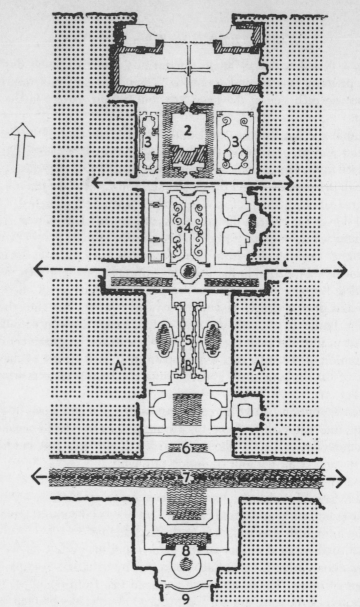

Fig. 5. Plan of Vaux-le-Vicomte. United by strong axes. The space division is a clear-cut distinction between dark massed woodland and light open space, in contrast to the Italian pattern of light piercing through dark, and the English tradition of misty tracery. The design progresses by increasing richness of detail near the house and depth of cross-axes away from it.

A. Dark enclosing mass of woodland. B. Open central space.

1. *Avant cour.*
2. *Cour d'honneur.*
3. *Parterre.*
4. *First terrace.*
5. *Second terrace.*
6. *Cascades.*
7. *Great canal.*
8. *Grotto.*
9. *View to hill and Farnese Bull.*

should waver. The men who had been so sure of their omnipotence and the rightness of their mastery over nature were replaced by those who said '*il faut ceder l'art à nature.*' There was compromise, and nature, or more often a parody of her, was readmitted. But however valuable compromise may be in politics, it is death to art. The classic formula lost its forcefulness and the gardens took on a self-conscious playfulness, which is their common fate when there is no longer conviction in their creation.

THE JARDIN ANGLAIS

The 'jardin Anglais' and 'Anglo-Chinois' bore little resemblance to the gardens of England and less to those of China. They were descended by tortuous routes from the originals. For the most part sinuous paths and beds of flowers and trees made a parody of the theory of both Chinese and English landscape design, which followed rules as strictly as did Le Nôtre himself. There were, of course, exceptions as there are isolated examples of successful gardens of the French tradition in England. But a comparison between the mock romance of the gardens of the Petit Trianon, and the pure, clear compositions of those of the Grand Trianon, reveal the difference between conviction and affectation.

The informal and landscape garden remained alien to the genius loci of France and to the qualities of the French mind, and in the nineteenth century there was a return to the Le Nôtre tradition. Duchêne brought back the rigid classic principles, and in hundreds of his restorations and in new work the typical French garden can be seen again and has not yet ceded to a new tradition. Does this mean that so far no other style has satisfied the French intellect and temperament? It may be so, for it responds to a love of form and logic and a hatred of compromise that is both their strength and weakness. Thus far the revival is justified, for, in gardens as in architecture, clinging to an old national tradition can have happier results than importing styles foreign to the land and people. But in both cases it is only second best to the vitality of a style which is both contemporary and local; for while it translates the constant factors of the genius of place and people, it ignores the changes of social life and outlook. To the extent that the classical French garden expressed the power and magnificence of the monarchy, so it must fail in truth to-day.

CHAPTER SIX

THE ENGLISH GARDEN

E VERY sphere of the nation's life is influenced by England's position
as the western outpost of Europe, receiving through the centuries
the last wave of each invading race and each movement of thought
which flows across the continent from the East; and the history of English
gardens has followed the general pattern. One after another foreign
influences have come in, and have each gone through the process of
selection and digestion, until from them has emerged something which is
typically English.

ROMAN AND MEDIEVAL GARDENS

The gardens attached to the Roman villas were an incident, out of the
stream of the country's history. They came, a fully formed tradition from
an advanced civilization, and were set down without context in a land
which, as far as we know, had no native gardens. As far as design goes it
is improbable that they left any mark, but they nevertheless made their
contribution by introducing new plants, among them the Sweet Chestnut
and the Vine. They also introduced topiary, but whether this tradition
survived or was re-introduced is not certain.

The Dark Ages following the Roman withdrawal were hardly
conducive to the peaceful arts, and it is not surprising that the next
appearance of recognizable gardens was within the shelter of monastery
walls. Throughout the centuries of barbarism the monks kept alive
learning and the arts, and since the monasteries were self-supporting
communities it was natural that husbandry should have been one of their
especial concerns. The essential needs were fish-ponds, vines, herbs
vegetables for food and medical supplies, flowers for the altar. These
suggest a garden of satisfying simplicity, and to its making would be
brought a love of good craftsmanship, a sense of unhurried continuity
and an atmosphere of meditation. In addition to these happy conditions,
the monasteries chose sites in the fertile sheltered valleys and, the Orders
being international, were able to draw on the accumulated skill and

knowledge of all Europe. In these gardens we probably have the first foreign influence which was to be drawn into the veins of the English tradition.

Outside the monasteries fenced plots about the Saxons' cottages started a purely indigenous tradition that has persisted independently of all imported fashions and has developed into the typical cottage garden; differing in size and in diversity of plants from its Saxon ancestor, yet clearly a lineal descendant.

In due course a secular parallel to the monastery garden developed within the defences of the medieval castles. It is easy to imagine what the lady of the castle required of her garden: first, herbs for her simples and fruits for her preserves, but also, and intensely, she must have desired a sweet-smelling place of solitude away from the stench and turmoil of the baronial hall. Above all in that age people craved security. The garden must be small, safe and enclosed. Only gradually, as confidence grew, did it expand and unfold, and each liberating step came as the result of some historic event. After Henry II had brought some sense of peace, the garden crept out from the castle wall and was enclosed by thorn or wattle, still on the defensive but growing in confidence. At the same time, in the increasing wealth and security of the cities, the first town gardens appeared.

The unrest of the Wars of the Roses brought a check and it was not until peace came again that the next step was taken which was to lead on to the typical Tudor garden.

Both monastery gardens and secular medieval gardens followed very much the same lines in England as in France. Simple in outline but not usually symmetrical, they were unrelated to the building and always enclosed, either by a wall or a thorn or wattle fence or, in later years, by trellis or pleached trees. The beds were filled with herbs and flowers; sometimes they were raised and turfed, with flowers growing in the grass, a method of planting not unlike the most modern school of Scandinavian thought.

The idea of using water decoratively was brought back by the Crusaders in very early days and forms a link between the garden of the oasis and the medieval cloister. This usually took the form of a well or fountain used as a central feature at the crossing of the paths. Turf seats were popular, where one could sit in the sun, and so were arbours of trellis and growing plants, to give shade. One of the first signs of a wish to look beyond the strict seclusion of the garden and view the hostile outside world from a safe distance was the formation of mounts. In the early gardens these were very simple affairs, but they were elaborated in Tudor gardens. Bacon in his essay, *Of Gardens*, describes one thirty feet high, approached by a bulwarked path up which four could walk abreast and topped by a banqueting hall complete with chimneys. In some cases these mounts stood within the gardens, in others they took the form of raised banks at the sides or ends. An old plan of Montacute, Somerset, shows one within the garden on the north side of the house, surmounted by a tree, and examples may still be seen in the gardens of Merton and Corpus Christi Colleges in Oxford.

Unfortunately, we can judge of the pre-Tudor gardens only from pictures. But from the examples in Chaucer's *The Romance of the Rose*, they must have been delightful places: un-selfconscious, and filling perfectly the needs of their owners.

THE TUDOR GARDEN

There is no hard and fast line between the medieval and the Tudor garden, but the trend of history after the end of the Wars of the Roses had produced, by Elizabethan times, a garden very different from the sheltered enclave of the Middle Ages. The first change, a natural result of internal peace, was one of expansion and a loosening up of the defensive wall. Then came increased trade, bringing not only greater wealth but ideas and craftsmen from abroad. Stone workers from Italy brought a belated ripple of the Italian renaissance to Tudor England, and the fountains and stone work took on a new richness. Gardens became more intricate; much use was made of topiary, and the plain beds gave way to knotts, whose interlacing geometric patterns were outlined in evergreen, the ground-work of the pattern being filled in with coloured earth or stones, or sometimes with simple flowers. These knotts are quite unlike the flowing parterres of the French garden or the parterres of Italy, and in some the strap-like interlacing patterns are reminiscent of Celtic design.

While previously all that men asked of their gardens was peace from a warring world, sweet scents and fruits and flowers, they now had energy to spare and exercised it in creation. What is left of Henry VIII's garden at Hampton Court, supplemented by a contemporary description of it, gives a very good idea of the stage which gardens had reached at this time. It was extensive, complicated and ornate. The beds were surrounded with low wooden fences, painted in the Tudor colours of white and green and decorated with carved figures of the King's beasts. There were covered walks of pleached trees, ponds, knotts and a mount.

Mazes were also a usual feature of the larger Tudor gardens.

But the most important of all changes during Tudor times was the arrival of the country house as opposed to the defensive habitation

Internal peace was accepted as an established fact, while new wealth and the break-up of the monasteries led to the founding of great country estates. As long as the ground surrounding the castle had to be circumscribed by wall or moat, the garden could not be related symmetrically to the building, but now that the defences were no longer needed the garden became an extension of the house.

We can see in Montacute, with the help of old plans, the essential lines of the typical Elizabethan and early Jacobean gardens. The forecourt is unchanged in outline, although its original use as an entrance court has been changed to that of a garden. The wall and balustrade surrounding

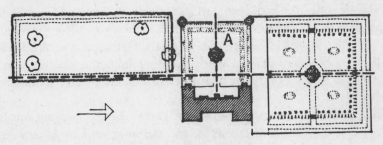

Fig. 6. Montacute. The seventeenth-century garden becomes an extension of the house. A. Forecourt.

this forecourt echoes in decorated form the idea of battlements. The castellations become richly wrought pinnacles, the turrets little temples (Plate 6). The wall itself is surmounted by a balustrade, through which the outer world can be seen. The defensive gate houses are transformed into enchanting gazebos. The whole faces onto open parkland across an intervening bowling green. At a slightly later date, it thrust its influence out into the surroundings with a broad double avenue. Originally the true garden lay to the north of the house and was probably bounded by the present raised terraces. A tree-topped mount and a rectangular pool were centred on the axis of the north door, while at one side was an area with the delicious name of the pig's wheatie orchard. An orchard formed part of almost all early gardens, and in some cases a grove of forest trees was also included.

The plan is extremely simple: the lines of the house are projected into paths, termed forthrights, while the architecture of the house is extended to embrace the forecourt and terrace. This strong linking of house and garden, and the fearless way in which it opens up to the surrounding country, makes it typical of its age and marks the final break from the medieval tradition of defensive enclosure (Fig. 6).

THE FRENCH TRADITION IN ENGLAND

As in all times of unrest, the development of gardens was checked during the Civil War and Protectorate. But with the Restoration of Charles II they received a new impetus, and a strong injection of foreign influence. Not only did it become fashionable to travel in Italy and see the gardens there, but also it was natural that Charles and his court, coming from France, should bring with them news of the great gardens being designed by Le Nôtre. Nor was the French style entirely alien to the existing tradition. Both were descendants of the Anglo-French medieval garden, with an admixture of Italian renaissance. But there were differences; the Italian influence had been far less strong in England, and certain elements of the Le Nôtre tradition—the tree and water allées for instance —were indigenous to France alone. It was, therefore, not surprising that the best results were obtained when the exact imitation was not carried too far, but was modified by the different conditions and traditions of England.

Both the hedged terrace at Polesden Lacey, Surrey, sagging into the trough of the valley as it crosses it, and the long walk at Albury Park, Surrey, attributed to Evelyn, show the happy results of allowing formal features to compromise with the lie of the land.

Kip's views give a remarkable record of the gardens of the seventeenth and eighteenth centuries, and it is interesting to compare them with de Cerceaux's views of French gardens of the previous century, to which they are analogous.

In Kip's views one can see some of the reasons why the style was not fundamentally so well suited to England as to France. Often the great patterns of radiating avenues are superimposed on the undulating English landscape in such a way that the pattern is distorted; in other cases, an unreal plain is shown covering the extent of the design and suddenly changing to the normal landscape (Plate 5). A further difference is that in most cases the surrounding landscape is one of open agriculture instead of hunting forests, with the result that the pattern of avenues becomes one of thin lines drawn on an open space, instead of the more solid French pattern of avenues cut out of the solid. This linear quality of avenues can be effective if it leads up strongly to a sufficiently important terminal, such as the main façade of the house, but repeated as a pattern, only held together by minor focal points, it lacks strength and character. Probably the most successful surviving garden of this period is Bramham Hall, Yorkshire, where the thickly wooded surroundings bring it nearer to normal French conditions.

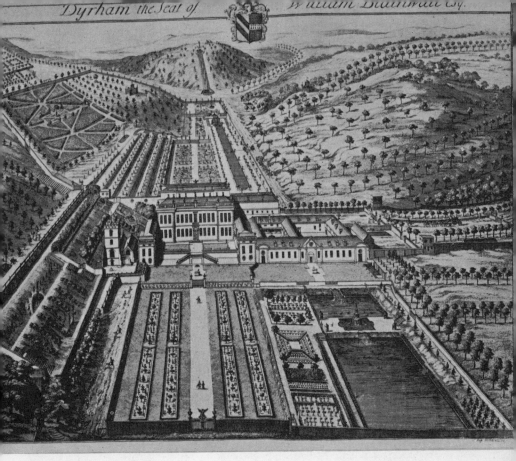

Dyrham the Seat of ... _William Blathwaite Esq._

5. One of Kip's views. The seventeenth-century gardens show the French style imposed on the English countryside, with its open undulating country in place of the thick forests of France.

6. Montacute, Somerset. Defensive battlements, no longer needed, are transmuted into decorative balustrades and gazebos.

7. The English lake. Water, which in Italy catches sunlight against dark shadows and in France gives precise reflections in a clean-cut frame, in England fades gently away into the mist and trees.

8. Stowe Park. The English version of the link between house and landscape. In its final stage of informality Stowe keeps its proportions of open and closed, its contrasts and its rhythm.

The greatest value which the tradition conferred on English gardens and landscape was its immense breadth of outlook. No English landscape architect has ever equalled Le Nôtre in courage, sense of proportion and certainty of purpose. But the works of de Caux, for instance, at Badminton were on a scale which widened the horizon of landscape architecture to a point where it was possible to lead on to the conception of using it for the planning of town and countryside.

The garden had indeed travelled far from the first tentative opening up of the Tudors. It had also changed radically in feeling. The Tudor garden was very much the simple extension of the house into the open air, the provision of extra rooms, furnished for one's individual enjoyment. The new gardens of the French tradition were both too big and too rigid to be comfortable to live in. They were rather places for the exercise of the intellect over the forces of nature. So much was this the case that often a hidden *giardino segreto* was introduced to give the intimacy and seclusion which the garden as a whole lacked, while a 'wilderness' supplied the touch of untramelled nature which was not allowed elsewhere.

In matters of detail there were parallel changes. The knotts, which had been small patterns on the floors of intimate rooms, became flowing parterres which were themselves part of the grand design, and the fountains forgot their ancestry in the Crusader's dipping wells and widened to the French tank and water allée. From this time dates the emergence of professional landscape architects, such as London and Wise, who laid out, among other gardens, the parterre and avenues at Hampton Court. (See *Gardener to Queen Anne*.)

But many of the gardens were laid out by the architect of the buildings, as the original gardens of Castle Howard, Yorkshire, and Blenheim, Oxfordshire, were by Vanbrugh. The preoccupation of landowners of this period with their gardens and estates is made wonderfully vivid in John Evelyn's diary (1640-1706). There we have a picture of an aristocracy intensely interested in 'new and curious things,' resembling their French counterparts in recognizing no bounds to the human intellect, but differing from them in their concentration on their own estates rather than on the court.

Plantations, great hedges of yew and holly, and terraces figure in these descriptions. For the first time we see the extension of gardening into the surrounding countryside. Not only was this so in the rather crude form of driving avenues across the landscape, but in the more constructive guise of Evelyn's advice on planting trees and woods to embellish gentlemen's estates and in his detailed instructions for setting thorn hedges to form the boundaries of newly-enclosed fields. Here was the seed which later was to turn all England into a garden, and it marks a turning point in the relation between landscape and garden, and in man's attitude to his surroundings.

The first gardens were places of refuge from a world where not only man was hostile, but also nature, in the guise of wolf-infested forest. Gradually nature was tamed, the forest reduced and the garden pushed its way outwards in the wake of the cultivated land. Now in the seventeenth century, the forest had almost disappeared and the land was wholly tamed. Men could not only look out from their gardens without fear of their surroundings, but they began to see the need to shape the whole landscape. At that moment in history they saw no reason to doubt that they could create a better landscape than nature's original. Doubt came later. For the moment man was in the full flush of creation.

The reign of the grand formal garden continued through the seventeenth and on into the beginning of the eighteenth century. The accession of William of Orange brought in certain Dutch features, but the influence showed itself as one of detail rather than of fundamentals. The long water canal, with its obvious derivation from the Dutch canals, the more extensive use of topiary and of clipped bays and oranges in tubs, brought, if anything, an increased stiffness to the gardens. Many orangeries date from this time, the most famous among them being that at Kensington Palace. There is a feeling of domesticity in the Dutch tradition as opposed to the greater breadth and magnificence of the French, but in its adherence to the formal and symmetrical it carried on the main stream of the classic tradition.

THE ENGLISH LANDSCAPE GARDEN

There can be no doubt that the years between Elizabeth and Anne produced in England some magnificent gardens; yet it is doubtful if they ever reached the status of a genuinely indigenous style, such as was attained by the corresponding gardens of France. It remained for England to develop her own garden, which should be as inevitable to her land, climate and spirit, as the gardens of Le Nôtre had been to those of France. But there was this great difference. Le Nôtre's garden had been the culmination of a steadily advancing tradition, while the English garden appeared as a complete break from anything which had gone before.

The Palladian Villa Rotunda, seated on its hill, with the magnificent yet humanized landscape of the Veneto flowing up to it, inspired the siting of the English eighteenth century mansion set in its own quieter landscape, but the strongest alien influence on the garden which developed round these country houses came, curiously enough, from China. From there the news of an ancient tradition of gardens based on natural landscape had come through in a fragmentary form and was referred to in the writings of Sir William Temple in 1685. Even before this, a precursor of the new trend is to be found in Francis Bacon's essay on gardens, in which he deplored the artificial extravagance of the gardens of his day and, among the attractions of his ideal garden, described a 'sweet wilderness.' Wildernesses were in fact often included in gardens from Elizabethan times onwards; there is still one in being at Hampton Court.

These were the first indications that man, having tamed nature, might crave to have her back again. In the seventeenth and early eighteenth centuries many men of letters wrote of the natural garden as their ideal. But although there is no doubt that the writings of Milton, Steele, Pope, Addison and Rousseau had a considerable influence on the changing fashion, it is probably truer to accept them as the voices of a force which was already there, rather than a prime cause of the movement. It was one of those moments in history when forces move from all directions towards a common objective and are manifested in every art. In the realm of painting, Claude Lorraine, Poussin and Salvator Rosa were undoubtedly the inspiration for many English parks, but they, too, had their roots in the same instincts which were responsible for the decline of the formal garden.

The old tradition had reached its final perfection and man's creative genius had to turn in a new direction. Moreover, the eternal struggle against nature appeared (deceptively) to have reached a point where nature was subdued and regulated; and, with the perversity of man, he proceeded to enthrone her as a goddess. In England these tendencies were reinforced by an obstinate individualism which disapproved of excessive regimentation in any form and saw a moral significance in imposing absolute rule even over plants. It was an illogical point of view, for in the 'natural garden' the designer imposes his will just as much as in the more formal. Rousseau had the heart of the matter when, in *La Nouvelle Héloise*, de Wolmar says, 'It is true that nature has done it all, but under my direction —there is nothing which I have not ordained.' The garden which strives to appear as an idealized landscape is more sophisticated than frank formality, which is man's first and natural treatment of his enclosed plot.

But, as in many English peculiarities, the apparent illogicality was based on a truth felt only instinctively, namely that Nature should be co-operated with rather than coerced; and the type of garden developed by the landscape school not only allowed for, but relied on, nature's collaboration. It was not a finite design, but one which grew slowly to perfection. There was every reason, historically and physically, why this type of garden should have grown on English soil. The slow growth to perfection was in tune with the English tradition whose very laws and constitution have grown in the same slow way, as opposed to the clear-cut code of Napoleon and the American constitution.

Land and climate were equally sympathetic. The small scale of the landscape with its gentle hills and little woods, the perfection to which trees would grow, the wonderful texture and colour of the grassland make it easy to see the whole land as an extension of the park. The climate with its misty lights and the infinite changes of the seasons gives interest and mystery to compositions which would appear dull and flat in a hard clear light. Water, which in Italy catches the bright sunlight against the black shadows, and in France gives precise reflections in a clear-cut frame, in England fades gently away into the mist and trees, blurring the reflections in opal tints (Plate 7).

Finally, the landed aristocracy were in a position to give full expression to their ideas. They were wealthy, their estates were large, and for the most part they had a strong attachment to their lands. The tradition which is revealed in John Evelyn's diary persisted in full force through the eighteenth century, and the improvement and embellishment of their estates was the first interest of many noblemen. In addition, many were men of cultivated taste. It was the age of the grand tour, when the young heir travelled Europe and saw the works of art of France and Italy. They came back enthralled with Palladian architecture and seeing visions of Claude's ideal landscapes in their own domains, where they proceeded to create an Elysium, their interpretation of the age-old ideal of the paradise garden.

The essence of the Landscape style was an idealized natural landscape, seen as a union of the Palladian architecture, which had so fired the English imagination, with the park-like countryside. It was intensely pictorial in conception and Sir Kenneth Clarke's analysis of Poussin and Claude's paintings[1] makes it clear how closely the tenets of these two artists were translated back into the medium whence they derived. Poussin's carefully constructed compositions of verticals and horizontals, based on the Golden Section, are reflected in the placing of Kent's temples and obelisks against the horizontal of the landscape view. Equally, Claude's atmospheric views of the landscape of the Golden Age, where man and nature dwelt in perfect harmony, are the very essence of the calm and gentle eighteenth century Elysiums of Kent, Brown and Repton. The elements in these compositions were land-form, water, trees and architecture, arranged with the utmost regard for pictorial composition. In them the genius of the

[1] *Landscape into Art.*

place was more respected than in any other garden tradition, except perhaps the Chinese. But this did not inhibit the most majestic schemes for local alteration to the land-form and the formation of great lakes and rivers from the smallest rivulets.

The breadth and freedom, which marked these compositions at their zenith, was not immediately achieved. The first departure from the formal garden was a tentative breaking down of the symmetrical plan into irregular gardens. Superficially, these bear little relation to the sweeping landscape parks which appeared later in the century, but they showed the way by substituting balance and a painter's composition for mathematical symmetry, and they paid due regard to the irregularities of the site and the genius of the place. Vanbrugh was an early exponent of this departure from the strictly formal and was responsible for the magnificent grounds at Castle Howard, a composed landscape on the grand scale with a strong architectural bias.

One of the first irregular gardens was at Chiswick House, Middlesex, where Lord Burlington, a man of taste and a patron of the arts, had drawn together a coterie of gifted men. His friends Pope and Gray gave the weight of their writings to the new idea, and indeed it owed much to literary inspiration, relying on association and poetic allusion to re-enforce the visual approach. Charles Bridgeman and William Kent laid out the gardens to the Palladian villa. Irregular paths wandered through the plantations between the still formal lines of the main vistas and the water took a slight meandering wave.

William Kent was destined to go further than his colleague in pursuit of a free style. He was both an architect and a painter, and although in the latter art he lacked technical skill, he turned his painter's eye to good account, and composed his ideal landscapes in trees, land-form and water, setting in them his architectural focal points of temples and bridges. The breadth and strength of his compositions can still be seen at Stowe, Rousham and Holkham.

His tradition was carried on by Lancelot ('Capability') Brown, who had been a gardener at Stowe, Buckinghamshire, while Kent was working there. He lacked Kent's architectural background and, at least sub-consciously, this may have influenced him in abandoning the last vestiges of formality in favour of the natural shapes of water, land-form and tree groups, although he too made use of buildings as focal points in his compositions and even designed houses. But in his compositions terraces were swept away and avenues broken up into groups. It is probable that he destroyed where he should have respected older work, yet there is no doubt that he left a legacy of superbly composed parks and that his skill in land-shaping and the management of water came very near genius. His setting for Vanbrugh's bridge at the entrance to Blenheim is one of the great landscape compositions of the world.

His successor was Humphry Repton. He was a less drastic man than Brown and was prepared to compromise with the convenience of his clients and permit them to retain the house terraces which Brown had banished in favour of a sweep of grass up to the house walls. He produced a series of little Red Books each containing his report to a client on the remodelling of his estate, illustrated with sketches and over-lays showing how they would appear after his improvements were effected. Fortunately a great number of these books are still in existence.

But perhaps his most far-reaching contribution was the tradition of bringing the principles of landscape into the urban scene. He worked in conjunction with Nash in the creation of Regents Park and their collaboration also resulted in some of the first tree-planted squares in London, considered by some to be our greatest contribution to civic design.

The legacy which the landscape park left has not only affected park and garden design in this country ever since, but its repercussions have been felt all over the world. Sometimes this has been in the rather unfortunate guise of the *jardin anglais*, but also, more profitably, in America and northern Europe it has been the inspiration for new and indigenous developments.

Nevertheless, in its original form it lasted a comparatively short time in full perfection.

Repton was its last great exponent and in his later years he was already trying to find a compromise with the forces which were eventually to destroy it. One of these was the desire for more flowers and more variety, and his solution for this was to conceal a series of gardens, for different kinds of flowers, within the belts of trees and shrubberies which gave the form to his main design. But at Nuneham Park, Oxfordshire, the poet Mason took the bolder but less successful step of including beds of flowers in the main body of his landscape garden, a forerunner of the decadent form of landscape garden which was to bedevil parks and gardens for the next century.

The reasons why the landscape garden could not digest beds of bright flowers are not hard to find. First, if the garden was an idealization of a natural landscape, flowers could only be introduced on a pattern recognized by nature, as, for instance, the daffodils are introduced at Stourhead, Wiltshire, or the Martagon lilies in the wilderness at St. John's College, Cambridge; flowers which are either native to the particular landscape or, by their type, arrangement and colouring, give the appearance that they might be so. Secondly, the soft tone of the English landscape was one of the bases of the landscape garden and to disrupt the tone scale with violent colour is to destroy the picture. Thirdly, the floor of the landscape park is formed by the unbroken carpet of softly-textured sward and to cut this with beds is to check the smooth flow of the design.

But while the landscape style was at its zenith, it had already been under attack from another quarter. Exponents of the picturesque, represented by Uvedale Price and Payne Knight, attacked Brown for the insipid smoothness of his ground work and the serpentine outline of his lakes, preferring the rugged bank and gnarled tree trunk to the smooth turf and well-groomed trees. Repton, with some justice, defended Brown's precepts.

The desire to create a landscape which was picturesque, in the sense that it was akin to a picture, was part of the whole conception of the landscape style, but the strength behind the landscape school was the idealisation of the normal in nature, while the picturesque and romantic movement seized upon the happy accident and the interest of deformity, which is an unsure basis for any art. There was a tendency throughout the landscape school to express this love of the picturesque in a fondness for sham ruins and even for sham hermits to dwell in them. From this cult can be traced a descent in decadence through sham bark and rustic work to the gnome-haunted rockeries of to-day.

But perhaps most potent force of all in the gradual disintegration of the landscape tradition was a general lowering of taste or, more fairly, the widening of wealth beyond the little coterie of gifted amateurs and their professional advisers. Formerly, it had been a closed society of men who admired the same pictures, read the same poetry and were steeped in the tradition of the countryside. Now, from the beginning of the nineteenth century, gardens were also required by the wealthy manufacturers, to whom Elysiums meant less than nothing. Fortunately, there are still examples of the great landscape parks sufficiently unspoilt to enable us to study them at first hand.

Stowe. (Plate 8 and Fig. 7). Of all the landscape parks of England, Stowe is perhaps the most typical of the tradition which it represents. Stourhead may vie with it as the perfectly composed landscape, but it lacks the relationship with house and countryside which was an essential part of the concept of the Palladian mansion set in an Elysian landscape and merging imperceptibly into the surrounding country. At Blenheim, Vanbrugh's bridge, set in Brown's landscape, is the supreme tableau, the stage-set which exemplifies all the magnificence and sense of form and

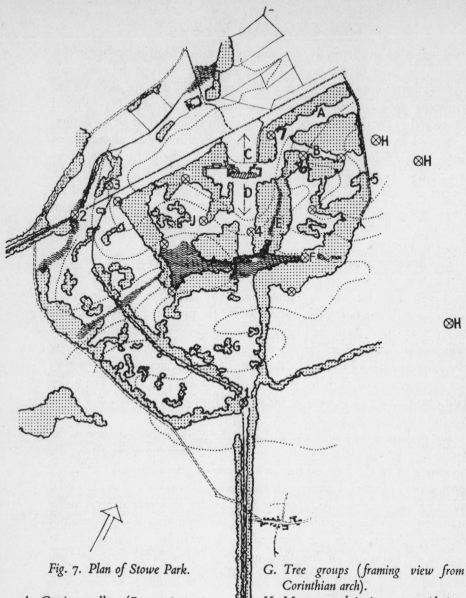

Fig. 7. Plan of Stowe Park.

A. Grecian valley (Progressive view, spear point).

B. Cleft view.

C. View over humanised country (wide open window).

D. View over idealized country (outlooking central vista).

E. Elysian fields (closed composition).

F. Palladian bridge (view disappearing into woods).

G. Tree groups (framing view from Corinthian arch).

H. Monuments bringing countryside into garden.

J. Rondo. Static view.

1. Corinthian arch.
2. Classic bridge (Oxford bridge).
3. Boycott pavilions.
4. Arch of Amelia.
5. Ha-ha.
6. Queen's house.
7. Temple of Concord.

of drama which the age possessed. But it is a static landscape. One sees, and admires, but one is not led irresistibly on, to enjoy the gradual unfolding of a landscape; and in this it lacks one of the most appealing attributes of English gardens. Stowe, on the other hand, is a landscape of movement, a garden in which life can be led and not merely a picture to be looked at.

Applying to it the test of whether it is the genuine creation of a certain way of life in a given place, it qualifies unreservedly as one of the classic gardens of the world.

The continuity of its development, the almost imperceptible stages of its evolution from Vanbrugh's original formal plan, through progressive stages of loosening up, first by Bridgeman and then by Kent, to the final idyllic landscape, follows the growth of the landscape movement in England and it epitomizes the society within which it developed: a society in which love of landscape and classical taste were general and whose members had considerable knowledge of the art of design. To this it owes the first of its many contrasts to Le Nôtre's masterpieces. These were far more the inspiration of one artist, produced for a society which could appreciate them, but could not have come within a hundred miles of creating them. Stowe, on the other hand, while mainly the creation of professionals, owed much to its owner, Lord Cobham, while Stourhead was entirely the work of an amateur.

Because of the high standard of appreciation of the men for whom it was made, Stowe renders up its full meaning only to the initiated. It is the pleasaunce of a coterie, sharing tastes, traditions and culture. It unfolds like a conversation of those times. Brilliant, lucid, laced with classical allusions, viewing the subject of discourse from all angles, discursive, yet never losing the main theme. Again, it was as complete a contrast as may be imagined to the clear, finite statement of Le Nôtre.

There is a quality of movement throughout which could have arisen only in a country where people had a love of strolling, of wandering round the grounds to admire, to discourse and to plan further improvements. There is no place in the composition where it can be said that finality is reached. Always there is the invitation to explore further, the glimpse of another temple on the far side of the water, another archway at the end of the vista.

The feeling of movement is vibrant in every part of the composition. In the Grecian valley, the gently rolling contours, punctuated by the accent of the dark groups of Scots pines, flow with the rhythm of a rippling stream. This is an understandable analogy, if the account by Marshall is true that Brown in his early days intended this valley for a river, but found, as many to their cost have found, that water will not stay on the slope of a hill. The planting, belonging to the era of Kent and Brown, contributes to the movement, the prevalence of beech with its flowing outline giving a soft, rolling background to the picture, while the ever-greens chosen are the Lebanon cedars with their spreading, interlocking habit of growth, yews, rounded and solid, and Scots pine, notes of accent, but accent in motion (Fig. 8).

In the original plan punctuation marks were provided only by the

Fig. 8. Fastigiate trees give static accent of finality, Scots pine an accent in motion.

temples and obelisks, not by trees which formed instead the massive background to the composition. Only the later plantings have introduced the fastigiate trees, disrupting the flow of movement by bringing the eye to a sudden stop with an exclamation mark. In gardens with closed vistas these fastigiate shapes can play an important part, but here they are curiously out of place. For this theme of continuous movement is perhaps the most striking characteristic of the garden. It is exemplified in the great South Avenue whose undulations are brillantly accentuated by the use of rounded static beech in the hollows, contrasting with the movement of the elms on the higher ground, while the folds of the ground which the avenue crosses at right angles are used to give a constantly changing view as one approaches (See Fig. 9).

First comes the view of the Corinthian arch, with a distant glimpse of the house seen through it; then the arch framing only the sky, then the portico of the house filling the arch. It is a brilliant series of allurements, with the great climax, when the arch is at last reached, of the house fully revealed across the park, with the stage wings of trees on each side framing and giving perspective to as finely composed a view as Claude himself could have devised. At this point the drive turns aside, a masterly stroke of stage management. To have continued on with the house still in view would have been an anti-climax, as well as transgressing one of the landscape school's dictums—'The foot should never tread by the same path that the eye has travelled over before.' Also, it would have involved cutting across the grass with a roadway and eventually bridging the water, which, while invisible from the Corinthian arch, must essentially remain as an unbroken stretch of water when seen from the house. Therefore, the drive turns away to the left and gives a preliminary glimpse of joys which are eventually to be revealed. It crosses the water by a classic bridge, climbs the hill between the two dramatic sentinels of Vanbrugh's Boycott pavilions, and arrives at the house on the north side. What more English method of approach could there be?

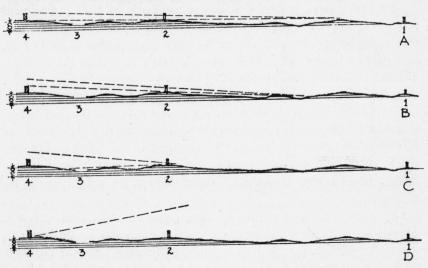

Fig. 9. Section of Stowe avenue. A. From a little distance up the avenue the house can be seen framed by the Corinthian arch. B. Further on, the sky only can be seen through the arch. C. From the Corinthian Arch, the house can be seen but not the lake. D. From the house both lake and arch can be seen. 1. Entrance gate; 2. Corinthian arch, 3. Lake; 4. House.

On a smaller scale this changing view from different points is followed out throughout the composition. The lovely little arch of Amelia when seen from below is a window opening on to the sky from the closed-in landscape of the Elysian fields, but at close quarters it is the frame for the smooth lawns leading up to the house. Equally, the treatment of the water is a poem in rhythmic movement. Springing from the dark recesses of the grotto, it flows small and narrow through the Elysian fields, expands to reflect the classic proportions of the Palladian bridge, widens again into the serene expanse of the central lake, shapes itself idyllically at the foot of the rondo, and flows away in a gentle stream under the Oxford bridge, contracting and expanding rhythmically throughout its length.

In tune with the movement of the composition, there is a sense of movement in time which gives a kinship with the ever-changing English climate and which recognises the element of growth which is an essential part of the typical English garden. The varying lights, the different seasons, are all as much a part of the design as the changing approaches to each view-point.

Historically it represents a gentle growth throughout the period of the great landscape gardens. The original outline, marked by a ha-ha and double line of trees, is shown in Bridgeman's plan of 1739 and remains there to this day. In the plan of 1763, showing Kent's idyllic landscape, the strong central vista of the earlier plan remains, but is flanked on each side by irregularities. The water has taken on a freer shape, but it still has its central obelisk. By 1777 there had been a further melting away of formality and the water had taken on its present free shape. But the bones of the design, with the strong central vista, and the distribution of closed and open areas, remains unchanged from the first plan. There are differences of opinion as to whether Brown had any hand in the later developments, but it seems probable that he did and that the considerable change between the plans of 1763 and 1777 owes something to his influence.

The progression was within a single phase of civilization and it is difficult to say now, with certainty, which part should be attributed to whom, for all is in tune and all is gently progressive, until the period is reached when the sure touch was lost in a general lowering of taste.

Almost every canon of the eighteenth century landscape design has its example here. The relationship between house, park and countryside is perfectly illustrated. On the north side the farmland comes close to the forecourt, subjected only to the slight sophistication of flanking wings of trees and the view of an obelisk. The house here is a part of the agricultural landscape from which it draws its being. But pass through the great hall of the building, out on to the terrace, and the natural countryside has vanished and is replaced by an idealized version of itself. It is sophisticated, improved, perfect in every detail and set about with the temples and arches of an Albano landscape. Straight ahead the grassy slope, flanked by dark trees, sweeps down to the central lake, then rises again to the Corinthian arch on the horizon. Beyond the arch the great avenue stretches away towards Buckingham. Yet it is a thin avenue compared to those which cut through the forest from Versailles; the country laps it about on each side, and in fact all the views out from the garden fade away into natural landscape, either as distant views or as wooded creeks. The masterful avenues of the French school mistrusted the countryside and overrode it, but here the countryside is recognized as an extension of the garden, the prototype from which Elysium is evolved.

If Stowe has a fault, it is the over-use of buildings to humanize and idealize the landscape. To-day the number of temples, arches, obelisks and bridges is not perhaps excessive, but since many have been destroyed there may well have been justice in Marshall's criticism that there was 'heaviness of planting and too many buildings. . . .' Nevertheless, there could scarcely be a more complete example of the way in which architectural features can be used not only to humanize but also to give cohesion. By them, distant views are brought into the composition, the eye is led to the desired position, and the feet are also led inevitably to the particular object which is dominant in each view. They are signposts which ensure that the symphony is unfolded in its proper sequence. They are also frequently used as the connecting links between changes in scene and mood. The Queen's House looks out in one direction to the Temple of Concord—a closed view of tranquillity; on the other side the view leads away to the open country, and is exploratory.

The architectural quality of these buildings, many by Kent and Vanbrugh, is not only a delight in itself, but they are atuned to the spirit of the place and suffer none of the common ills of garden buildings, for they are neither pompous, facetious nor apologetic.

Their siting is brilliant. Most are given a setting of trees, but others make full use of the dramatic possibilities of siting against the sky. Thus, as the approach drive climbs the hill the Boycott pavilions are seen silhouetted on the crown of the hill. Most of the temples are on slight knolls, to accentuate their importance as focal points. The land-form throughout is beautifully managed and illustrates its informal use as opposed to the terracing of the renaissance gardens. It is a tribute to the designers that it is now impossible to say with certainty where the contours are contrived and where natural. The existing ground form was used to the greatest advantage and the general lines of the hills and valleys have obviously dictated the design. But there are places where major artificial contouring has evidently taken place and others where there has almost certainly been at least local shaping. The rippling formation of the Grecian valley may have been suggested by the natural ground form, but there must surely have been some skilful accentuation of it, in addition to its exploitation by rhythmic planting. On the great south avenue there is a skilful treatment of cross-falls, successive folds falling in opposite directions, in such a way that they balance each other and guide the line of vision down the centre of the avenue (See Fig. 10).

Beyond all these characteristics which make it the embodiment of the

English landscape school, Stowe has also in the strongest degree the virtues which make a masterpiece in any tradition. In spite of the apparent freedom of the treatment, it is bound together by a strong sense of unity and is as strictly composed as a sonnet, contrasting in this respect with the lax and formless creations that are sometimes called landscape gardens to-day. The parts are in exact relationship to each other, each movement leading on inevitably to the next. For this reason, in spite of its size and complexity, the plan is easy to grasp.

Fig. 10. The Great Avenue, Stowe. Cross-falls balance each other and guide the eye down the centre.

The house itself is carefully placed at the critical point on the brow of the hill. The broad, open magnificence of the central vista is flanked on one side by the closed-in, intimate composition of the Elysian fields, on the other by the series of idyllic views looking one to the other across the rondo. Both are in-looking as opposed to the out-looking central vista, but of completely contrasted characters. All three movements are bound together by the theme of the water. On the west side the feeling of rounded enclosure is continued—by the encircling stream, the entrance drive and the tree belt—and on the south-east side woods close in beyond the Palladian bridge and the Elysian fields. But to the north-east the Grecian valley thrusts out again into the surrounding country, so that we have the contrast of the wide open window straight on to the country at the north front, the magnificent classical view of the south front, and the narrow intriguing spear-point of the Grecian valley. Thus within the cohesion of the general design there is that variety of individual parts which is an essential quality of a great garden.

The third great quality which it possesses is 'proportion in all its parts' and proportion with man himself. This is undoubtedly one of the reasons for the deep sense of contentment which it brings. It is magnificent but not overpowering. The invitations from one view to the next do not ask for undue exertion. The extent of the central vista is nicely held within its flanking woodlands; nowhere is there an open space large enough to give a feeling of exposure, while in the closed areas of the Elysian fields there are frequent windows out into the open glades beyond, so that there is never a feeling of oppression. Thus, although the contrast between the closed and open spaces are kept always distinct, there is never too much of either.

In detail, the south avenue is an essay in proportion. The trees are now about 80 feet high and are spaced 30 feet apart along an avenue 150 feet wide and over a mile long. This belies the statement sometimes made that an avenue cannot be achieved across the width of a modern road. But it does show that for success the trees must be close together, big enough, and the avenue long enough. It is a different type of avenue from the tall narrow approach as exemplified by the famous beech avenue at Savernake. In the latter, the telling feature is the trunks of the trees, but in the Stowe avenue it is the trees as a whole which frame the avenue and, to get its effect, it must, therefore, be seen on a long perspective (Fig. 10).

There is still another quality which a garden should possess to earn the highest place in history as a classic design. Although conceived for a particular age, it must have the power of survival into another age. The great gardens of the renaissance undoubtedly have this power. Although they may lack the final touch of the people for whom they were created, they are, nevertheless, still great works of art. The thronging crowds of tourists at the Villa D'Este, however different they may be from the cardinal's entourage of the fifteenth century, cannot rob it of its quality. The Belvedere in Vienna is great enough to accept the little children's play-places within the shadow of its bosquets. For the English garden, with its emphasis on growth and movement rather than on finality, the case is more difficult because the framework is less strong and rigid. Nevertheless, Stowe undoubtedly survives by the strength and grandeur of its original conception. Probably its finest time was a hundred years ago when the trees planted by Kent and Brown must already have achieved some stature and before too much damage was wrought by changing tastes and finally changing uses.

The ground form, the disposition of mass and void, the relationship of the garden to the house and countryside, the composition of one part with another, and, in most cases, the architectural features remain and are sufficient to preserve the entity. But the planting, more transitory than any of these, has lost some of the unity which was essential to perfection. We have already referred to the fastigiate trees whose unwanted punctuation disrupts the rhythmic movement. But, equally, the colour harmony has been disrupted by the introduction of glaucous trees. *Cedrus atlantica glauca* now replaces part of the great peripheral belt of *Cedrus libani*. The varying greens of the deciduous trees, changing in every light and season and given weight and solidarity by the black-green of the conifers, form a symphony which does not want glaucous blue, nor gold, nor plum purple. To use these as replacements for the original trees is like restoring a Rembrandt with Picasso blue. These misplaced innovations are due only to so complete a change in the climate of taste that the original intention of the artist is not grasped, and once this is realized there is no impediment to replacing the old trees, as they die, with the same species.

But other changes which have come to Stowe, as to so many other of the great landscape parks, raise genuine difficulties. That the use has changed from a great household to a school is an unavoidable accident of history and in many ways a fortunate one, since it has preserved the house and its grounds in good order. But it has meant that new buildings of some size have had to be built. At least one of these occupies a place of such importance that it vies with the house itself as the dominant feature of a view. The temples are in some cases in places of great prominence, but by their nature and small size they never leave one in any doubt that they are subsidiary to the landscape; only the house itself was allowed to dominate it.

In still another direction Stowe must have lost some of its perfection. As in all other parts of the country, the water level has fallen and in many places one can trace the larger areas of lake which were once there. In particular, the Elysian fields have suffered, weeds now covering much of the remaining water surface. More clear water space would give greater simplicity to an area which now errs on the side of fussiness, and indeed throughout there is a tendency to overgrowth and lack of clarity.

But while the problem of maintaining the gardens of a bygone age are many, yet Stowe, with its clear-cut composition and its lucid lines, should prove no more impossible to preserve as a work of art than the more rigid, but no more coherently designed, gardens of France and Italy.

NINETEENTH CENTURY GARDENS

We have seen how towards the end of the landscape period there was a return to formal lines in the shape of terraces and of enclosed gardens within the still informal plantations.

But in 1820 there was a far more fundamental return to formality. The Italian revival headed by Barry re-introduced old elements of the Italian garden—the axial design, the terraces, the balustrades, the urns and the parterres. It was a natural reaction to the extremes of the picturesque and the decline of the landscape gardens, but it was devoid of any fresh impulse which could have given new life to the old formula. It had in it all the features which we have seen in Italy and later in France, but they were repeated without the joyous invention and magnificent craftsmanship of the renaissance or the lucid classicism of the French. Moreover, they were combined with a new factor which was to influence gardens with increasing force for the next century. This was the huge influx of plant material and the desire to have more and brighter flowers.

Flowers as individuals had been eclipsed since medieval times. In the landscape garden they were not used at all in the main picture, their place being in the walled kitchen gardens, screened from general view. They were almost as hard to accommodate in the formal French and Italian gardens. They were too insistent as individuals and swamped what should have been the dominant pattern of parterres and terraces. But all through the nineteenth century the flood of plants grew. They came from the hybridisers and were brought back by explorers from the New World and the East.

There was also a growing fashion for heated greenhouses in which to raise the brilliant tropical bedding plants; and having raised them, beds must be found in the garden for setting them out in summer. All these factors coincided with the general lowering of taste and a growing desire for ostentation.

As in many other walks of life the nineteenth century in gardening was a time of muddle. The landscape tradition deteriorated into winding paths, snaky shrubberies and beds of flowers, while the formal tradition took its uninspired way through the Italian revival. Finally, the two styles met in an unhappy marriage. Determined to have the best of every possible world, terraces, sunk gardens, parterres and urns struggled for supremacy against winding paths and cut-up grass. These gardens show a curious lack of understanding of the principles which underlay either of the great traditions. Certainly they did not begin to solve the problem of making good use of the new plant material, which had been partly responsible for the departure from the old styles.

Perhaps the best gardens of this period were those where the exotic luxuriance of some of the new plants was used to create a romantic landscape far more lush and closed in than in the eighteenth century style and often combined with rocky streams reminiscent of the picturesque tradition. They suggest a painting by Douanier Rousseau rather than by Claude. Some charming gardens in this style are attributed to Joseph Paxton.

The first man who seriously tackled the problem of using a wide range of hardy plants was William Robinson. He cannot rank as one of the great garden designers, because it is doubtful if he saw the garden as a whole, but he was a supreme plantsman and his influence in teaching the right use of plant material places him as the forerunner of modern planting design.

Like most pioneers, he was highly prejudiced and would have banished bedding plants, topiary and all formality, allowing only plants hardy to the soil and climate, and insisting that these should grow in their own natural way. His influence at that time was entirely salutary and his broad commonsense was combined with a natural sensitivity which showed in his use and grouping of hardy plants.

His own garden at Gravetye showed the possibilities of creating landscapes with the use of a great variety of hardy plants, provided they were given the right setting and planted in broad and simple masses. The sheets of lythrum beside the lake, and the English version of an alpine meadow with anemones and tulip species grown in the grass, were forerunners of a modern tradition of planting which has spread all over the world.

A healthy sign that genuine interest in gardens was beginning to reawaken was the virulent battle which was joined between Robinson, the advocate of informality, and Blomfield, the champion of the architectural garden. Neither would admit that there could be compromise, but in fact a compromise was reached by their immediate successors, Gertrude Jekyll and Edwin Lutyens.

Gertrude Jekyll carried on the Robinson tradition. Her eye for plant grouping has never been bettered and she combined this with a deep personal knowledge of plants and a winning pen which brought her theories to a very wide public, particularly to the owners of country houses. She was largely responsible for the cult of the herbaceous border, which at its best has enriched the tradition of English gardens. Her writings and those of William Robinson, in the *English Flower Garden*, brought about an enlarged version of the old cottage gardens, which had continued their quiet way since Saxon days, oblivious to fashion's changes except for the introduction of a few new plants.

Sir Edwin Lutyens carried his architectural style into his gardens, creating formal extensions of his houses which, while based on the old classic formula, may be considered as a style of their own; albeit one which was short lived, for the era of architecture to which it was attached was near its end. Unlike Blomfield, he recognized that the informal might also have its place, at a distance from the house, and called in Gertrude Jekyll to plant his formal gardens and add to them her delightful excursions into woodland gardens. The partnership resulted in some very pleasant gardens of distinctive form. They were curious in consisting of two quite separate influences—the architectural garden forming an extension of the house and the informal linking it to the surrounding country and sending its outliers into the house's domain.

This was the general pattern of domestic gardens from the end of the nineteenth century until the second world war. Its weakness lay in its lack of unity and in the fact that it was possible only for gardens of a certain size; for the break between formal and informal there had to be room for an area of transition. Copied on a smaller scale in thousands of villa gardens it produced the unrest of warring features. It was at best a working compromise for an age of transition.

During the last fifty years a second type of garden has evolved, in which the richness of the new plant material is held within a framework of open air rooms. Sissinghurst, Hidcote and Tintinhull are all variations of this theme and they all succeed because the architectural form of the enclosures is strong enough to contain the plants. The arrangement has something in common with the Spanish garden, where the most luxuriant flowers cascade within the firm outline of a box hedge.

That, perhaps, is the last style which can rank as historical. The modern tradition which is evolving has not yet crystallized, but certain trends can be discerned and to see them at their clearest, we should look to Northern Europe on one hand and to America on the other.

Hidcote—The Plantsman's Garden. The garden at Hidcote Manor, Gloucestershire, has the right to a place in garden history, because in it an aspect of contemporary life has found expression as a work of art.

No completely satisfying garden style has evolved in England since the great landscape parks and gardens of the eighteenth century. Their greatness lay in the perfect synthesis which they achieved between the English countryside and the philosophy and way of life of their owners. Ever since these perfect but flowerless landscape compositions ceased to satisfy the Englishman's ideal of a garden, there has been a groping after some new form. There have been attempts to compress the landscape garden's spacious lines into cramped spaces and to enliven its austerity with beds of flowers. When these expediencies proved unsatisfactory, efforts were made to find what was missing by bringing back the motifs of Tudor and Renaissance gardens. But since these motifs were lifted from their context without any understanding of their underlying reason, they could not be made to fill a need which was the result of changed conditions.

One of the greatest of these changes was the influx of new plant material which encouraged a love of growing and collecting plants for their own sakes. In catering for this new class of plant enthusiasts, gardens had to serve a new function.

They were no longer only places of peace and seclusion, as the medieval gardens had been, even less were they places of display like the French gardens of the Renaissance. Instead, they were primarily workshops, in which the owners could enjoy their hobby of collecting and growing plants. Thus they became the creations, not of artists but of gardeners. As a result their value as pictorial compositions tended to be subordinated to the individual interest of the plants.

These purely horticultural gardens are commoner than any other type in England to-day. The individual plants and sometimes the groupings of colour and texture often give pleasant enough pictures, but in general they suffer from lack of stability, form and repose, and the very diversity of their planting is monotonous because its contrasts are on too small a scale and too often repeated. They have none of the clear distinction between open space and dense planting which is seen in the French gardens, with their open avenues and flat parterres cut out of a background of thick bosquets, and in the English landscape gardens, with their trees set in clumps and belts against a background of open sweeps of grass. They also lack any clear rhythm of progression or sense of space enclosure.

It is true that these shortcomings can be overcome by restraint in the selection of planting material whereby the plant-forms themselves can be used to create the mass and void, the space enclosure and the large scale contrast of colour and texture. But this places a limit on the choice and variety of plant material. Large masses of a few selected plants must be used and the introduction of endless variety must be sacrificed in the interests of the picture as a whole. Therefore, while in many cases it is the right solution, it is only a partial answer to the needs of a real plant enthusiast, who requires that no bounds whatever shall be placed on his freedom of choice.

At Hidcote an attempt has been made to solve the problem on quite different lines. Here no limit is placed on the variety of plants grown, but the flowering plants are used as the furnishing for a series of open-air rooms and passages, enclosed by high hedges and trees. These green walls give the composition a solid and permanent framework. There is a rhythmic progression in the way the enclosures lead into each other, great use being made of contraction and expansion, the in and out principle of architectural composition. The pattern of solid and void is given by the contrast between the close planting in some rooms and the emptiness of others.

The plan is dominated by a long central walk, which gives cohesion to the whole design. On the south side is a series of enclosed gardens leading one into another. The layout on this side is intricate, small-scaled and closely planted. But to the north there is the complete contrast of a large, simply shaped lawn having as its only features two groups of great beech.

Beyond the lawn is a beechwood, still simple, but contrasting in its fine dappled texture with the smooth green of the lawn.

Thus we have a clear pattern of progression: first, the small enclosures, filled with detail and carved from the surrounding walls of green; then the vertically cleft opening of the long walk, richly designed and full of interest, but larger in scale; then the complete openness of the big lawn; and finally the closure of the beechwood.

This contrast in treatment between one space and another, which gives the plan as a whole its virtue, is repeated in the detailed design. This is well shown in the sequence of gardens containing the round pool. Leading off from the main walk there is first a small enclosure filled with an intricate box-edged parterre. Steps down from this lead to a roughly circular hedged garden almost completely filled with a large, still pool. Because the space is filled only with water and the massive shapes of the surrounding foliage plants, the effect is rich yet peaceful (Plate 9). Had the pool been in a more orthodox proportion to its enclosure, the simplicity would have been lost, and the garden would have become patterned and lacking in contrast to its parterred predecessor. Beyond the pool garden is a small round of grass surrounded by yew; an empty room completing the progression from intricacy to simplicity.

It is this application of the universal laws of composition which lifts Hidcote so far above a mere plant collection and makes it something more than a re-hash of other garden styles.

There are elements in it reminiscent of many other countries and ages, but the way in which they are used welds them into a fresh and individual creation which could have developed only in its own place and context.

The good soil and climate, encouraging easy growth, combined with the need for shelter at an elevation of 500 feet, make it reasonable that the solid planted area should dominate, the open spaces being carved out from the background of sheltering trees and hedges. This sense of enclosure, of the dominance of vertical over horizontal, is one of Hidcote's most characteristic features. To some it is oppressive, yet it is founded on sound reasons and to it the garden owes much of its curious individual attraction.

The contours of the site are reflected in the many steps and changes of level from one garden to the next, but their most striking use is in the gradual stepping up of the main vista and its termination in open sky. It is an effective device which kindles the desire to know what lies beyond that empty space, and it is led up to with great skill by the building up of the flanking hedges and massed trees and by the use of a receding series of projecting walls and hedges in the form of stage wings. It would require a superhuman act of will to refrain from walking up it (Plate 10).

There are variants of this theme throughout the design and it marks a departure from the classical conception of a vista. None of the main vistas at Hidcote is terminated by a feature. Instead of giving the eye something on which it can rest and be content, they lure it on by an air of mystery, by the knowledge that there is something round the corner. The great cedar, which is perhaps the finest tree at Hidcote, is just off centre, both from the main walk and from the cross vista. This unorthodox treatment suggests that classic features have not been blindly copied, but have been adapted to serve new ideas. It is the psychological and practical reasons behind the design which give to it significance as a work of art. Hidcote is the creation of an active man and of one to whom a garden is an end in itself. It is not only a place in which to stroll and sit, but a place in which to work. If it is somewhere in which to talk with one's friends, the talk will be mostly of the garden itself and the plants in it. It is a world self-contained and absorbing, having curiously little connection with the house, nor much with the surrounding country. It is a garden to be looked at from within, not from without. In other days a garden has been a setting for a man's life, an extension of his house, an adjunct to the other arts, rather than providing a complete interest in itself. The great classic gardens are finished compositions: one can admire them and philosophize in them, but one cannot play with them; whereas the hedged enclosures of Hidcote are a series of rooms in which the furniture can be endlessly rearranged.

If the garden is to be a place in which to sit and meditate on other things, then ones eyes must rest quietly on the static view and closed vista. If it is a place in which to stroll and philosophize, then one needs the long, unbroken walk, like John Evelyn's great terraces at Albury. But Hidcote is for neither of these things. It is for those who want to be led on by the interest of the place itself, to proceed slowly plant by plant. Apart from one long grass ride, which is the least satisfactory feature of the garden, there are no straightforward walks, nor any static views. Even along the main walk the path divides and turns aside, while its whole design is an invitation to explore. Once off the main walk, there are constant interruptions of steps and sudden turns in the paths. The great lawn has no straightforward access at all from the rest of the garden. The openings between the small gardens are often so narrow that two could not walk abreast and sometimes even one must squeeze through. The in and out motif is played almost to excess. But it is understandable when it is related to the natural desire for a small enclosed space in which to pursue a hobby.

Just as the old motif of the vista is given a new twist, so is topiary used in an individual way. Here the quality valued is solidity, not intricacy, and

9. The pool at Hidcote. Because the space is filled entirely with water surrounded by the massive shapes of foliage plants, the effect is rich yet peaceful.

10. Hidcote. The main vista is stepped up and terminates in open sky.

11. A Scandinavian Garden (Eywin Langkilde).

12. American landscape architects show the imaginative use of materials in garden design—a garden by Lawrence Halprin.

instead of being used as formal punctuation marks set down on a background of open space, it is combined with the hedges and trees to form a solid background out of which the open spaces are carved. This gives a sculptural quality to the garden. There is a comfortable solidity about it. The asymmetric build-up of hedges, *Quercus ilex* and cedar looking east down the main walk, is a notable composition in mass. Within the small gardens the massive, solid forms of clipped box and yew, with their rich, dark, even texture are the ideal foil for the loose textured and often rather fussy flowering plants. But they have another role, as well as that of steadying down the more varied planting. In the gardens of all ages men have felt the need to introduce some symbol of conscious art. Hitherto this has taken the form of statuary and architecture. But the subtleties of classic sculpture call for the simplest settings. Statues are seen to perfection against the dark ilex of the Boboli and classic temples on the smooth green hills of Brown and Repton. Their place is not among the spraying foliage of an English flower garden. At Hidcote this is recognized and the only urns and statues are kept away from flowers and used to light up a niche against a dark hedge. But among the flowers, the conscious form is supplied by the topiary, sometimes clipped to an architectural form, or a conventional bird, sometimes to a freer shape, akin to the more massive style of modern sculpture. But the great bulk of these yews gives a sense of scale which could not be achieved by even the largest piece of sculpture. The fearlessness with which plants are used as architectural forms is a significant feature in a garden whose informal planting is in direct descent from the purely naturalistic school of Robinson and Jekyll.

Not only is the scaffolding of the garden built with walls and buttresses, arches and pilasters of living material, but there is an ingenious use of the trunks and branches of trees as architectural elements.

One of the best known features in the garden is the double colonnade of the grey trunks of hornbeam flanking a section of the main walk. It is the theme of the central nave and side aisles. Elsewhere, limes are trained to make a low, wide, vaulted passage with splayed sides sweeping together in a Tudor arch. Close by, a complete contrast is given by a view down a high narrow cleft, formed by tall clipped yews, springing outwards from a narrow base. One of the most successful arcades of all is the path through the beechwood leading north from the big lawn. It is flanked by close-spaced slender grey trunks of young beech and combines a satisfying approach to the garden with an easy transition to the natural woodland.

The parallel with architecture in the use of hedged rooms is emphasized by an interesting use of texture on these living walls. Some hedges are entirely of yew, some of beech, other of box, contrasting with one another, but each in itself providing an unbroken background. But where the hedges are of great height and stand clear of other planting, they are given a mottled texture and change of colour by combining beech and holly, or holly and yew, in one hedge.

This care for texture is apparent in the best examples of the detailed planting, for the division of the garden into a series of rooms enables the planting of each section to be selective.

One small enclosure relies for its character on spikes of thin, grey leaves, of yucca piercing through a fine-textured silver hypericum. In the pool garden great care has been taken to keep all the foliage in scale and to use plants with a dignified and sculptural quality, such as magnolia, mahonia and osmanthus. A very simple passage garden is planted entirely with a groundwork of iris foetidissima and hellebore, a shrub layer of species of hydrangeas and a background of cerasus. The device of giving harmony by allowing only a few plants to dominate any one scene is carried through the larger framework of the garden, which is dominated by the hedges, the *Quercus ilex* and the beech.

This use of selective plant composition on two levels, the higher one on a large scale and the lower level on a small scale, is dependent on the space enclosures being above eye level; another reason for Hidcote's vertical emphasis.

Hidcote, because of its strong permanent framework, has a greater prospect of endurance than most plantsmens' gardens, and yet its full beauty is dependent on the rightness of the furnishings within the walled rooms. The subtleties of texture, the contrast between the contents of one room and the next, are an essential part of it. If it is no longer used for the purpose for which it was made, and ceases to be the plaything of one who combines a love of plants with an artist's eye, it may lose its place as an outstanding work of art. Its intricate space division, robbed of the reason which gave it validity, might become tiresome. Will it be like a house for the dual purpose of housing a collection of beautiful furniture and making a home for its owner? Without the right furnishings, the design becomes pointless; without the owner, it becomes a museum.

CHAPTER SEVEN

THE CONTEMPORARY GARDEN

THE most recent of the long historic line of garden traditions which is now evolving in America began to emerge in Northern Europe during the first half of the century. It shows distant descent from the English landscape garden, overlaid with the Robinson-Jekyll tradition of planting, and a strong strain of Japanese influence, while the impulse of the Bauhaus school of architecture gave it a twist towards a new use of free form.

From this sprang a recognizable type of garden associated particularly with Scandinavia, remarkable for its domestic quality and its deceptive air of casualness. These are comfortable, unassuming gardens, relying, as cottage architecture does, on simplicity and sensitivity to organic growth. Ostentation or a heavy hand destroys them. Historically they are important because they set a standard of attainable excellence for the small and modest garden (Plate 11).

In Switzerland, gardens by Gustav Ammann and his colleagues show clearly how the comparatively rigid design of the classic gardens has been broken down into a liquid pattern of informal shapes, interpenetrating on different planes. A series of sketches by Amman shows the process of a design evolving from a formal classic pattern based on the golden mean through gradual stages of disintegration to a purely informal arrangement of planting. (See Fig. 11.) This is the point of evolution at which for the moment the European garden has paused. Its success depends on the translation of the classic proportions and spacial relationship into organic forms and on the introduction of sculpture or its equivalent to re-assert the human influence.

In Brazil and North America the tradition is carried to its next stage. The organic pattern is organized back into formal shapes. No longer is there the geometric shape of the classic tradition, but the free, floating shapes of abstract painting. This process of relating first the classic pattern to the organic world, and then re-imposing a formalized pattern, is in

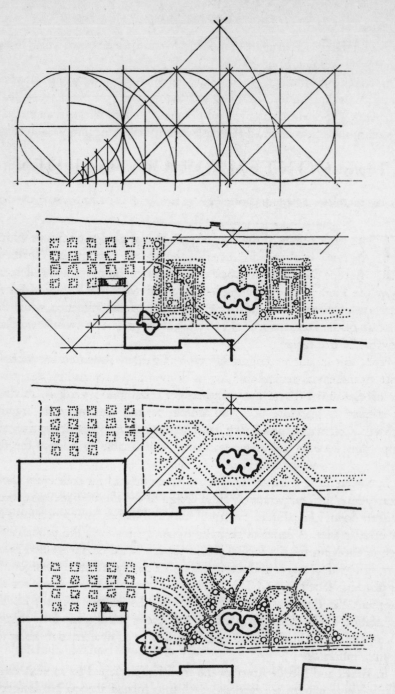

Fig. 11. *Three stages in the development of a design by Gustav Ammann. The proportions of the golden section persist through the gradual breaking down of the formal pattern to an informal expression.*

74

tune with the eternal struggle of the artist to relate the physical world to the conceptions of men's minds (Fig. 12).

In treatment, modern Californian gardens show a strong Japanese influence in their austere restraint and the concise compositions of rock and plant. The Spanish colonial tradition has also played its part and a look of spaciousness, even in small gardens, seems to reflect the sunny Californian skies.

The preciousness of grass in a dry climate is shown in its treatment as a

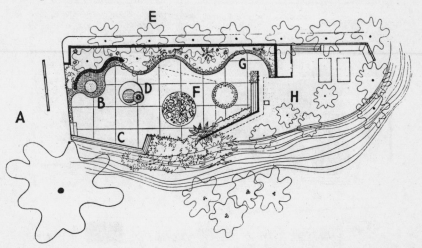

Fig. 12. *In this garden by Lawrence Halprin of California, informality is organized back into formalized shapes.* A. House; B. Barbecue; C. Seat; D. Pool; E. Road; F. Rocks; G. Arbour; H. Service area.

contained shape, a panel of green texture against the background of dry surface. One of the greatest contributions of modern American landscape architects is the imaginative use of new materials, showing how wood, concrete, metal and glass can create forms of new vitality, far preferable to a stale and impoverished caricature of the classic use of wrought stone (Plates 12 and 13).

But it is perhaps in Brazil that the modern garden has crystallized into the most definite style. Here it is evident that, although it is the offspring of history, a new expression has evolved from the fusing of the old traditions with the spirit of the age in a distinctive land and climate.

Here, too, the garden has come in the wake of new architecture. Rooted in the exuberant baroque of Portugal, it spanned the intervening centuries, isolated from the changing influence of the old world, and found new expression under the influence of Le Corbusier in the possibilities of concrete construction with all its freedom of line.

To this new expression of garden design, Burle Marx has brought a painter's eye, a fertile imagination and a love and understanding of plants. Although his feeling for plant form is reminiscent of the English gardens of Robinson and Jekyll, plants to him are purely the artist's material, sometimes colour wash and texture to be used to fill in the shapes of his design, sometimes the living sculpture of his compositions. Their division into qualities of massed colour and texture on one hand and individual shapes on the other is more pronounced than in any other garden and

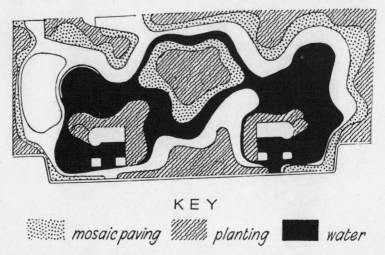

KEY

mosaic paving   planting   water

Fig. 13. In a garden by Burle Marx the abstract shapes of modern painting are translated into blue pools, paving and flowers.

contributes to the clear-cut pattern in contrast to the Scandinavian garden, where the tone, texture and form of the plants are themselves the basis of the design.

In these Brazilian gardens the abstract forms of modern painting are translated into landscape in the form of blue pools, coloured foliage plants, and different shades of grasses (Fig. 13). The brilliant colours, the scale and free sweeps of the designs are in keeping with the size and brilliance of the Brazilian scene. The strong pattern of the sculptural plants are natural in a country where the cactus and the agave grow, and the clear-cut patterning is an attribute which has always appealed in a climate of strong sunshine.

They are the gardens, too, of extroverts, pictures at which one looks rather than gloriettas in which to lose oneself. While their strength as works of art is dependent on their being the natural offspring of Brazil, they, like all the other great traditional gardens in the long line of their ancestry, will contribute a new creative wave to design all over the world.

The danger of their influence lies in imitations, which render the shapes anaemic or arbitrary, whereas their success is in the dynamic and individual form, which can only issue from the spirit of an artist. Perhaps their greatest contribution is that they have brought the vocabulary of garden design into concord with the contemporary spirit of the other arts and have re-affirmed the close sisterhood of painting and landscape.

13. Clearly defined ground planting contributes to the abstract pattern—a garden by Lawrence Halprin.

PART TWO

PRINCIPLES OF DESIGN

UNITY

SCALE

TIME

SPACE DIVISION

LIGHT AND SHADE

TEXTURE

TONE AND COLOUR

STYLES

14. In the memorial garden to the Danish Resistance in Copenhagen, unity is given by the ground work of setts, the vertical pattern of tree-trunks and the overhead canopy of trees.

15. An interesting composition of tree-trunks and foliage forms the focal point of a small garden (George Boye).

CHAPTER EIGHT

PRINCIPLES OF DESIGN

THROUGH all the variations, due to climate, country, history and the natural idiosyncrasy of man, which have appeared in the evolution of the garden through successive civilizations, certain principles remain constant however much their application may change.

UNITY

Perhaps the greatest of these, and the one most lacking in the average garden to-day, is a sense of unity. It is a quality found in all great landscapes, based on the rhythm of natural land-form, the domination of one type of vegetation and the fact that human use and buildings have kept in sympathy with their surroundings. When we say that a landscape has been spoilt we mean that it has lost this unity.

In the same way, all the great gardens of the world have a unity both of execution and conception which shows that they were created in singleness of thought. Their makers knew what they wanted and were able to express it as a complete whole. This quality can be seen in the progressive water-theme of the Villa D'Este, in the clear-cut compositions of Le Nôtre, and in the sweeping landscapes of Kent and Brown. It is equally apparent in the early gardens of every country; from the oasis garden of the East to the medieval cloister.

In the case of primitive gardens unity is achieved in the simplest possible way, first by limitation of materials and secondly by the strength of a single purpose, whether that purpose was to grow food for a monastic community, to find a place of seclusion in a warring world, or refreshment from the desert heat. But as desires and the means to satisfy them become more complex, this automatic unity has to be replaced by deliberate design, and the really great gardens all bear the impress of a mind or tradition which was strong enough to select only the forms and materials which would express one over-ruling idea. The result is that indefinable attribute called style.

In the Le Nôtre garden the strong axial and radiating pattern extending outwards from the house unites the design. In the English landscape garden the smooth flowing ground-form and the containing tree-masses are the unifying factors.

Given a great enough artist, almost any site may be designed for almost any purpose; but the general run of pleasant gardens owe their success to the acceptance of certain limiting factors. The site itself imposes a discipline. A garden whose design is based on the shape of the ground and the character of the surrounding landscape may or may not achieve the highest standards of beauty, but at least it will have the restfulness which comes from compatibility, and the more difficult and unusual the site conditions are, the stronger this virtue will be.

Land-form gives basic unity to a garden, just as it does to a landscape. The sweeping lines merging gently into each other unite the ground-plane of the English landscape garden. They must not be broken by a harsh bank, nor a rock wall, nor by the sudden level rectangle of a tennis court. In contrast, the perfectly proportioned terraces at Vaux-le-Vicomte, with their clearly defined transition from one level to another, make a composition of even planes. (See pp. 40–42.)

Unity may also be imposed by climate. The garden of Arnold Forster at Zennor, Cornwall, is an example of the unifying effect of exposure to the full force of the wind. The wind-clipped shape of the sheltering shrubs makes a pattern which gives a consistent character to the whole garden.

There is the same homogeneity in a garden on poor sand or chalk, provided it keeps strictly to the flora natural to the soil. But if the nature of the soil is changed and plant communities alien to the site are introduced, the natural unity will be lost and will have to be replaced by the far more difficult method of unifying design. The garden will have passed from the artless to the sophisticated. Where the site does not itself impose a unifying discipline, one may be created. Congruity in planting and other materials is part of this discipline. Hidcote owes much of its unity to the repetitive use of box and yew, and Tintinhull to the recurrence of senecio and other grey foliaged plants.

Even more important is congruity of form: the quality which brings the parts of a design together into one whole so that no part can be altered without reference to the rest. For example, a serpentine path at Vaux would be as unthinkable as a geometric bed cut in the grass at Stourhead or Stowe. In the English landscape garden a groundwork of grass flows like a sea through the composition. The continuity of this background is essential to the unity of the design. The Californian garden is less a pattern built up on a background than a mosaic of congruous shapes; the grass, the pool, the terrace, all closely related in form and interlocking to make one composition (Fig. 12).

At the Tivoli gardens in Copenhagen, unity is given by the repetitive pattern of bubbling fountains in wooden bowls, and this repetition is strong enough to carry the varied and informal planting in the individual beds. In the Villa D'Este, water is the unifying theme. The Villa Lante is united by the proportion and logic of its progression from the woodland to the open parterre, and by the congruity of workmanship which gives a preciousness to all the elements and which would make a plain or coarse object out of place. In some of the modern Brazilian gardens, on the other hand, the surfaces are either plain or of coarse texture, and here a finely-carved fountain figure would be equally incongruous.

Lutyens often used his ground pattern to unify his design as in the Great Platt at Hestercombe, Somerset. The Danes achieve the same end in a different style. In the Resistance garden at Copenhagen the honeycomb pattern of setts let into the grass binds the design together like a spider's web. In this same garden are two other unifying elements—the tree trunks with their simple recurring vertical pattern, uniting as the parallel strokes on an etching unite; and the overhead canopy of the trees, bringing the scene together under one ceiling (Plate 14). A woodland has a more strongly unifying pattern than any other natural environment. The success of the Swedish urban landscape owes much to the fact that it is held within this light yet pervasive framework.

Tone and colour unify landscapes just as they do paintings. On a small scale it is often effectively used in grey gardens or, less happily, in blue borders or, with outstanding success, in Sorenson's all-yellow garden at Hellerup. On the larger scale it is one of the great factors in the English landscape garden, and at Stourhead the quiet greens are an essential part of the garden's beauty. Here the azaleas set within the framework of the woods are acceptable, partly because they are contained and muted by the wood and partly because they are on so great a scale that they light up the entire view in their season of flower, almost in the same way that the whole tone changes with autumn colour. It is a general intensification which does not spotlight one particular feature. On a quieter scale the same effect is given by the mantle of pale yellow cast over the hillside by the wild daffodils in early spring. On the other hand, isolated groups of colour, particularly if they are in the open and not within the woodland, destroy the unity of the composition.

In addition to the unity given by a pervading quality, it may also be imposed by a dominant feature to which all else is subordinate. The house to which the garden is attached may set the tune to which all parts of the garden must conform. This is so at Montacute, where the garden is clearly an extension of the house both in the setting of its forthrights and in the strong echo of the architecture which is carried throughout the balustrades and gazebos. In other cases it may be the view which dominates. Sir George Sitwell, in his *On the Making of Gardens*, gives the sound advice that the finer the view, the simpler the garden should be, and attaches so much importance to the setting of the garden that he considers one should be sited only where there is a beautiful prospect; a counsel of perfection which can seldom be followed in these days. Where it is applicable, the garden may serve simply as a transition between the house and the country beyond. It will be a forecourt whose composition is related to the view, giving it the right foreground, supplying the balance, the framing, the vertical accent or the horizontal mass which may be needed to complete the picture. Equally, the garden's colouring can be a completion of the view. In open country, or overlooking the sea, the prevailing tones will be grey, blue, purple and green, and for harmony these colours should be repeated in the garden, in perhaps more intense shades, with the complementary colours used only sparingly at carefully selected points. A band of brilliant colour, interposed between the foreground and the view, disrupts the harmony and checks the eye, while a quiet stretch of unbroken green will lead it gently on.

More often the modern garden has to be in-looking rather than out-looking and must supply the main interest within its own boundaries. In a small garden a fine tree or piece of sculpture may be enough to form the focal point to which all else is subordinate (Plate 15).

One of the simplest forms of garden, especially suitable for long, narrow sites, is the main walk with a strong terminal feature and subsidiary interest on each side. It is the final simplification of the Le Nôtre tradition, the strong axial design. The usual failure in translating it into small gardens is that the subsidiary interest is allowed to be too strong in relation to the main axis. It is true that at Vaux the cross axes reveal gardens of a size and richness which are marvels in themselves, but the main axis is some 1200 yards long, and can hold its own. Hidcote, the skeleton of whose plan is based on axis and cross axes, never allows lateral interest to compete with whichever main axis one is looking down.

Equally satisfying, but perhaps harder to achieve, is the design based on the central open space. Basically this is the form of many small gardens whose chief function is to be open-air rooms. They are similar in intention to the Spanish patio, but instead of being circled by the building and shaded from the sun, they are pushed out from the house to get as much sun as possible.

While in the axial garden the eye is led along to the far end, in the patio garden it is brought to rest in the central space. The features are used as furnishing for the room. There may be a view beyond, but one should not feel impelled to get up and immediately walk to it, but rather be content to sit and admire or, at the most, to wander on after a due rest. This difference in design between the static room and the long walk is a fundamental one, and although in a large garden both moods will occur in different places, there should be no doubt when looking at a particular view, whether the design is static or progressive. Repetition of objects along the line of vision impels the eye forward, as the serried tree trunks do down the lime walk at Sissinghurst, Kent (Plate 16) or the urns along the terrace at the Villa Lante. But repetitive objects arranged in an apse, like the caryatids at the end of the exhedra at Chiswick House, Middlesex, suggest finality.

All gardens which show the greatest richness of design combined with simplicity have a common characteristic in the way in which the elements of their pattern interlock and overlap with each other. This not only gives them a close-knit unity, but imparts the quality of movement, one of the most emotionally stimulating attributes of a design. This interlocking can take place both in the ground pattern and on the different planes of elevation.

In the Alhambra, it is revealed in the flow of landscape through the architecture of courts and colonnades (See p. 26).

At Vaux, the cross-axes interlock with progressive depth, into the framework of the woods. At Stowe, it is most evident on two levels, the ground plane flowing under and interlocking with the canopy of massed trees.

At Tintinhull, the pattern of internal free planting, and the composition of the big trees, overlap with the architectural divisions (See p. 183).

In Burle Marx's gardens, the free shapes float across each other in an interlocking pattern, like the shadows of clouds on the hills (See p. 76).

At the Tiefenbrunnen swimming baths at Zurich, the free pattern of the buildings, the slender lines of trellis, light standards and slim, straight trunks of trees, form a framework of linear pattern which penetrates and holds together the informal landscape design, much as the fine lines in a Paul Klee composition form the framework for his clouds and knots of colour (Plate 17).

The lack of unity, which has disrupted the majority of gardens of the last century and a half, is due to the same causes which have made chaos of our landscape; too many new things, ill-digested; new plants which we have not yet learnt to use; materials, such as Westmorland rock and crazy paving, which are transported to all parts of the country and used in positions to which they are unsuited; foreign influences, copied without being assimilated or understood. But, above all, there is a lack of decision as to what each man really wants in his garden.

Decisiveness of intention was another factor which permeated the classic garden. The quiet refreshment of the oasis garden, the magnificence of the French, the spacious, ideal landscape of the leisured English land-owner, were designed for one purpose and one way of life. This was so well understood that if, in certain moods, a contradictory use was required, it was carefully concealed within the framework of the main theme, tucked away like the *giardino segreto* or, like the English kitchen garden, walled-off or embowered within the woods.

To-day, because there is not the same solidarity of taste, and also because gardens are spread through a far larger section of society, there is a greater diversity of needs. For this reason, a modern garden style, showing the same uniform characteristics as previous traditions, is unlikely to emerge and should not be encouraged, for it would contradict one of the bases of a true garden, in that it could not genuinely represent the character of its owner. Instead, the need of each owner should be developed into a garden individual to himself, and in the sincerity which such a garden expresses, it is likely also to give pleasure to others.

The very diversity which this would produce reflects the true need of our present society. Mass production and centralization have smoothed out too many of the idiosyncrasies which gave savour to the less comfortable world of the past, and if gardens are to fill their historic role of compensating the individual for the incompatibilities of the outside world, the private garden must be more individual than it has ever been before.

There are, however, two types of pattern which may be considered typical of this century. One is the composition of free forms, floating over each other and interlocking in different planes to form the rhythmic pattern of the abstract garden (See Chapter 7). The other is the cellular, honeycomb design which has been developed to a high degree in Scandinavia. It is a true expression of the age because it allows diverse and small-scale uses to be welded into a unified composition, thus solving the modern problem of maintaining individual values within a world of crowd-organization.

This cellular construction also allows for that variety within the design which has always gone hand in hand with unity, for if lack of unity brings discord, lack of variety brings boredom. All the greatest gardens have shown that the two are not incompatible. Vaux shows endless invention in the design of the lateral gardens leading off the main axis while at

Stowe the proportion and character of each view is different, the architecture of each arch and temple individual and distinct.

Surprise and hidden depths are part of the attribute of variety, whether it is the magnificently conceived hidden canal at Vaux or merely a curving path disappearing into the shadow of trees in a small private garden. A garden without mystery is not one to live with, although it may serve as a setting to some great building, to be seen purely as part of a view and not felt as an environment.

This difference between the introvert garden, to be experienced from within, and the extrovert garden, to be admired from without, is a psychological factor of design whose influence has varied from age to age. The Baroque were the most extrovert of gardens, but even in them a *giardino segreto* or *Kamer Garten* was felt necessary in which to find intimacy and seclusion. There is a touching contrast between the sensitive scale of the little *Kamer Garten* at Schönbrunn and the vast clipped avenues stretching in every direction in the great main garden. The introvert influence reached its zenith in the deep shady walks, the mysterious caves and dark ravines of the romantic period, but in a less extreme form the desire to feel oneself contained within a garden is evident in England to-day. A garden is quite as much a place to live in as to look at.

SCALE

Scale and proportion are themselves attributes of unity, for without them there can be no harmony of design. The universal laws of proportion embodied in the classic tradition and the golden mean naturally apply to garden design as to all else, but their application is subject to some special considerations. Perspective, in landscape, plays an even greater part than it does in architecture. Very few features in a garden read as elevations, and even on levelled ground, allowance must be made for the foreshortening of shapes, while the undulating land-form of an informal garden distorts drawing-board patterns into unrecognizable shapes. Atmospheric perspective will also play its part in all but the smallest gardens and is influenced by the relative tone and colour of foreground and distance, blues and greys adding to the apparent distance and hot, strong colours reducing it.

Scale in landscape has to contend with the limitless expanse of sky and horizon. This scale of the open air must either be taken as a standard or the boundaries of the composition must be defined as some lesser space. But even within the defined space a more generous scale is needed than in buildings, for objects are still in contact with the sky and half-way to the landscape. Moreover, gardens are places of leisure, of expansion and release. The steps and paths are for strolling with ones friends and need more ample proportions than their counterparts within the buildings. Garden features are far more often too small than too big.

In the French gardens the space in which the garden is contained is clearly defined by the solid walls of the surrounding trees, while the ceiling is indicated by the cornice formed by the free-growing tree tops above the line of the formal clipping. In this way the exact dimensions of the space is delineated and the parterres, fountains and statues within relate to it, as the furnishings do to a room.

The failure of many imitations of the French style is due to the omission of this definition of scale. In all gardens, of whatever school, there is a sense of bleakness if there are neither trees nor high surrounding walls to bridge the gap between man's stature and the sky. The garden, after all, is a humanized, protective shell against the unmanageable immensities of the outer world.

In the English landscape garden, the definition of scale and space enclosure is equally important, although less rigid and immediately apparent than the French, for in this case it is merely indicated by the placing of the tree groups and the land-form, both rising in carefully composed scale from the lowest level set by the sheet of water.

These gardens often relate in scale to the surrounding landscape and not only to a scale created arbitrarily for themselves. This is one of the reasons why the landscape style can only be wholly satisfactory set in a landscape of naturally small and humanized scale. Where the surroundings are not right in scale and character, a buffer has to be interposed in the shape of a tree belt, or a composition of tree groups and land-form, allowing the garden to become self-contained.

The garden must also relate to the human scale. There is a school of thought which contends that man's mind has an infinite capacity for expansion or contraction; that he can, like Graham Sutherland, see the vast complexity of the Alps in one small stone, or bring down the immensity of the universe to that of his own stature. This is true, but it is only valid while man is alone. If other human figures appear in his giant or pigmy landscape the true human scale is revealed. For this reason, the garden, at least of the average man, must still keep man as its measuring rod.

The classic gardens of both France and England were created at a time when men had overcome their fear of nature and welcomed wide views physically and mentally. There was, therefore, no curb to their spaciousness. The Englishman looked out and saw the whole world as his garden; the

Frenchman saw as his garden as much of the world as he desired, and his desires were large, for his life was a life of crowds, and his garden must be his concourse.

But both these outlooks are unusual. Men have more often felt the need to reduce the overpowering size of the universe, to bring it down to more cosy proportions. The medieval gardens show this clearly with their high enclosures, and Hidcote and Sissinghurst are in the same tradition to-day in an age when the desire for a small private world has again become a natural craving.

But whether the garden is on a large or small scale, it must still relate to the human form in one way or another. The great French gardens need their crowds, without them they have a feeling of emptiness. This is not

Fig. 14. *Trees forming a grouped composition.*

so in the landscape garden, because the mind relates the scene to an agricultural landscape and accepts the fact that it is thinly populated. It was in any case designed for a small coterie of friends, not for a parade of courtiers.

In the intimate type of garden which seeks to create a small-scale humanized setting, there may be scaling down, yet paths, steps and openings must still be large enough for their human use. Parts of Hidcote have almost reached an Alice in Wonderland point where a human being is made to feel an over-sized intruder. But here and at Sissinghurst there are also masterly examples of reducing scale to give significance to some feature which would otherwise be trivial (See Plate 18).

A garden where there has been lack of decision on the relative proportion of one thing to another has a nondescript appearance. Either the parts should fit together to make one indivisible whole or one element should be dominant over all others. In the case of planting, for instance, trees may be composed into a mutually supporting group, or there may be one large tree to which other planting remains subsidiary (Fig. 14).

Or in the case of a high wall, either the terrace or border in front of it should be wide and dominant, using the wall as a background, or the wall should dominate and the treatment at its foot be kept subsidiary in the form of a plinth. In the Dutch Garden at Holland Park, the high brick wall, the border at its foot, the wide walk and finally the low, broad wall of clipped lavender on the far side, together combine into a well-proportioned composition, restful and satisfying (Fig. 15).

Many devices have been used in the past to increase the apparent size of gardens, from the painted *trompe d'oeil*, which suggests a non-existent view or extension of the garden, to the false perspective which increases the appearance of length in an avenue by narrowing the end. Perhaps only

Fig. 15. At Holland Park, wall, border and walk together form a well-proportioned composition.

Le Nôtre dealt with such vast distances that he had to employ the opposite deception of foreshortening the view.

The false perspective is of little value where the view may be looked at in reverse. But losing the boundary in shadow, or making it recede into the surrounding landscape, were favourite devices of the English landscape school, while the trees planted as stage wings framing the house as seen from the lake at Stowe adds both distance and emphasis to the view. (See Plate 19.)

Both these principles are among those which can be used in the small gardens of to-day. Others are the facts that the apparent size of a lawn is increased by close-mown grass as opposed to rough, and that shadows and openings at the side will increase the apparent width, while a smooth boundary will make it look longer. The static appearance of a lawn is increased by dishing the ground towards the centre and by high, solid boundaries. Distance is added to a view looking downhill, and conversely one looking uphill is foreshortened—a useful fact in giving emphasis to objects sited on hills, but one which adds difficulty to the design of small gardens sloping steeply up from the house.

Avenues, which played a part in all the great formal gardens of Europe, owe their attraction to the emphasis which they give to a view and the seductive power with which they draw the eye and feet along their length. This is due partly to their canalization of the view and partly to the rhythmic repetition of the tree trunks. To be effective there must be a strict relationship between the proportions of their width, height and spacing. The great avenue at Stowe is broad, long and majestic. The trees are allowed to develop their full spread and stature. Such an avenue can only be achieved with forest trees in a position where they can have unlimited spread. In contrast, the little avenue of limes, planted by Lady Holland in Holland Park, is only 10 feet wide (Fig. 16). The trees, 6 feet apart and crowded by the woodland behind them, do not register as individuals, but rely for effect on the aisle of the close-spaced trunks and the interlaced upswept branches. This is the Gothic pattern of avenue,

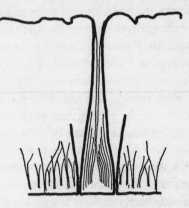

Fig. 16. The cleft pattern of a slender avenue of limes in Holland Park.

using the natural growth of the branches to form the tracery of the arch. The Savernake avenue of beech is the same basic proportion on a larger scale. The cypress avenues of Italy have the same narrow, close planted pattern, but instead of meeting in a Gothic arch, they pierce upwards towards the sky, while the French avenues have a more classic architecture, the straight clean columns of their trunks supporting the squared and solid

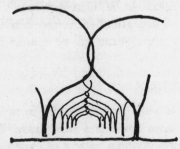

Fig. 17. The Tudor Arch of the chestnut avenue—Holland Park.

wall of their clipped foliage. The chestnut avenue in Holland Park forms a series of Tudor arches (Fig. 17).

All these patterns succeed because they carry out a definite intention, worked out in correct proportions, between the size of the trees and their spacing, and all have the necessary continuity. These factors are all lacking in the so-called avenues which are planted down modern roads, consisting of small trees too far apart, and with their continuity interrupted by lamps and telegraph poles.

TIME

There is one way in which landscape design differs from all other arts, and that is the part which time must play. There is no garden which can spring to life as a fully finished work of art, although some are far more dependent on time than others. Those gardens which rely on a clear-cut pattern, outlined by structures and clipped trees and hedges, must still wait for the growth of trees to attain their true form, but having reached that stage, they can continue for centuries with a minimum of intelligent upkeep, in a state of static perfection. Even when, like the Villa D'Este, they have grown far beyond their creator's intention, the basic soundness of their design, and the strength of their architecture, keeps their spirit alive; and the prodigality of their growth may to us be more attractive than the austere pattern of their early days. The English landscape garden must have taken far longer to reach perfection and it requires the skill of an artist, not only a craftsman, to maintain it in the spirit of its creation. That the first owners saw the picture so clearly, in spite of the lack of maturity, was due partly to their imagination and good taste, partly to the large part played by land-form, water, trees already mature and architecture in the composition and partly to the fact that a well-proportioned design will show itself in promise to a seeing eye, even when the element of plant form is only in an embryonic state.

The English plantsman's garden, relying only on the natural beauty of plants, is the most dependent on a period of growth to reach its intention and the most vulnerable to time and neglect. In William Robinson's old garden at Gravetye, only the architectural strength of the terrace provides a foil against which some of his plant groupings can still be appreciated.

SPACE DIVISION

The fundamental pattern of landscapes and gardens results from the distribution and proportion between open space and solid mass. The solids divide the land into space enclosures giving a pattern of closed and open, of in and out, of dark and light. The solids may consist of hills, trees or other strong plant growth, or architecture. To be effective, space divisions must be above eye level. The spaces consist of open ground, or water.

The great schools of landscape have each had a particular way of creating their space division, with a different proportion between the closed and open areas. The French tradition may be likened to a structure of rooms and corridors; a rigid and symmetrical series of spaces, enclosed by walls of trees, bosquets or hedges, with floor patterns and furnishing within the ooms. Our own Tudor gardens, and many town gardens, are a simplication of this plan. Hidcote and Tintinhull also have the room method s their foundation, but instead of the French carpets and formal furniture hey have a secondary, informal pattern of open space and solid, in the orm of plant material, built up within the rooms and in some cases over-lapping the walls. This latter type of garden is successful only if t makes a good composition with both the formal walled spaces and he informal planting. When it does so, it has the added enrichment of wo interlacing designs, one firm and architectural, the other loose and organic.

The Alhambra is an illustration of the colonnade method of space division. Less rigid than the French, the mass and open space flow one into the other. A woodland garden, an orchard, and the spaced trees of Hyde Park, all follow this pattern.

The Villa D'Este's pattern is a solid mass pierced by openings. Most talian gardens show this emphasis of cutting out of the solid rather than building up from the open. It is natural to hot climates, but also derives from the strong sculptural feeling of the Italian tradition.

The English landscape school is the most subtle and least defined of all he space divisions, being that of open space punctuated by solid groups. t is a method followed in the majority of informal gardens, and its danger ies in its lack of definition, which gives rise to the idea that no particular elationship is necessary either between one mass and another or between he proportion of space to solid. Yet as we have seen in the case of Stowe, he laws of proportion and composition are just as exacting, if less rigid han those of the French school.

This space division by tree-groups and land-form is often combined with the colonnade method, where the trees thin out into typical parkland. As an adjunct to firm massing the colonnade can be very successful, just as the outriders to a wood add to its beauty. But colonnades are not features which can continue vaguely and indefinitely over the whole area. If they are to make a pattern, they must be related to more solid objects and also to some clear open spaces. The beauty of English parkland scenery is the lacy composition of single trees weaving through the firmer pattern of copses, hedgerows, and open fields. Lack of this principle is the chief fault in Hyde Park which achieves composition only where the spaced trees are seen against a background of solid mass, or in relation to the clear, open space of the Serpentine.

In Scandinavian gardens, the colonnade of tree-trunks is often used as a framework to contain solids and focal knots in the shape of buildings and sculpture.

The same principle applies with smaller plants; a group may be improved by outriders, but never by consisting solely of spaced plants. The Japanese garden has a compact and more rigidly designed form, and by its discipline and clarity shows even more clearly that the informal grouping of mass can be as definitely proportioned as the composition of the classic formal gardens.

LIGHT AND SHADE

Closely related to the distribution of mass and open space in a garden is the use of light and shade.

We have already seen how the need for shade in hot countries, and for sunlight in the cooler, has been one of the factors in developing national styles and, similarly, the visual effects of lighting will vary from country to country. In the shaded gardens of Italy, play can be made with the sudden blaze of sunlight appearing at the end of a dark chasm of evergreen, or the window of blue sky above the cypress tops. In England, on the other hand, the most telling effects will be the gentle diffusion of light filtering though open-foliaged trees; or a foreground silhouetted against the backcloth of the misty and atmospheric distance, which in Italy would appear hard and clear.

But there are some effects of light and shade which transcend all climatic conditions. There is always a delight in looking out on to the sunlight from within a dark wood, or from between the columns of an arcade, whether they be the pillars of an Italian pergola or the trunks of a lime walk, and there is the unfailing effect of light falling on some special spot from surrounding shade. The open glade in the wood, the statue at the end of the avenue, the pool reflecting the sky from between the tall cypress, all give this pleasure. In the placing of features in relation to the light, it must be remembered that texture and modelling show to advantage only when the light falls on them, whereas silhouetted form should have the light behind it. Thus carving should face the light, whereas wrought iron will be most effective against it. Evergreen oak, whose beauty lies in its modelling and texture, will look finest to the north, while ailanthus and cedars are trees for silhouetting.

TEXTURE

The importance of texture in a garden increases as the pattern becomes more elusive. In the French gardens, with their strongly defined formal patterns, it is relatively unimportant. In the Spanish, with their insistence on the value of the individual plants and the contrast between wall surface, foliage and ironwork, it takes on a greater importance, while in the English landscape park it becomes an inseparable part of the composition. Whereas in Spain the textures tend to be hard and clear-cut, iron grille against the smooth wall, and the shiny leaves of orange and aspidistra reflecting the hard sunlight, in England the textures are soft —grass, deciduous trees, yew and box. Such buildings and statues as there are take on the gentle patina of the damp climate. Hard and shiny surfaces, whether of marble or of foliage, are out of key, unless used as deliberate accents of contrast.

Probably only in the gardens of Japan, with their contrasts of rock, mounded plants, patterned sand and water, has texture played so great a part in the pattern of gardens, as it does to-day. The textural possibilities of all the garden materials are explored, and there could be no greater contrast between the smooth stone, quiet floor, and massed plant form of the classic garden and the juxtaposition of coarse walling, wood, glass and concrete, which may be found in a modern Californian garden. In the classic garden, the strong formal pattern needed the utmost simplicity of surface. In the modern garden, the textured surfaces themselves build up into the pattern. It is a technique particularly suited to the small garden, where the elements of design are seen at close quarters.

TONE AND COLOUR

It is paradoxical that while so much effort has been put into increasing the colour range of garden material in the last century, so little is understood about its use.

The problem of colour in relation to plants is dealt with in Chapter 10, but some references must be made here to the wider aspect of tone and colour in all garden materials. The classic gardens have each their own character in this respect. The Italian gardens are almost designs in black and white, with only occasional spots of intense colour. The cypress and the *Quercus ilex* merge their dark greens into a homogeneous background silhouetted against a blue sky and lit by the white focal points of statues, terrace walls and fountains. The ground, in general effect, is white or golden in the sunlight, black in the shadow. It is only necessary to picture one of the long dark allées disrupted by light green trees to realise that this limitation of tone range is essential to the picture.

The French garden is less black and white, but is no less simplified. The general tone of the surrounding trees is all of the same quiet green. One type of edging surrounds the parterres, one type of surfacing covers the paths. Any variation would throw out the clarity and symmetry of the pattern, which is defined by the dark of the trees and hedging against the lighter groundwork.

The English landscape garden is by comparison varied in colour, but it is a variation within well defined limits and used as a component of the composition. The ground work to which all else relates is grass. The limit of lightness is the surface of the water and the usually grey sky, which is picked up with a warmer glow in the weathered stonework of the architectural features. The trees, which form the mass of the composition, vary in tone to a degree which is not seen in either the Italian or the French gardens, for their variation contributes to the modelling which is an essential part of the composition. But the degree of light and darkness is sufficient only to give depth to the groups, it never disrupts them. The later additions of golden or glaucous varieties destroy the composition by breaking what should be a coherent whole into unrelated fragments.

It is no mere chance that most great garden designers have also been artists. It is impossible to compose a picture in the infinitely varied and subtle colours of plant form without at least understanding the principles of colour harmonies.

In considering the colours of an English garden, it should be remembered that, except in the case of small town courtyards, the dominating colour will be that of grass, and all other tones and colours should be related to it. It is a lovely green, but a very vivid one and by no means compatible with all flower colours.

It is not only in the matter of colour that the artist's eye is needed in garden design. More than in any other art it is essential to be able to visualize the final effect. Sketches of as many view points as possible are helpful, but they supplement and do not replace the ability to walk in imagination through every part of the projected garden, to see it not only as a series of static views, but as a complete landscape in the round, unfolding and progressive, something to be within, even more than to look at from without. The designer should feel the form of the garden; it must exist for him as an actual place in which he walks, exploring every path, looking at every view, before it is ever made.

STYLES

The particular style in which a garden is designed is immaterial. The present fashion for free forms is neither better nor worse than the geometric shapes of Le Nôtre or the free-flowing lines of Capability Brown; those who feel in the vernacular of their day should express themselves in it, provided it is a genuine expression and not the imitation of a fashion, for if it is copied without conviction it is as lifeless as the reproduction of a dead age.

It is natural that the tendency to abstract forms which has appeared in painting and the free shapes which have been accepted into the vocabulary of architecture should also find their way into garden design. We have seen (Chapter 7) with what success they have been used by Burle Marx in Brazil and they can be found in gardens in all parts of the world designed in the last few decades. The creative skill required in their use is probably higher than that needed to create a reasonably good garden in either the formal or naturalistic styles. For if the free shapes do not make an entirely satisfying pattern in their own right, they have nothing to fall back upon, but when successful they strike a chord of sympathy in the modern mind. One of the most usual subjects for an abstract shape is a swimming or paddling pool. The clarity of the water and clean outline lend themselves to the treatment, which, if applied to planted elements of the garden, tends to become confused unless the planting is limited by strong discipline as in Burle Marx's gardens. The happiest use of these forms is where they are clearly defined themselves, but are associated with free plant-form on another plane. Their least happy use is where they are combined with naturalistic shapes so that one is left in doubt whether a pool, for instance, is intended to be natural or abstract. If doubts of this kind are raised in one's mind, it is certain that the garden design has failed, for the really great gardens have an air of inevitability; they are so because they could be no other way.

16. Repetition along the line of vision impels the eye forward. The lime walk, Sissinghurst Castle.

17. In the gardens of the Tiefenbrunnen, Zurich (Architects: Schütz, Roost and Dürr), the free pattern of the buildings, the slender lines of trellis, light standards and tree-trunks form a framework of linear design.

PART THREE

MATERIALS OF DESIGN

LAND-FORM

PLANT MATERIAL

WATER

SCULPTURE AND STONE WORK

GARDEN BOUNDARIES

GROUND PATTERN

18. Scaling down from the immensity of the open-air to the intimate proportions of a room—Sissinghurst Castle.

19. Receding wings of trees give distance and emphasis to the view of the house Stowe.

CHAPTER NINE

LAND-FORM

THE shape of the ground is the foundation of all landscape. The steep crags of Cumberland and the soft swell of the Downs are the basis on which these two distinct and characteristic landscapes are built.

Equally, land-form is the basis of most of the great gardens of the world. We have seen how the Italian garden evolved from the terracing of the hillside, how Vaux-le-Vicomte used the valley and cross-fall of the site, while the English landscape park idealized and accentuated the undulating land to form its composition of gentle hills crowned with trees or temples, overlooking the lake-filled valleys (Plate 20). The Japanese, while not necessarily using the land-form of the actual site of their garden, transfer to it a distillation of the mountain scenery of their country.

In these divers ways the classic gardens illustrate certain simple laws of manipulating land-form which are applicable to every size and style of garden.

The line of sight, like the flow of water, tends to travel along a valley and can, therefore, be canalized by framing the view on each side. For the same reason, ground falling away to one side of the view will give an impression of side-slipping unless there is some counterpoise to arrest the eye and guide it back to the centre. Any object to which the eye is guided, and which then arrests it, gains in importance.

The simplest exploitation of this fact is the statue giving a vertical stop at the end of the canalized avenue. In the landscape park, the same principle places the temple on the hill with the ground sweeping gently up to it. It explains the added emphasis given to a group of trees sited on a hill-top. By its means, the eye may be diverted occasionally from the main vista, to travel to a subsidiary point of interest, but it must be kept subsidiary while at the same time either forming a sufficiently satisfying stop to send the eye back to the main view or giving a hint of the unknown, to be explored later. This principle is illustrated by the cleft view to the obelisk branching off from the Grecian valley at Stowe.

The art of centralising the view is beautifully illustrated in the south approach to Stowe, first by the counter-balanced folds of the ground between the great avenue and later, beyond the Corinthian arch, by the placing of tree-groups in the form of stage wings, to lead the view on to the house (See pp. 55–62).

In a very different style, we have seen how at Vaux-le-Vicomte the transverse fall of the ground has been both used and counteracted so that there is added interest in the flanking gardens, yet never a tendency for the eye to side-slip from the central vista.

At Chatsworth, Derbyshire, on the other hand, the formal garden stretching out from the east wing, gives a feeling of discomfort because the ground falls away to the south without a counterbalance, and the far horizon slopes away in the same direction. For the same reasons, while a slope along the line of sight is permissible in a formal design, a true level across the line of sight is essential.

A second tendency, to look straight down the side of a hill, at right-angles to the contours, and across to the opposite hillside, is also illustrated by both the formal and informal schools of design. The towering cypresses at the Villa D'Este form a cleft through which the eye looks down the steeply falling contours, and at Vaux-le-Vicomte the fall to the valley, and rise to the hill beyond, is as compelling as the canalization down the central parterre. At Stowe it is equally well illustrated in the view from the house terrace, which plunges straight down the hill to the lake and then sweeps up to the Corinthian arch on the horizon.

The traditional terracing of Italian gardens follows both principles; the main view is usually out across the terraces which run parallel to the contours, while subsidiary cross-vistas open up along each terrace, the side-slipping here being counteracted by the balustrading, the tall hedge or the planting on the outer edge of the terrace.

The Villa D'Este is unusual in having its terraces set obliquely to the hill, but the same principle is followed, partly by artificial correction of the cross-fall, and even more by the heavy tree planting which keeps the central vista canalized.

The forming of artificial hills goes back to prehistoric days and has given us such familiar landmarks as Silbury Hill, Wiltshire. In gardens, too, the mount was one of the earliest features, and there can be no question of the fascination which a sudden eminence holds for most of us.

The exaggeration which the eye gives to height in relation to breadth means not only that anything placed on a hilltop will gain in importance, but also that the slopes themselves appear exaggerated. In frankly artificial ground form, this fact can be used to advantage. The amphitheatre constructed by Sorensen from the foundation excavation for flats near Copenhagen rises in drama to give a setting in scale with the great point blocks. But in naturalistic shaping the tendency is to make the slopes too steep and too sudden. They should be gentle and continuously flowing, convex and concave curves merging into each other without intervening flats or angles, and the transition to the surrounding ground should be imperceptible. If natural ground form is studied, it will be seen that a convex curve never runs straight into level ground; there is always a reverse concave curve uniting the two. Only knowledge and love of natural land-form make it possible to use informal contouring in landscape compositions. One of the finest examples of the art is the hill in Asplund's crematorium near Stockholm. This is a created landscape in the finest sense and suggests the immense possibilities of composing with land-form on a large scale with the help of modern earth-moving machinery (Plate 21).

It is particularly necessary to be able to handle contours when artificial lakes are to be made. Capability Brown was a master of this, as he was of all problems of contouring. His critics' complaints that his slopes were too smooth for a natural effect may surely be discounted, when we see how the easy, graceful sweeps and slopes have stood the test of time, in a way that a picturesquely crumbling bank could never have done. His sheets of water lie naturally within the land-form. If there is a headland, the slight swell on the ground suggests it as a natural formation, if the water widens out, it does so into a gentle basin. These seem self-evident points, but they are constantly neglected in the ponds which appear to have been shaped with a pastry-cutter on dead level ground and, more regrettably, in reservoirs where headlands have been blasted away to form an unnaturally shaped sheet of water.

Contouring the ground can add immensely to the interest and apparent size of a landscape. New view points are revealed by the unfolding undulations of the ground and there is the added pleasure of an object suddenly appearing over the brow of a hill, a pleasure often found in the countryside, where one breasts a hill to see a church tower suddenly revealed on the far horizon.

Changes of level are one of the classic means of introducing surprise and variety. We have seen (p. 59) how the undulations of the south drive at Stowe are used to give a succession of different pictures, while at Vaux the same principle provides the optical illusions in the position of the fountains (See p. 41).

A whole garden may be hidden from view, to be suddenly revealed from a chosen spot; and even on a small plot, gentle contouring can be used to conceal some part of the garden. Sometimes a small garden of the in-looking type can be made more interesting, secluded and self-contained by raising the sides and back in a horse-shoe formation, which gives background to a saucer of garden in the centre. Or a gentle mound may be brought a little forward from the far boundary, allowing the garden to continue round the back of the hill, perhaps in the form of a small woodland.

One of the reasons for the failure of the many imitations of the English landscape garden is that the contouring, which was an essential part of the design, is omitted. The grouping of the trees and the course of the paths then become meaningless. A path which winds gently between hills has a look of inevitability, while one which serpentines over level ground is merely irritating.

Even where the ground as a whole is not to be contoured, an effect of unbroken grass can be given by slightly sinking any paths which must cross the lawn.

Where a garden is to be based on contouring, land-form and planting together should make a balanced, sculptural composition. For studying this art, there can be no more fruitful source than the Japanese hill gardens. To our eyes their actual form is too artificial to have a place in the average garden, perhaps because they are related to the steeper landscape of Japan and so strike an alien note in our own more gently sloping land. But their very exaggeration makes them a clear pattern for general principles. (See Chapter 2.)

In working out the composition of ground form on a small scale, a plastic model is helpful. The clay can be laid down to existing ground levels and then formed into the desired composition. This method also ensures that the available amount of cut and fill is used. Designing informal ground form is closely allied to sculpture and it is as reasonable to employ a maquette in one art as the other. In judging the effect, the model must always be looked at from the correct eye level, otherwise the usual fault will be made of exaggerating the steepness of the slopes, which appear flattened when looked at from above. It is even possible to survey the model and transpose the corrected level to the actual ground site.

The type of shaping used in landscape parks is based on the natural flow of contours found in the landscape, but it may be desired to use ground-shaping in a purely formalized and artificial way. There would never be any doubt, in looking at the shaping, as to whether it is intended as an adaptation of the natural or as a purely architectural expression. The clean-cut banks holding the fountain basin in the garden of the Belvedere in Vienna (Plate 22) is a good example of the use of architectural ground-shaping. So are the amphitheatres of Rome and Greece. On a smaller scale, if a grass bank is used to support the terrace of a house, it should be on clean formal lines if the part of the garden surrounding the house is formal; while if the landscape is to be brought informally up to the house walls, it can either be shaped to merge into the surrounding ground or it may be used as a transition from house to landscape by descending in gentle steps, or in the forceful glacis of the old castle. The prehistoric lynchets of the chalk downs show how admirably clean-cut land-carving can harmonize with soft natural contours.

Swiss and Swedish landscape architects use informal contouring with great skill to blend their buildings into the natural surroundings of their often hilly sites.

All changes in level should be welcomed as creative opportunities, particularly now that recent introductions of grass cutting machines for banks have made the use of sculptural land-form a practical possibility. In public work vast quantities of material are available from excavations and spoil heaps, which can be used to create new landscapes and pleasure grounds far more interesting than those on level ground.

CHAPTER TEN

PLANT MATERIAL

༼ᦦᦦᦦᦦᦦᦦᦦᦦᦦᦦᦦᦦᦦᦦᦦ༽

THERE are two attitudes to plants in gardens. One is that the purpose of a garden is to grow plants, the other is that plants are one of the materials to be used in the creation of a garden.

The first attitude goes back to the early history of gardens. The gardens of the oasis and the cloister were primarily places in which to grow plants, but even in ancient Greece other aims were becoming predominant, and the development of garden design in almost all countries has been in the direction of considering the garden as a whole more important than the individual plants within it. In the renaissance garden, plants are used almost entirely as adjuncts to, or as an extension of, the architecture on one hand and the surrounding landscape on the other. In the patio garden, while the plants retain their individuality, they are selected for their contribution to the composition. In the Japanese garden, they are more strictly selected and controlled than in any other tradition. In the English landscape park, trees in their natural form play the important role, yet their species and grouping are dictated by the pictorial needs of the landscape. In the English garden of the past hundred years we get, almost for the first time, an attempt to create a picture out of plants grown primarily for their own sake. It is perhaps not surprising that this new fusing of two hitherto distinct ideas has led to some confusion.

The diversity of plant material now available to us is often blamed for the lack of design in the majority of English gardens. But the real fault lies in lack of discrimination and restraint.

It is impossible to have too great a range of plants to choose from, provided a choice is made. The qualities of plants are so complex, and their cultural requirements so diverse, that even with our present vast choice it is not always easy to find the exact plant for each position. Burle Marx, with his painter's approach to garden design, is constantly enlarging his palette of plants by collection and hybridization, yet in his gardens he selects for each one only the very few plants which exactly translate his intention, and those, too, whose cultural requirements are suited to the site.

To choose rightly, one must be quite sure what qualities the plants possess and what role one wants them to fill. The first essential is the ability of a plant to grow and thrive in a given position. Without this, it can only be a disappointment. So the first selective process is to choose the plants hardy to the climate, tolerant of the amount of sun or shade, dryness or moisture which they will encounter, and suited to the soil, acid or alkaline, heavy or light. These conditions should be known before the first designs evolve, for it is useless to conjure up pictures of stately parkland trees in a windswept district where only close planted shelter-belts will survive, or to imagine glades of rhododendrons on a soil which proves to be alkaline.

Planting may be either part of the structure of a garden or its interior decoration. Its structural role is by far the more important, just as the walls of a house, both for the protection they give and for their visual proportion, are more important than the wallpaper.

Physically, the function of planting is to give shelter, shade and protection; visually, it determines the proportion and form of the garden, the contrast between closed and open and the division of space. It provides texture, framing, background, tone and sculptural form.

WIND SHELTER

In the climate of the British Isles, wind shelter is often more important than shade and its provision not only makes greater use of the garden possible, but gives it an obvious relationship to the forces of nature which brings with it a unity of composition.

The planting of shelter belts should never be regarded as an evil necessity, but rather welcomed as giving special character to the garden. In extreme cases the small enclosures protected by over-lapping baffles and the wind-clipped shape of the trees and shrubs will produce a garden carved out of protecting plant form. There is no type of planting in which reference back to natural plant communities and to farming practice is more rewarding. The first point to decide is the minimum width of shelter belt necessary to obtain adequate protection. This naturally depends both on the area to be sheltered and the strength of the wind. On the Russian steppes, 88 feet has been given as an optimum figure, but in the kind climate of Kent and Worcestershire a single row of poplars is all that is required to shelter a fruit orchard.

The determining factor in deciding the width of the belt is whether the strength of the wind will allow the protecting trees to reach adequate stature. In exposed coastal districts the angle at which the wind cuts the growth can be seen, the outer defence being very low, but providing shelter for gradually heightening growth, so that the stronger the wind, the greater width of shelter is needed to reach a given height. The outer slope also improves shelter by guiding the air currents upwards, instead of causing turbulence by the sudden check of a vertical wall. But under normal inland conditions, a wall or hedge will provide adequate shelter for five to ten times its own height.

In cold coastal districts typical outer edge plants are ligustrum, hippophae and gorse, with sycamore and Austrian pine for the taller growing trees. On the south-west coasts there is a far wider choice, including the maritime pine, and in more sheltered inland districts suitable species range from the beech belts of the Cotswolds to the willow and thorn of East Anglia and the spruce of north-west Britain. Examining these shelters pictorially, they have one thing in common—they are always homogeneous. They may be all of one species, or a combination of several, but they are never scrappy or spotty. Their contribution to the landscape is a unifying one, they echo both the land-form and the climate in their own shape.

In a garden, they should follow this model and express a definite character, rather than appear as an indeterminate mixed border. If the are to take the form of a hedge, then let them be firm and solid, but if a looser boundary is wanted, which will give a penetration of shadow, the shaws of Kent and Sussex provide a good example. These are strips of the original woodland left as divisions between the fields. They may be of hazel with oak standards or of coppiced ash or sweet chestnut. Fifteen to thirty feet wide, they give adequate shelter and, carpeted with woodland flowers, they are one of the loveliest features of these countrysides in spring. In translating natural prototypes to the garden, they may either be copied exactly or other species and mixtures chosen, provided always that their character and simplicity is maintained. A good mixture where winter effect is important is holly and *Cornus sibirica*, the strong red stems of the cornus making a fine contrast to the dark green, strongly-patterned holly. A quick growing mixture suitable for difficult soils, and for positions where there is no objection to rampant growth, is *Cotoneaster frigida* and grey poplar. The harsher evergreens such as spruce will give the effect of a hard black wall, without the play of light and shade or the opportunity for underplanting. They must, in fact, be treated as background rather than as a picture in themselves. But as a background they can be most valuable, showing up the stems of silver birch or the white thickets of *Rubus giraldianus*.

SECLUSION

In the urbanized state of England, seclusion is one of the most important structural uses of planting. The form which the screen should take largely depends on the space available for it. There may be room for a spinney or woodland or there may be room only for a hedge. It can usually be combined with wind shelter and should always be part of the design of the garden. If there is space only for a straight line, this should be accepted as a virtue, rather than disguised. Pleached trees with recurring vertical stems, a high, close-clipped hedge, a line of Lombardy poplars are all arrangements whose essence is linear emphasis. To attempt a mixed or informal planting along a narrow defined line is to contradict the character of the site and to confuse structural planting with interior decoration.

The plants which will provide seclusion all the year around in reasonably short time are limited. Pleached beech and hornbeam hold their leaves in winter and are quicker growing than most evergreens. For informal grouping, the larger and more densely growing evergreen cotoneasters are a good choice.

SHADE

Even in England planting for shade should not be neglected, for it is on the hottest days that the garden is most used. In the southern countries shade, usually dense and extensive, forms one of the chief reasons for the garden. But in northern lands it becomes incidental, an occasional change from the sunlight of the open garden. The most pleasant shade trees are those which throw a dappled shadow, and they should be planted in grass to give full effect to the pattern of the leaf shadows on the ground and to allow the pleasure of lying in the shade on a summer afternoon. The plane, the lime and the maple are all excellent for this purpose, but the lime should be one of the species, such as *Tilia euchlora*, which does not shed too much honeydew. Arbours contrived in thick evergreens are far less pleasant than open growing trees, for they can be close, stuffy and infested with insects. They are, however, beloved by children and for this reason should be perpetuated.

The pleached alley with over-arching branches was used in Tudor gardens for a shady walk, for, as Bacon says, 'You ought not to buy the shade in the garden by going in the sun through the green; therefore you are, of either side the green, to plant a covert alley, upon carpenters work, about 12 feet in height, by which you may go in shade into the garden.'

SPACE DIVISION

Besides these physical needs for planting, there are the needs of visual structure. There are the green walls which will define the space enclosure, or the free growing groups which will serve the same purpose in a less formal way; the trees which will give perspective, balance, height and background.

In every case the primary needs of the design must be kept in mind. Decide what shape, colour and texture is needed, what size the plant is to grow, how long one is prepared to wait for it to attain the size; then choose the plant which comes nearest to this specification, without being diverted from it by considerations of novelty or the hope of getting some extra advantage, such as bright flowers on a plant which is needed primarily as a background.

We have traced the part which plants have played in the design of the great historic gardens. The use of trees has varied from the French high-pruned trees with an overhanging cornice, defining exactly the dimensions of garden space, to the free but none-the-less calculated grouping of trees in the English landscape parks. Hedges have been used as the high dividing walls of Hidcote and the low, steadying surround for the beds of luxuriant flowers in Spain.

The qualities needed for these plants are simple and easily grasped. In every case a mass effect is desired of a certain tone, stature and form, and in the case of the French trees and of hedges, the form is artificially obtained. But in a garden such as the modern Scandinavian, in some of the Brazilian and in the best type of English informal garden, the design is constructed from the character of the plants, and it is in these that the most exact knowledge of the individual plant is needed. The plants are used as sculptural compositions, contrasted and related to each other in form, colour and texture, and often the groups themselves must form the space division and bones of the garden, thus differing from the hedged beds of Spain or the formally contained borders of the Hidcote tradition.

Hedges. Hedges have always been a structural component of the garden, but in the last fifty years they have suffered from the modern weakness of impatience which has caused various substitutes to be used in place of the relatively slow box and yew. *Cupressus macrocarpa* was planted in thousands until it was discovered that it died out except in coastal or very mild districts. Thuja and certain of the cupressus are still used and in some positions are quite satisfactory, but they cannot compare with the yew in texture or depth of colour.

As in all other parts of the design, there must be a clear idea of what is required of the hedges. We have seen, in going through the great gardens of the world, what an important part hedges play. The wall-like hedges of Italy require height, solidity, depth of colour and evenness. At Hidcote height again is needed, but because the garden is one of detail interest, more variety of colour and even a mottled texture in the same hedge is used. If the eye is to be carried down a long alley to a statue at the end, then the Italian type of hedge should be used, all of one material and closely clipped. But if the hedge is to form not only the background, but also part of the planting composition of the garden, then it may have the mottled texture of the Hidcote hedges or the swelling buttresses of Owlpen, Gloucestershire.

In some positions a very high yet narrow hedge is appropriate and for this nothing is better than hornbeam or beech; both keep their dead leaves through the winter, the beech a bright russet and the hornbeam a sadder brown.

The disrepute into which privet hedges have fallen is partly deserved, but also partly due to their misuse. They are not interesting either in colour, form or texture and they impoverish the soil. But they will grow under almost any conditions and for an evergreen hedge under the shade of trees it is hard to find a substitute. It is much more interesting when clipped either into a tall tapering hedge or a low and very broad one. The usual nondescript size and shape adds considerably to their depressing appearance and is made worse by occasionally breaking into pretentious battlements.

GROUPING AND COMPATIBILITY OF PLANTS

The use of plants in sculptural compositions is part of the Japanese tradition, where the low mounds of azaleas contrast with the gnarled pines and upright bamboos. The same principle is being used to-day in modern gardens where the rigid demarcation of hedges and shaped beds has been replaced by groups of plants which, at the same time, give the main space division of the garden and provide in themselves compositions of form, colour and texture. In different scales this type of grouping applies to all sizes of plants—trees, shrubs, herbaceous and ground plants. The basis of these groups is the classic combination of upright, recumbent and prostrate forms, or sometimes a simpler contrast of vertical and horizontal, or static and dynamic.

A few examples of these groups will illustrate how they can be carried out on different scales.

A waterside grouping of Lombardy poplar and weeping willow combines with the horizontal line of the water to form the upright, recumbent and prostrate combination. A close, rounded clump of gorse beside which grows a gnarled thorn represents the static and dynamic.

Tall leaves of *Iris dalmatica pallida* and flat leaves of bergenia form the vertical and horizontal composition (Figs. 18, 19 and 20).

To select the right plant for each position one must not only know the general appearance of the plant, but recognise the particular characteristics which make each one of different value in a garden composition.

The first broad classification is of stature. As in the wild landscape there is the tree-layer, the shrub-layer and the ground-layer, so in the garden we have trees which will give stature, scale and framing; shrubs which will

Fig. 18. *The static cushion of gorse contrasted with the dynamic thorn.*

give space division and enclosure at a lower level; and the herbaceous and ground plants which form the ground pattern and interior decoration.

The plant may be deciduous or evergreen. The texture may be close, matt and dense like the yew, box and evergreen oak, or coarser and shiny, like the laurel and holly, or gaunt and open like the ailanthus.

Professor F. Robinson, in her book, *Planting Design*, gives a grading of ... fine and light, fine and heavy, medium, coarse and light, coarse and

Fig. 19. *Vertical Lombardy poplar, recumbent weeping willow, horizontal water.*

heavy,' and she shows how a diagrammatic analysis of a Japanese garden on this basis results in a good abstract pattern.

Texture is important in choosing plants for backgrounds. It is their close, matt texture which makes box and yew hedging ideal as a foil to flowers and statuary; whereas the broken light reflected from the shining leaves of holly makes it a poor background, but pleasantly enlivening when used as an outer boundary hedge and seen against the misty blue of a winter woodland.

20. The English landscape park formed its compositions of gentle hills crowned with temples overlooking lake-filled valleys Castle Howard.

21. The artificial hill created by Asplund at the Stockholm Crematorium. One of the finest modern examples of a designed landscape.

22. The clear-cut basin to the fountain shows the architectural use of land-shaping—Belvedere, Vienna.

23. The strong foliage of Hosta as a foil to smaller flowers.

In the grouping of plants the relationship of one texture to another is quite as important as the more obvious factor of colour. It is particularly so in ground planting where the plants have little variation of size and form, and the best effects can often be obtained by the pattern made by one texture intermingling with another. This pattern of foliage can often be seen in nature; ivy leaves lying on a mat of fescue on a stone wall, or the starfish of bog violet against the cushion of sphagnum moss, or pinnate fronds of silver weed against the fine-foliaged wild thyme. In all these

Fig. 20. Flowering cherry and pine, a dynamic group.

examples success depends on simplicity, one plant supplying the quiet background, while the other stands out clearly against it.

Form and habit are important in all plants, but perhaps most striking in the case of trees. The extreme shapes, which should be used only where special emphasis is needed, are the weeping, the fastigiate and the tabular. But every tree has its characteristic shape, whether grown as an individual or as a group.

The beech has a graceful flowing line; a single specimen will sweep down to the ground with its branches, a group will appear softly rounded, in the familiar form so well suited to the chalk downs.

The oak is rugged and elbowed, its outline bounded by lines and angles rather than by curves. The sycamore is strong, solid and heavy, echoing the billowing mass of cumulus clouds.

Some trees are at their best in masses and as backgrounds, others as single specimens and foreground groups. Scots pine, silver birch, cedar of Lebanon and ailanthus are examples of foreground trees; their chief attraction lies in their pattern, their individual shape, the beauty of the trunks and habit of branching. All of them can be used to frame views of buildings beyond them, because they are open textured. The oaks, sycamore, yews and spruce are suitable for backgrounds because they are massive with dense or heavy foliage.

There are certain coarse textured and strongly patterned trees, such as the horse chestnut and the catalpa, which are seen at their best as focal points, at close enough range for their pattern to be appreciated.

In addition to its general outline, a plant has a pattern which is formed by its shape, the arrangement of its leaves, branches, buds and flowers. Those plants with strongly marked patterns are valuable in giving strength to a composition or as adjuncts to architecture. Typical examples are the acanthus, the vine, the yucca, aralia, hosta and magnolia (Plate 23).

One of the more subtle qualities of plants is a certain relationship in colour and proportion between the stem, the leaves and the flowers, and the poise of the flowers upon their stems. It is these qualities which give the plant species a grace often lacking in the garden hybrids. Compare, for instance, the tightly packed truss of flowers in some double lilacs with the delicately poised flowerlets of *Syringa persica*, and the loss of the hooked keel of the type delphinium in the solid spire of the modern elatum varieties. The flower-heads of lace cap *Astera macrophylla* are in scale with the foliage and with other plants, while the heavy spheres of *H. hortensis* are by comparison clumsy and usually look right only in conjunction with architecture and not among other plants.

The intensifying of flower colours by hybridization can also throw out the subtle harmony of the wild plant. Compare the harsh colour combination of rose Fashion and its leaves with the harmony of *Rosa rubrifolia*. This loss of quality by hybridization is not invariable and depends on the features chosen for intensification. The long-spurred hybrid aquilegias, for instance, have accentuated the most characteristic feature of the plant, whereas in many other cases finer points have been sacrificed to mere size, or to doubling, which extinguishes the beautiful pattern of the single blossom and its central boss of stamens.

Colour is often considered only in relation to the plant's flower. Yet the general tone of the plant and its appearance when out of flower is quite as important, or even more so, since the flowering period may be short. The most carefully chosen flower colour will not compensate for leaves which are out of key with their surroundings.

These attributes taken together—stature, form, pattern, texture and colour—add up to the plant's character; that indefinable personality which decides whether plants will look right together, and whether they will fill the particular place in the design for which they are intended. The best associations are between plants which have one element in common and another contrasted. Complete contrast in all elements can be used for special emphasis, but repeated too often the effect is restless, lacking the unity given by a connecting link of similarity.

In the gardens of the Alcazar in Seville, there is an example of extreme contrast in the size and texture of foliage; the huge glossy leaves of a banana against dense, small-leaved box (Plate 24). In this case the unifying factor is the similarity in the shade of green. An English example is that of the sword-like leaves of *Iris dalmatica pallida* contrasted with the rounded leaves and horizontal growth of *Senecio greyi* and yet brought into unison by the grey-green colouring. Equally the contrast may be in colour and the uniting factor one of texture.

The same principles can be seen in natural groupings. One of nature's most beautiful compositions is that of the chalk-land plant community, containing beech, yew, whitebeam, viburnum, wild privet, dogwood, dog rose, mullein, potentilla, thyme and fescue. In stature we have the clear division between the trees, the shrubs, the herbs and the ground plants, together giving composition in height and mass. The three tree species are compatible and yet contrasted. They have in common a roughly rounded outline, the beech and the yew markedly so, the white-beam less so. In texture they are graded from the fine, dense yew, the less dense but still fine textured beech and, in contrast, the coarse, open-textured whitebeam.

In tone and colour, the yew gives depth and a dark accent all the year round. In winter the other trees fade to a misty grey-purple, but in spring there is the lively contrast of the fiery green of the beech and the shining silver of the unfolding whitebeam buds. The shrub layer carries on the theme in a modified form, the privet echoing the yew, the viburnum the whitebeam and the dogwood the beech, but added to them is the detail interest of the dog rose, a plant of delicate pattern and a prototype of the foreground plant.

Of the herbs, the mullein and the potentilla are both pattern plants, well contrasted, the potentilla with spreading leaves and habit, the mullein strong and vertical, a plant of accent, not to be used too often nor in mass. Its value is shown to advantage because it stands up clear from a flat cushioned ground-pattern of thyme and fescue. These last by their difference in texture, and the occasional accent of silver weed, supply the quiet interest of the ideal ground pattern.

The whole is a composition in smooth rounded form, relieved by minor notes of strong pattern.

In contrast to this is the typical pine/birch wood. There are no rounded forms, both trees are open in texture and there is no shrub layer to make the transition from tree to ground, the open pattern of the trunks goes straight down to the herb layer, which consists this time of ling whose jagged habit of growth echoes that of the Scots pine. Below the ling is the hard, smooth layer of moss. The character throughout is hard, open and strong-patterned. The delicate pattern of potentilla would be lost here, and the most telling contrast is the smooth, rounded form of a toadstool, one which would be meaningless in the chalkland community.

Passing from the natural plant associations to those of gardens we can again decide why the planting in certain cases satisfies us. In the Italian renaissance gardens the species used are few and they are used with a clear intention. At the sides, the bosquets are there simply to contain the garden and to unite it with the landscape. They must be massive, dense and homogeneous. They can be of *Quercus ilex* or of plane. They would fail in their purpose if they consisted of an unconsidered mixture of trees, because they would lose their homogeneity, or if they were of small trees they would not carry the desired weight, or if they were of highly coloured foliage they would distract attention instead of concentrating it on the garden.

Within the garden there may again be quiet trees such as *Quercus ilex* where solidity and a calm background is wanted; but where there is to be emphasis, along a terrace, up steps, to crown a hill or at focal points in the design, there will be *Cupressus sempervirens* with its strong fastigiate accent. At the Villa D'Este these are contrasted with the delicate umbrella shapes of the stone pine to form a silhouetted composition on the skyline (Plate 25). In this same garden the quietly nondescript plantings which cover the banks between the terraces fulfil their purpose as a background to the displays of water in a way which could not be achieved by a planting of individually interesting trees and shrubs.

Hedges, often of *Quercus ilex*, in Italian gardens serve the same quiet purpose of background to the statuary, the fountains and the occasional bright flowers. Flowers are rare and their bright colours are intensified by their dark surroundings. Orange trees in tubs are the typical foreground pattern plant.

At Vaux-le-Vicomte again the trees are used as background and frame and their value lies, not in their individual form, but in their massed and solid effect, cut, in this case, to make a formal frame to the garden. The hedges are purely architectural outlines to the pattern of the garden, and within them the flowers in the parterres are used, not as compositional patterns in themselves, but purely as colour, just as park bedding is, but in the case of Vaux-le-Vicomte the use is justified by the merit of the pattern which they fill.

At Stowe the trees are not only the frame and structure, they are a component throughout the whole design. They must have a certain variety and individual character, which was not needed in the two previous examples. But yet there must not be too much variety. The beech is

24. Foliage contrast—Box and Banana in the gardens of the Alcazar, Seville.

25. Umbrella pine contrasted with Cypress. Rome.

26. The gardens of the Generaliffe, Spain, are sprayed and patterned by the interlacing jets.

27. Stone echoes the ripples of the water. Villa Lante, Italy.

dominant, holding everything together with its rounded sweep, but within it are the darkenings of the yews and cedars and against it the stately groups and single specimens of lime and plane.

In the Spanish garden the box hedge is used to contain luxuriant plants, free-growing, but lacking in any compositional relation with each other. In contrast to the carefully chosen individual plants of the patios, they are like vases of flowers related in shape and placing to the general design.

In the Scandinavian garden the plants themselves supply the form of the design.

COLOUR

There are perhaps three successful ways of dealing with colour in the garden. One is the Italian method of designing a picture in monotone, enlivened only with high notes of colour. The second is to observe the laws of nature, while the third, the hardest of all, is to treat the colour of plants as if they were the colours on a palette and paint pictures with them. The last is probably the method which appeals most to modern English taste, but to do it needs the rare combination of an exact knowledge of plants with a painter's eye; and for the general run of human beings, nature will prove a safer guide.

Nature provides us with some daring colour schemes and it is worth enquiring why they are always successful. The answer seems to be that she either keeps one colour, or harmony of colours, dominant over a wide area, or, if startling colours are mixed together, they are broken up into kaleidoscopic patterns. There is on one hand the bluebell wood, with the blue dominant over all the other delicate spring colours, and on the other a hayfield (before the days of selective weed killers) where the orange of hawkweed, the deep purple of self-heal, the blue and pink of milkweed and the magenta of knapweed are mixed together into a rich mosaic of colour bedded into a background of green and honey. The garden equivalent of the hayfield is the cottage garden, which by its same inconsequent mixture achieves the same happy result. But if these colours are separated out into beds or solid drifts, the individual colours clash and jar with each other, as may be seen in the blocks of different coloured tulips in municipal parks. Nor should the mixture consist wholly of the bright colours and omit the quiet background of the hay stalks.

Unless the majority of cultivated flowering plants are to be banned, nature's methods must be translated rather than strictly adhered to. For instance, almost all wild trees and shrubs have either green or white flowers, and these are undoubtedly the best with nature's early spring colour scheme of intense green, white and pale yellow. The exception is the wild crab, whose pink is soft and broken, and which flowers a little later than the cherries, when the green is beginning to darken. But against the singing green of the early beech leaves nothing can be more lovely than the white of the wild cherry. A pink tree against this background throws out the harmony. But within the garden, it is possible to build up a setting where the cherries and the flowering peaches can be seen to the best advantage. Groves of cherries make their own colour dominant, so that one walks through a world of pink and white. Almond comes before the green and finds its complementary colours in the blue sky and grey winter woods. The intense spring-flowering trees such as *Persica* 'Clara Meyer' are too strong either massed or singly against the spring green, but they can look right against the background of a grey wall or blue-grey foliage.

Even more difficult in the early spring is the rather hard orange of *Berberis darwinii*, and the egg yellow of some varieties of forsythia, whereas the primrose of the variety *Forsythia ovata* and the soft colour of *corylopsis* are perfect. As the greens darken with summer, practically no colour is too strong in itself for use, provided it is used in the right place and quantity.

A very small amount of strong colour will tell as contrast in a misty atmosphere. To realise this one has only to remember the intense brilliance of coloured lights seen in a fog. Sunlight has the effect of lightening colour. For this reason brilliant colours can be more freely used in a sunny climate without appearing gaudy. But it must also be remembered that many people feel a great craving for colour after the dark of winter, particularly a winter spent in towns. The English countryside is never colourless and the deep blues and purples of the winter woods can be infinitely satisfying. The aim should, therefore, be to provide colour in the garden without producing a confused glare. The general ground colour in England is grass green. This is an intense colour, which must be taken into account in choosing the flowers which are to be seen against it.

No colour in the garden registers as a pure colour-card; it takes its value from the surroundings, the lighting, and the texture of the surface. Given the right setting, the smallest spot of strong colour will have more effect than a great mass of it nullified by its neighbours. One of the most brilliant effects is a touch of orange, seen through the green depth of a wood. Here the heightening effect is the contrast of the complementary colours, green and orange. Similarly the pink of an almond looks at its best against the mist-blue background of a winter wood. But in these examples of contrasting colours the quieter colour should be the prevailing one, with the bright one as a spot of contrast.

The science of colour and its relation to music is mentioned by Repton in *The Art of Landscape Gardening* as an exciting new discovery which may explain our preference for certain combinations of colour, and if these preferences are analysed it will often be found that they are based on the harmony of triads in the spectrum—red yellow blue: orange green violet: citrus slate russet: sage plum buff (See *Planting Design by* F. Robinson).

Because of the effect of the sun in lightening colour, white and pale flowers are best in shade, where they will light up the dark recesses of the shadow. *Rhododendron ponticum* looks its best in a shadowed woodland; in the sunlight it is unpleasantly insipid.

The use of coloured foliage holds many dangers, but properly used it can help to solve the problems of giving flower colours their best setting. Grey foliage is particularly valuable in this respect, and the popularity of lavender and pinks is as much due to the foil they give to other flowers as to their own sweet-scented blossom.

But there are many gardens to-day which have been spoilt by the introduction of purple, golden and glaucous blue foliage. The colours are not necessarily bad in themselves, but where trees form the green framework of the garden or the link between garden and country, a sudden spot of purple or gold destroys the composition just as surely as the appearance of a Georgian house would be spoiled if a small portion of the brickwork were painted bright green or blue to relieve the monotony of the old red brick. The introduction of glaucous trees into the main tree groupings at Stowe and Stourhead is in the same category of vandalism. The function of a background is to harmonize the view; it must be restful and it must recede rather than jump forward to the eye.

The coloured foliage trees are so dominant that they can be used only in a scene composed especially for them. They can either themselves become the background or become the focal point in a composition harmonized to them. It would be possible to plant a glade of glaucous trees with purple foliage as a foil. For example, *Cedrus atlantica glauca* and *Corylus purpurea* carpeted with ajuga. Or a golden garden could be designed for the winter and early spring where, beside the gold, only brownish greens would be used, such as box and cryptomeria. A whole landscape of such colours would be tiresome, but as a small enclave they could be delightful.

TREES

Trees are both the most important and most permanent of all garden plant material. However precious the small individual garden may be, it is of limited value unless it is set within the larger landscape of the town and country, and given a context of scale and continuity which can be supplied only by forest trees.

For this reason, trees, long-lived and slow to mature, should be the first consideration in all landscape and garden planning. The smaller and quicker growing trees have their place, particularly in the private garden, but they can never be a substitute for the stature and solidity of the large trees. These must make the framework and the smaller trees be used only as accessories. To overcome the long wait while such trees as

Fig. 21. *Planting of silver birch and Scots pine merging into each other.*

oak and beech come to maturity, faster-growing, shorter-lived trees can be used as temporary fillers. The danger of this practice is that the permanent trees may be sacrificed to the fillers, which should be ruthlessly removed as soon as they interfere with the larger trees.

In grouping trees, it should be decided whether they are intended to develop each into a perfectly shaped specimen, in which case their spacing must allow for their eventual spread, or whether they are to grow together into a solid group, when their spacing may be far closer. Where they are to form space division or background they should be close planted, while the fully developed specimens should be reserved for the focal point, or the outriders coming forward into glades and parkland from the more solidly planted backgrounds. Many trees thrive best if they are close planted and thinned out later.

Some trees are naturally light-loving, other shade-bearing. Those which show individualism in nature should be allowed to keep it in the garden. For instance the *Sorbus aria* is always seen as a lone tree in the downlands as the *Sorbus aucuparia* is on the mountains. The silver birch is happiest in light, informal groups or open woodland where the lovely shape of the silver trunks can be seen rising from grass or fern.

In grouping, two or at the most three species are enough to form the composition of each group, and these should follow the same laws of contrast and compatibility as all other plants (See pp. 111–116). But in the case of large groupings, the contrast must be between a group of one species and another, rather than between individuals. Thus, in a mixture of Scots pine and birch, the pine should thicken into solid groups, and then thin out among the birch, to make a connected pattern of evergreen, rather than be evenly scattered (Fig. 21). Or if the pyramidal shape of red-twigged lime is to be contrasted with the round solidity of horse chestnut, the two species must be grouped separately to give a clear distinction between their shapes.

Similarly, if smaller trees such as thorn are to be grouped with forest trees, they should be planted in solid drifts where their change of scale will register in relation to the taller trees, instead of becoming confused with them (See Fig. 14).

The clean trunks of trees are things of beauty which should be masked only when it is desired to bring solidity down to ground level, and even then the undergrowth should be drifted among the trees, as it is in a natural woodland, allowing the sight of occasional tree-trunks and the penetration of light and shadow.

SHRUBS

During the last century, flowering shrubs have become a major material of garden design and, well used, they can contribute both to the framework of the garden and to its interior decoration. Their solidity down to ground level makes them effective for space division at a lower level than the trees, a valuable quality but one which precludes their use on lawns which are intended to read as a continuous sweep of open space. On contoured ground, restrained use of broad masses of a few species only, carefully contrasted in form and texture, can make a small scale composition on exactly the same principles as tree groupings.

Shrubs can also be used to form sculptural groups either by themselves or combined with other types of plant or, as they are in Japanese gardens, grouped with rocks. Used in these ways shrubs are part of the structure of the garden composition. But they may also be purely internal decorations, like the hydrangeas in the fountain garden at Tintinhull. Or they may be used singly as focal points, like the *Cornus kousa* in the same garden.

HERBACEOUS PLANTS

The herbaceous border is a very English institution with its roots in the old cottage garden tradition. It was lifted into society by the writings of Gertrude Jekyll and William Robinson during the last century; and, like most things which are taken up violently by fashion, it has been abused: yet at its best it can be an endless joy to the plant-loving owner of a garden. Perhaps the first rule of success is to ensure that it shall not be strictly herbaceous, for if carried to extremes this not only excludes spring bulbs but dwarf shrubs such as lavender. A truer name for it is the continental one of the 'mixed'.

Its most usual faults are lack of form and of contrast in habit and foliage. Many of the herbaceous plants, which are popular on account of their showy flowers, have undistinguished foliage and a bushy, nondescript shape. This is true of the great family of asters, the heleniums, erigerons, rudbeckias and phloxes, while although the lupins and delphiniums have interesting shaped leaves, they are too sparse and short-lived to tell in the jungle of the border when not in flower. Added to this is a similarity in habit of growth and scale of flower, which contributes to a general mushiness. Also, many of the plants die off before the end of the summer, leaving gaps or untidy thickets of dead stalks.

The first care in designing a border is to give it a backbone of strong form so that the shape of the border will take its place as part of the garden composition quite apart from the flowers.

It is difficult to design a satisfactory border except against a good background of wall or hedge, preferably over 6 feet high. A double border has to be so wide if it is to accommodate the larger plants, which alone will give it form, that it assumes a scale out of keeping with this type of planting, which is essentially domestic.

Given the background, the border should be bound to it by an indication of buttressing. This may either be done by formal buttresses of yew, for example, or informally by planting shrubs of some solidity at intervals against the wall and coming out across the border. But if the informal method is adopted, then the spacing of the groups and their relative weights must be informally balanced, not arranged symmetrically as in the case of the formal buttresses. Some suitable shrubs for these strengthening groups are osmanthus, elaeagnus, *Mahonia bealei* or *M. japonica*, *Spiraea lindleyana*, *Viburnum rhytidophyllum*, *Magnolia grandiflora* and eucryphia. That is, plants which either have great solidity or whose foliage pattern is strong and distinctive, with a leaf scale larger than that of the average herbaceous plant. The feeling of solidity, which this buttressing will give, must then be carried forward to the front of the border using smaller plants, but again those which have either strong large-scale leaves or the simple solidity of yew or box.

In the first category are yuccas, *Phormium tenax* (where it is hardy), *senecio greyi*, *Viburnum davidii*. In the latter are box, lavender and rosemary. These permanent subjects form a satisfactory pattern in themselves having a certain rhythm and balance and should be strong enough to maintain the interest of the border through the winter, providing a framework to the drifts of spring and winter bulbs which otherwise will appear lost in the bare ground. This winter pattern can be added to by a foreground covering of ground-planting such as dianthus, thymus and achillea King Edward VII, through which the smaller bulbs can grow. There are also a few of the so-called herbaceous plants which normally hold at least some of their leaves during the winter, such as iris, bergenia and *Stachys lanata*.

Within this framework can be grouped the more transitory plants, but with these, too, the form and composition of the grouping should be considered as of even greater importance than the amount of flower and colour. There are certain plants which are invaluable in giving contrast of form and leaf. Of the taller growing species, bocconia, echinops and cynara have a carved quality, which shows up particularly well against the background of wall or hedge. Acanthus, eryngium, hosta, some of the stronger leaved iris and bergenia play the same role among shorter plants. A plant such as eryngium, whose chief beauty lies in the strong yet delicate pattern of its leaves and bracts, should be silhouetted against a simple background, rising clear-cut out of a low ground cover such as armeria. The strongly vertical leaves of iris should be given the foil of a horizontal or cushioned growth.

There are several methods of overcoming the difficulty of bare and untidy patches when plants have died down. A roaming plant such as *Vitis coignetiae*, which matures late in the season, can be planted to grow over and cover the dead stems, or late flowering plants with good covering capacity can be interplanted or drifted in front of lupins or delphiniums. Useful plants for this purpose are *Anthemis tinctoria* and *Aster cordifolia*.

There are certain plants which never lose their good appearance, being decorative in seed as well as flower. *Achillea eupatorium* is an outstanding example, which also plays its part in giving strong form to the border. Paeonies are another whose leaves and seed heads are always decorative.

The arrangement of colour in the herbaceous border is more difficult than in any other part of the garden, because the range is more varied. Fine effects can be achieved by confining the choice to a certain range of colouring. A border of white and green can be effective, especially in the half shade.

At Hidcote there is a border of red and deep orange flowers, not normally an easy range of colours to deal with, but placed against hedges and foliage of strong dark green and purple/green the effect is magnificent.

An all-yellow scheme is also good. A blue border is apt to look dead without a touch of complementary colour, and is at its best with pale yellow, strong purple, grey foliage and a touch of orange. The grey, white, clear blue and yellow border at Tintinhull is particularly good against its dark green background. A complete range of purples, on the other hand, can be perfectly satisfying because the warmth is supplied by the darker reddish purples. The michaelmas daisies are probably more effective grown massed together than in any other way.

It is also possible to get results without the self denial of keeping to one colour range. The colours, however, should never be arranged in solid blocks, but should either be on the principle of richly woven tapestry or a medieval stained glass window or, on a larger scale, there may be a gentle transition from one carefully composed colour group to the next. In either case a plentiful use of background plants is needed, whose tone will harmonize with the other colours and give homogeneity to the whole. Grey foliage is a valuable harmonizer and lavender, stachys, *Artemisia ludoviciana*, rosemary and *Senecio greyi* can all be used for this purpose. The greys harmonize with the blues and provide a complementary colour for the pinks. The Hidcote border, with its strong oranges and reds, correctly uses dark green as the complementary background. One of the most useful flower colours for giving depth and strength to a border is the deep garnet red of *Pentstemon rupicola*.

The colours should be planned to give a balanced composition throughout the season, so that an abstract of the flowers out at one time, whether few or many, makes a good pattern in itself; the weight of colour effect will, of course, shift its position from season to season, but there must not, at any one time, be a solid block of colour in one half of the border and a blank space in the other.

There are many ways of growing herbaceous plants other than in the border. Those which do not object to shade may be naturalized in light woodland. They can be grown in grass as they were in medieval days. They can be grouped with shrubs and ground plants in those informal compositions where plants themselves form the shapes of the garden, or they can be grown as individuals at vital points in a patio garden, or at the foot of a wall. Or they can be used as filling to the beds of a parterre whether it be of the traditional type or the free shapes of Burle Marx.

In old gardens the scent of plants was rightly counted as one of their chief beauties. Possibly smoking and petrol fumes have dulled the modern sense of smell, for many people can no longer appreciate the subtle scent of box in the sun referred to by Bacon. Yet to anyone living in a garden, and not merely looking at it, scent is still the most evocative attribute of a flower. The essence of a summer day or the rare warm evening is the gentle scent-laden air which no true garden must withhold.

There are certain plants, magnificent in themselves, which constantly suffer misuse, and perhaps chief among them are azaleas and rhododendrons. The wonderful colours of azaleas have made them immensely popular, but because of this colouring they need very careful placing.

28. The gardens of the Belvedere, Vienna, draw the horizon into themselves.

29. In the colder climate of Copenhagen the water bubbles sedately from the wooden bowls in the Tivoli Gardens.

30. The central fountain, lower parterre, Villa Lante.

31. Water gives the setting for some of the most beautiful garden features. The Sea Horse, Villa Lante.

An indiscriminate mixture can have the most painful results and both their neighbours and general setting must be chosen with discrimination.

The orange of Ghent hybrids and the pink of *hinomayo* are particularly unfortunate together and should never be allowed to appear in the same view. A woodland glade is their best setting even if it is on the reduced scale necessary in a small garden; it gives them the conditions of half shade which they like, and provides a cool deep green background and the dapple of shadow, which is the best foil for their brilliant tones.

But even here the hotter colours should be used with discretion. The cool yellow of *A. pontica* and the various cream shades, on the other hand, can be used extensively and even combined with a carpet of bluebells without appearing too gaudy. Perhaps the most lovely of all settings is a wood in which there are natural outcroppings of grey rock, which will not only steady the colours, but give form and reason to the drifts of planting.

Just as green woodland supplies a complementary colour to the orange shades, so grey rock and dark blue-green conifers will form a background for the pink and purple varieties. The great virtues of the Japanese azaleas are their habit of growth and beautiful evergreen foliage. In the case of some varieties with the cruellest colours one could wish they would never flower, but be content to form the entrancingly shaped mounds of bronze green which compose with the shape of rocks more perfectly than any other plant. They are plants to be used as individuals or in carefully composed groups where their shapes can be appreciated. The worst way to grow them is in a solid mass of mixed colours. The salmon and orange pinks are the hardest to place and if used at all should be in small quantities grouped only with dark green or grey. *Malvatica* is one of the kinder colours and is particularly good with the grey of rock. The fiery red of *hinodigiri* can be used effectively as a minute spot of discord.

Rhododendrons, except the alpine varieties, are essentially forest plants and to be seen at their best should be grown in the half-shade of trees as they are in the glade at Kew. Here also the changes of level give an opportunity to observe the magnificent leaves of *R. sinogrande* and to appreciate the beauty of their stems and the occasional flower truss seen against the sky.

In any large planting of rhododendrons, the cool colours should predominate, the white, blues, mauves and lilacs shading to the deep purples and clarets and the dark reds as accents. The strong pinks are better kept out of the picture, for here again they are neither complementary nor in harmony with the background of green, but the softer pinks are lovely if their neighbours are chosen with care.

The indiscriminate mixing of azaleas and rhododendrons leads to deplorable results, for in the main the colours are incompatible. There are exceptions, however, such as the use of cream, buff and tawny-orange azaleas with rhododendrons of lavender-blue and deep purple, such as *augustinii* and Purple Splendour.

CONIFERS

Conifers on the whole are not easy mixers, perhaps because they have too many points of difference from the softer deciduous plants. They associate naturally with the ericaceae, because the growth of a heath is not unlike that of a conifer in miniature—evergreen, hard and scaly. On the same principle, the asymmetrically branching conifers, such as *Pinus sylvestris* and *Cedrus libani*, are more at home with deciduous trees than the symmetrical spruce, because they are more nearly related in their habit of growth. Where there is no factor of similarity, the success of the grouping usually depends on either the conifer or the deciduous plant being entirely dominant, with the other merely an incident. In the case of birch grown in the foreground of a wood of spruce, the birch forms the picture, the spruce merely acts as a background. In the classic group of upright cypress, the recumbent pine and the flowering almond, the group is coniferous, the almond is an incident. The odd cupressus rising from a flowery and deciduous English garden is sometimes a success as an accent of vertical emphasis, or a group can be used to build up a shape and background which dominates the scene, but a sprinkling of them is distracting and weakens the composition.

The planting of the conifers near the lake at Kew is an excellent example of their proper use. In their own area they are dominant over the deciduous trees and, growing cleanly from the grass, they are composed with the contoured mounds and valleys to show their character of growth to the best advantage.

While the picea are usually associated with mass-produced forests, many of the pinus are strong charactered individuals; they produce such well defined shapes that they can be used most effectively as a composition of form, restricted in colour to varying shades of green, with at the most the incidental touch of colour which might be given by a group of foxgloves in a woodland glade, some spikes of mullein, or a spray of wild rose.

Another misused family is that of the rose. They are flowers for individual enjoyment and, pictorially, the worst way to grow them is in beds by themselves. Some varieties, either naturally dwarf or pegged down, can be used as colour filling, like bedding plants, but most types do not show at their best grown in this way. Their flowers are too individual and their colour effect spotted rather than massed. But grouped with other plants, either as the main interest with the other plants as foils and background, or as foreground incidents, the individual beauty of their flowers can be appreciated. The wild rose of the hedge poises its flowers against the solid background of the field hedge or flings an elegant spray against the sky. But roses lack solidity; they are the typical foreground plant, the furnishing within the structure of stronger, denser planting. In Spain, where roses are one of the most popular plants, they are planted in box-edged beds and allowed to spray out freely among other plants.

Some of the rose species are exceptions and can stand by themselves as flowering shrubs. The Scandinavians have recognized the landscape value of the more compact *rugosa* varieties, such as Schneezwerg, and use it perhaps more than any other single plant in the landscaping of their housing schemes. It is still weak in character in winter, but in summer the strong firm pattern of its foliage and its rounded sculptural growth places it high in the ranks of good landscape plants. *Rosa rubrifolia* is also valuable as a massing plant, where the plum and grey of its foliage can make the most valuable foil for other colours.

There are families of plants which, on the other hand, are exceptionally versatile. The cotoneasters are a vast family which are constantly being called in to fill varying roles. Their wide tolerance of soil and climate and their ability to look after themselves, once established, make them invaluable, and although they can be spectacular in berry and some even in flower, they have a quiet restraint and a scale comparable to the general run of indigenous plants, which makes them good mixers in almost all positions. They range in habit from the 15 to 20 feet high *C. frigida*, which is unrivalled for making a quick screen on heavy clay, to the completely prostrate *C. dammeri*, one of the best of all carpeting plants.

The points to observe in selecting cotoneaster varieties for different purposes in the garden are their habit of growth and foliage value.

Some, although evergreen, are of little value in the winter because of their open habit and the sparseness of their leaves. Others, like *C. salicifolia*, present a winter appearance of real solidity. One of the most lustrously evergreen is *C. conspicua*, whose prostrate variety *decora* is a fine subject for clothing banks. *C. horizontalis*, although deciduous, has such a wealth of well-shaped, good coloured branches that it is still of value in the winter, but where a true evergreen is wanted, *microphylla* is probably the nearest in form. *Congesta* has a delightful habit of wrapping round objects on the ground and forming itself into mounds like the shapes in a Japanese garden. It is most useful for composing on a small scale, in a courtyard, or to diversify ground pattern.

LANDSCAPE ARCHITECT'S PLANTS

Where the plantsman will classify plants botanically, in accordance with their families, or ecologically, in accordance with their preferences of soil and climate, the landscape architect will add another classification according to their visual values, and it may be interesting to consider a few plants grouped together under this heading.

Aralia, Fatsia japonica, Rhus typhina, Spiraea aitchisonii, Mahonia japonica and *M. bealei* are suited to varying positions, but they all have in common a strong individuality, big scale leaves and a well-marked pattern, which makes them valuable as special accents in positions where their form will show up against a simple background or where they will give stiffening to groups of softer texture.

Bocconia cordata, Thalictrum glaucum, echinops, cynara, eryngium and acanthus carry something of the same character into the herbaceous field. They all have strongly patterned foliage and a certain rigidity which gives stiffening and accent to less distinctive plants. But to be seen at their best they should stand out clearly as sculptural groups, rising from a horizontal base, and either standing alone against a simple background or grouped with one contrasting form. For instance, the deeply-cut leaves of acanthus can be contrasted with the large entire leaves of *funkia robusta glauca*, the similarity in colour serving as the uniting factor. Or bocconia may be grouped with *Elymus glaucus*, whose vertical leaves will contrast with the indented rounded pads of the bocconia.

Viburnum rhytidophyllum, heracleum and *Achillea eupatorium* all give, in their varying scales, the pattern of the horizontal, plate-shaped inflorescence held on strong, upright stems and contrasted with leaves of marked pattern. They contain within themselves so fine a contrast of form that it is sufficient for them to stand alone, but they are also good as contrasts to low rounded masses or as stiffeners among plants of less determinate character.

Cornus kousa, C. florida and *Viburnum mariesii* are distinguished by a tabular pattern, flat flower heads held on horizontal branches, which makes them a foil for the vertical tree-trunks of a woodland.

Bergenia, hosta, *Sedum spectabile* and *Saxifraga peltata* are examples of plants whose simple broad leaves form a contrast to vertical spikes or finely cut foliage.

The stronger growing irises, veratrum, sisyrinchium, tritoma and verbascum are type plants of the vertical spikes which compose so well with the horizontal habit of the foregoing group. This form is repeated on the largest scale by *Cupressus sempervirens* and Lombardy poplar.

Yucca and *Phormium tenax* supply a form which is rare in temperate gardens, the strong group of spikes radiating out from a central point. Because of its exotic form it should be used with discretion, usually as a point of emphasis; it is at its best either rising from a smooth surface or contrasting with a low rounded or horizontal form. In Holland Park there is an extensive planting of *Yucca gloriosa*, grouped on a contoured lawn. It makes a lovely and exotic picture, enhanced by peacocks and a background of bamboo.

Equally exotic and to be used only in the most carefully chosen positions is the gunnera with its immense leaves, and on a diminishing scale rheum and rodgersia. It is fortunate that gunnera's cultural requirements make it a waterside plant, for the broad open plane of water and the vertical contrast of giant reed are its best neighbours.

Euphorbia wulfenii is an accent plant both in form and colour. Its colour is so striking that it should either be led up to with other glaucous plants or stand alone, related to architecture, at the corner of steps, or rising from the paving of a terrace.

Anemone japonica, *Spiraea aruncus*, paeony, hellebore, royal fern, Solomon's seal, *Thalictrum adiantifolium* and epimedium represent the type of low-growing or herbaceous plant, which is decorative even when not in flower. Restrained, well-bred, by their perfect form and pattern they will fit in quietly in any situation, and only ask that they shall not be overwhelmed by more rampant and formless neighbours.

Their equivalent in shrub form is found in *Viburnum davidii* with its quiet but decisive leaf pattern and invariable air of well-groomed health; in skimmia with rather similar qualities and the zenobias where peaty conditions make their use possible; or *Choisya ternata* where climate allows its use; or on a larger scale *Arbutus unedo*.

Senecio greyi, *Phlomis fruticosa*, rosamarinus and lavender, and among herbaceous plants *Stachys lanata*, *Artemisia ludoviciana* and *Cineraria maritima* combine good foliage and habit with the grey colouring which is so valuable in garden colour schemes.

There are certain plants which stand out as aristocrats by their sheer quality. They have a perfection of flower, form and foliage which lifts them into a class by themselves. The whole family of magnolia comes into this category and the magnolia grove at Kew shows one of the best ways to use them, planted in drifts on gently contoured ground, turf below them, sky above and a backcloth of forest trees at a respectful distance.

Equally effective is their use at Bodnant, to light up the darkness of a wood, or as single specimens to give distinction to a courtyard or terrace. On a smaller scale, the tree paeonies have the same quality, a perfect relationship of flower, leaf-form and colouring. They, too, look their best in grass or standing up from quiet carpeting plants, grouped under the half-shade of birch or other light woodland trees. Eucryphia is another of these aristocrats. Among herbaceous plants, romneya fills the same role and is finest against a wall and grouped only with restrained plants of clear form which will not confuse the pattern of its leaves and flowers. *Iris dalmatica pallida* is a suitable neighbour. Its flowers are over before the romneya is out, the leaf colours harmonize and the straight spears of the iris are a good foil for the cut leaves of the *romneya*.

CLIMBERS

At the other end of the scale from the aristocrats is a certain class of climbing plants typified by *Polygonum baldschuanicum* and rambler roses, which may better be described as scramblers, for they have a smothering effect which can be valuable in covering ugly structures and banks, but which is death to good architectural elevations. But there are some climbers which, used in the right place, can become an adjunct of the architecture. *Hydrangea petiolaris* and *H. quercifolia* have a robust pattern and gnarled habit of growth which is full of character. All the vitis are good, but none better than *V. vinifera purpurea*, perfect both for pattern and colour. Its use in conjunction with *Fatsia japonica* against the old brick wall in Holland House gardens shows the possibilities of leaf design against the right background. *Vitis henryi* is less strong in pattern, but nearly as good, and is one of the most accommodating of all climbers, self-clinging and thriving in shade. The ivies have probably fallen into disrepute because the more rampant large-leaved varieties form themselves into a solid mass where the effect of their individual leaves cannot be seen. But the infinite variation of the native English ivy provides sprays of a chiselled perfection which is not bettered by any cultivated plant.

Paradoxically, there are two approaches needed to improve our use of plant material; one is an ability to see each plant as a whole individual, with all its characteristics, and the other is to be able to subordinate the individual plant to the picture as a whole.

CHAPTER ELEVEN

WATER

ᙯᖇᖙᖇᖙᖇᖙᖇᖙᖇᖙᖇᖙᖇᖙᖇᖙ

ALL the great gardens of the world have made use of water in one form or another and its use has been adapted by each country according to its needs and climate. It exerts an immense fascination, focusing attention on itself as few other garden features do.

Playing water is the only element, besides birds and human beings, which brings life and movement into the garden, while an expanse of still water gives a unique sense of space and unity. It clarifies a design by accentuating the basic level to which all else relates. In the landscape parks the lakes form the plane of reference on which the pattern of land-form and trees is built up.

Any opportunity to use water should be taken, provided it can be suited to the particular circumstances. On the practical side, one must ask whether there is an adequate supply and whether it can be kept clean. For private gardens there are now electric pumps which can circulate a small supply of water and make it do many things. In public parks, a through flow is desirable to keep the water pure.

Where water is both practicable and desirable, there are many factors which decide what form it should take. It is no use repeating in a dank London courtyard a motif of dripping water which was designed for refreshment from the hot Spanish sun; but in that same courtyard it might be possible to devise an eye of water which would reflect back the scanty light from the sky like a bright mirror.

In a hot climate, you cannot have too much water. The Generaliffe and the Villa D'Este play with it in every conceivable form. It sprays and drips, flows in cascades and shoots into the air in a pattern of interlacing jets (Plate 26). The sound, the sight, the smell of the damp-sprayed air are all a refreshment from the heat. But in a cool, damp climate, such copiousness would be depressing and the damp air would strike chill. A cascade or a single playing fountain is welcome even in England for the fascination of the moving water, but too much of it only echoes the too frequent rain. Moreover, the sun, whose sparkle on the droplets is one of the joys of water jets, is too often missing from the English sky.

Perhaps it is for this reason that you never see in England the same exuberant invention that the Italians display in playing with the water and rejoicing in the feel of it. There is a water runnel at the Villa Lante which gives this impression of rejoicing in the touch and shape of water. The rill spouts out from a dolphin's mouth and swirls down a long trough, which is itself carved into a series of rippling swirls like petrified water; while by the side a flight of steps echoes the ripples in a more sober form (See Plate 27).

It is significant that in the Tivoli gardens in the colder climate of Copenhagen, although water is used as the recurring motif of the design, it is quiet water making a sculptural form as it bubbles sedately from its wooden basins (Plate 29).

The moods which water can serve are as varied as the human temperament. It may be a sombre serenity. It may be *joie de vivre*, with copious far-flung jets; or frivolity, shown at its crudest in the water-jokes beloved of the late baroque period, and, more gently, in the intermittent jets at the Villa D'Este with their fascinating beat of 1, 2, 3, plop; or, to come to modern days, the elaborate and entertaining water-toy designed by Huys for the London South Bank Exhibition.

Contentment is the note of the bubbling fountains in the Tivoli; inspiration in the jets flung from the star at the apex of the parterre fountain at the Villa Lante; majesty in the tremendous fall of the Organ at Villa D'Este. Voluptuous pleasure in the coolness of water in an arid climate is translated by the slow plop of water falling in large drops in a pool and in the endlessly gushing waters of the Generaliffe.

If the water is to serve as a pool of light to draw the sky down into itself, then it must be still and open to the sky—held to it like a mirror. The water should lie high in its container, brimming up to the edge, or cupped only in very gentle banks. The dew-pond high up on the Downs is the natural prototype. The upper basin at the Belvedere in Vienna does the same thing on the grand scale; by drawing down to its surface the sky and the far horizon, it makes itself the focal point of the surrounding landscape and the skyline of Vienna (Plate 28).

Or the purpose of the water may be for its reflection. Then success will lie in the correct placing and level of the water in relation to the object to be reflected and to the eye of the observer, a matter which can be worked out on sections remembering that the angle at which the line of sight strikes the water equals the angle of reflection. The care which Le Nôtre took to ensure the correct reflection in the pool at Vaux-le-Vicomte was mentioned on page 41 and Repton showed equal skill in his informal lakes. (See *The Art of Landscape Gardening*.)

32. The line of urns at Villa Lante forms a progressive pattern.

33. The smoothness of Epstein's Dove is accentuated by the background of bamboo.
34. Yuccas contrast with Barbara Hepworth's vertical feature.

35. (*Left.*) The siting of the little lion at Villa Marlia pulls the eye upwards.

36. (*Right.*) Steps may be narrow, steep and exciting (Pietro Porcinai).

Or, again, a particular effect of drama may be sought—darkness or depth of colour. Sir George Sitwell, in his *On the Making of Gardens*, sets out the whole art of shadowed water, pointing out the value of dark evergreens as a background to the water and how cutting off the lateral rays of the sun will concentrate the reflection on the deep blue of the zenith. Conversely, Repton shows how a stream with gently sloping banks appears wider than with steep ones because the shadow is reduced and a greater area of water reflects the sky.

Where reflections are wanted the greater part of the water should be kept clear of aquatics, which should be used only with great discrimination and as a definite contribution to the composition. For instance, a still dark pool in a wood, or set about with evergreens, may be improved by the flat pattern of lilypads and the pure white star of their flowers; or the calm surface of a large lake may be emphasized by the piercing stems of the reeds, but often a sheet of water is rendered no different from dry land by its covering of plant life.

While the full joys of playing water can be appreciated only in a hot climate, even in England water in movement has its place. The great cascade at Chatsworth, Derbyshire, is a fitting echo of the hilly northern landscape and in public places cheerful spraying jets add to the gaiety of the scene. It is unfortunate that when we use them we show so little invention and sense of their possibilities, both in the shapes the water can be made to take and in its container. For whatever role the water itself may play in the scene must be matched and contributed to by its surround. The statues for fountains, the moulded copings of basins, the spouting beasts and the simple lotus fountains of the East have given us some of the most beautiful garden features of the past.

The Villa Lante shows enchanting examples of these conceits. The spirited sea-horse rising from the water of the basin near the entrance (Plate 31); the rolls of stone echoing the ripples of the runnel down the centre of the garden (Plate 27); the magnificent centre piece of the lower parterre, spouting water from the raised star (Plate 30), each confers a special character to the water which plays round it.

Even the humblest village fountain in a French place or Italian piazza is beautiful in its own right, quite apart from the water. It is as if water, the central necessity of life, were given a fitting setting, second only to the church as the centre of communal life. But perhaps naturally there is no sign that, in England, water has ever received particular reverence. It is perhaps because of this lack of tradition that the standard of most ornamental fountains and pools is mediocre if not shoddy.

The modern cost of the equivalent of the stonework at the Villa Lante might be prohibitive even for a public park. The small community and the private individual at least will have to look for something a great deal simpler. But it is revealing that the wooden bowls of the Tivoli in Copenhagen, which form so attractive and distinctive part of the design, were made of wood only because the war made other materials unobtainable, and there are doubtless equally good solutions to be found for our own shortages.

Where the water and not the container is the chief object, it is possible to reduce the construction of a formal pool to a vanishing point of simplicity, by using a metal container and bringing the turf up to the water's edge.

Concrete construction is most often used for pools, and it is capable of special effects which should be exploited, instead of an attempt being made to imitate stone. While the beauty of stone surrounds lies in their moulding and carving, the beauty of concrete lies in the clear lines and free shapes which it can take. The pools designed by Church get their effect from the interesting shape of the water, where a renaissance fountain would rely on the beauty of the container.

If fountains are not seen at their best in England, still water comes into its own. In climates of more constant light large sheets of water may be lifeless or too glaring, but in England there is no need for the water itself to move. Instead, the still surface reflects the changing lights of the sky and the changing seasons of the trees. It can be lovely in rain and more beautiful in mist than in sunlight. So it is that although water in all its forms may be found in English gardens, the really memorable examples are of placid water; the lakes of Stourhead and Blenheim; the quiet river at Wilton and the misty Cambridge Backs reflecting the pale spring green of the weeping willows.

The waters *par excellence* for the English climate are the placid lakes winding mysteriously away into misty inlets, reflecting the rich yet gentle colour of the trees through the constantly changing lights and seasons.

This was the type of water exploited by the landscape architects of the eighteenth century. The smallest streams were dammed to create lakes and the semblance of winding rivers. Their apparent extent and their sense of mystery were increased by the water winding out of sight round some gentle headland or into a wooded creek. If the effect of a slow flowing river could not be achieved on one level, the intermediate cascade from one level to another might be concealed in a wood, and to all appearance the same stretch of river widened out again into view beyond. The drama of a cascade was sacrificed to the appearance of space and tranquillity, for these were the particular virtues which the water was to provide. In many of

Repton's slides the transformation includes one of these placid sheets of water lying below the gentle grass slope surmounted by the mansion, reflecting groups of trees and quietly browsing cattle. It was the gentle smoothness of these artificial rivers which was criticized by the upholders of the picturesque and to them a preferable use of water was the cascade and the rugged stream; both are emanations of the northern forest, suited alike to our climate and our love of pottering about with plants.

The delight which can be added to a garden by even the smallest stream

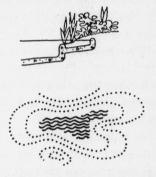

Fig. 22. A stepped-back shelf will allow the concrete edge of a pool to be hidden. Ground shaping allows the water to lie naturally in the land-form.

is expressed in Getrude Jekyll's *Wall and Water Garden*. Where a rill runs through a garden it can be dammed to make a series of pools and falls and boggy areas.

In a large informal lake, puddling can be used, with natural banks of grass and waterside plants. This was the method used by Brown and Repton. But nowadays, particularly with smaller ponds, concrete construction is more usual and raises the difficulty that an unsightly concrete rim is often allowed to show. Efforts to hide this rim by balancing bits of rock or crazy paving on it are worse than useless. In a large enough lake, the rim can be concealed by gently sloping the ground down to the water and out into the lake, forming a natural beach which will cover the concrete. But in a small pond there is not sufficient space to do this without reducing the depth of the water to a mere puddle, and the same principle can be followed by constructing a shelf in the concrete wall just below water level with a beading in front to retain the soil or shingle, and the water-retaining concrete carried up the back (See Fig. 22). Either grass or planting can then be brought to the water's edge, with the added advantage that a moist planting space is provided for waterside plants, which are now often planted outside the concrete where they obtain no benefit from the water. There are cases where, although the water is informal, there is no objection to showing a definite edge. The piling along river banks, for instance, is a pleasant sight and the Thames-side gardens are delightful with their shaven lawns finishing neatly at the top of the riverbank boarding, or in some cases at a white-painted concrete wall. Examples of this treatment can be seen at two extremes in the English village pond with its wall or wooden piling supporting the bank on either a straight line or a simple curve, and in the immensely sophisticated Japanese pool with its piling following a convention as rigid as all its other laws.

Perhaps the most important of all points in designing informal water is to ensure that it lies naturally in the land-form and takes the form which the shape of the ground dictates. From the smallest garden pond to the great reservoirs in the hill lands, there are examples of water artificially retained in a position it would never have taken naturally. In reservoirs the effect is caused by arbitrary blasting away of headlands and building up of embankments without relation to the surounding land form; but in gardens the land-form itself can be organised to hold the water in a natural cup.

Some modern examples of pools of abstract shape appear to flout this rule, but in fact they are not intended to appear natural and must be judged on the criterion of all abstract design: do they give a pattern which is pleasant to the eye irrespective of reference to natural objects?

The placing of water at the lowest level in relation to its immediate surroundings is a general rule almost inviolable in the case of natural ponds, and usually desirable in formal ones, but there are occasions when the raised bank is dramatic and gives special effects of reflection. It cuts out any reflection except that of the sky, so that the water appears as a mirror of burnished steel.

In whatever form water is used, it should be treated with respect, as an important part of the general design. The small muddy pool tucked away in the corner takes on a depressing air, which is directly contrary to the light reflection and compelling interest which are its true characteristics.

CHAPTER TWELVE

SCULPTURE AND STONE WORK

T HE art of garden making and the sculptor's art have been
complementary to each other ever since the days of
Rome.

Some of the earliest gardens of the renaissance were designed expressly
for the display of statues and until the last century sculpture of different
kinds was an essential part of the design of all the great gardens of the
Western world. Statues have been used in many different ways, but the
underlying reasons for their use have been the same. They are the great
humanizers, by which man projects his personality and his love of creation
into the realm of nature. Lovingly he turned the tree trunk and acanthus
leaves into the column and carved capital. In the classic statues he expressed
his ideal of the human body, into the voluptuous curves of the baroque he
put all the self-confident joy of life of the seventeenth century, and to-day
the sculptor reflects the modern groping for the underlying unity of the
world. Statues have always been an expression of man's mind and because
of their obvious human origin they at once draw attention to themselves
and stand out from their natural surroundings. For this reason they are
natural focal points. From afar attention is projected to them, so that all the
ground between them and the beholder is at once recognized as man's
domain.

The English landscape gardens of the eighteenth century used this device
to embrace the whole park and even the intervening farmlands into their
picture by the placing of a temple or an obelisk on a distant hill. In the same
way the statues in the rondells at Versailles make it plain that the allées
and bosquets are part of the civilized world.

Just as a statue at a distance has an irresistible pull, making the eye and
thoughts travel to it over intervening ground, so it allows the attention to
rest in peace once it is reached; and this is the role it plays as the terminal
feature of a classical vista or as the focal point of a small garden.

One or both these two qualities, of drawing the eye irresistibly over
intervening ground and of allowing it to rest content, can be seen in almost

all well-placed statues and the neglect of them is the cause of most ill-siting. At the Villa Lante the line of carved urns draws the eye along the length of the terrace (Plate 32), while the semicircle of caryatids at Chiswick House gives satisfying finality to a shortened view. Because a statue is a natural focus of attention, it brooks no competition and either one piece should hold the attention at a time or several together should form a complete and unified composition, or a natural progression.

The long vista at Bramham Park, Yorkshire, looks across a pool and the end is marked by a huge urn. The two do not compete, but are complementary, forming together one composition. The dominant vertical figure is completed by the calm horizontal pool which does nothing to prevent the eye travelling easily on its way to the terminal point.

But at the Villa Medici, in Rome, the dominating figure in the pool, which should be the focal point of the view, is confused by the second overpowering figure at the far end of the garden.

There are good reasons why the classical statue is an attribute of the Italian garden. The climate, with its bright light, not only conserves the whiteness of the marble, but shows it to the best advantage, especially when seen against the background of sombre evergreens. In England the climate discolours the stone and the misty light tends to blur the outlines. For this reason the bolder lines of the temples, bridges and obelisks of the eighteenth century gardens are more effective than the statues, while the massive forms of some modern sculpture, whose broad planes might be overpowering in bright sunlight, are better suited to our misty climate and a better foil to the open texture of deciduous trees.

It is natural that abstract forms, which modern painting and sculpture have made familiar, should find their way into the garden, either in the selective form of *objets trouvés* or in the creative form of sculpture. There is historic precedent for the *objets trouvés* in the Japanese use of carefully selected stones for their garden compositions and it is not only in this field that modern art has reached something closely akin to the art of the ancient East.

A seeing eye may recognize in many unexpected objects some form which evokes pleasure and expresses the feeling of the garden's character, bringing to it a point of interest and emphasis. Italian oil jars have a traditional place in the garden, but many of our native objects are quite as beautiful in form, including, for instance, certain types of buoy which might find a fitting place in a sea-side garden.

The opportunities for siting sculpture in gardens are more diverse than in any other environment and ideally there should be complete unity of intention between the sculptor and the garden designer. Either may take the lead or they may work in unison from the first. Usually it will be the garden architect who desires a particular type of work for a particular place, but it may equally well be that a garden is required as a setting for a predetermined work. In either case the background with its tone and texture, the lighting and the shadow, will become part of the composition of the sculpture, which in its turn may become the heart of the garden design.

The clear-cut, gleaming statues of Italy find their perfect foil in the dark, matt, low-toned walls of clipped *Quercus ilex*. And, in the same tradition, yew has long been recognized as the perfect background plant. Where the effect is to be light against dark, modelling against a flat surface, this is a sound choice. But sometimes a different effect may be sought. It may be that the work should be seen as a dark silhouette, in which case the sky makes the ideal background. A magnificent example of this is the fountain group at Villa Lante (Plate 30). Or where broad mass is more important than fine detail, it may be better to replace the matt-surface background with a strong mosaic of patterned foliage. For instance, Henry Moore's reclining figure would look well against a background of *Viburnum davidii*, and the smooth form of Epstein's dove is accentuated by the interlaced pattern of the bamboo leaves (Plate 33). From its earliest days sculpture has derived patterns from plant form, and an alternative to using plants as a purely recessive background is to let them contribute to this pattern. The choice of a group of yuccas as the setting for Barbara Hepworth's vertical feature was inspired (Plate 34).

The colour relationship of sculpture to its setting may be either the simple contrast of light stone against dark foliage or some more subtle affinity, such as the green of bronze, harmonized with a background of glaucus foliage.

The position of a statue in relation to eye level can give completely different effects. Just as the eye is carried forward towards a man-made object, so it can be led upwards. The little lion perched high on its pillar at the Villa Marlia accentuates the depths of the hedged enclosure and pulls the eye and spirit up to the opening of the sky above (Plate 35).

Unless there is a deliberate intention to create some such effect, the sculpture should be placed at natural eye level. Scale-relationship to the human figure has a strong psychological effect. A statue far greater than life size is extrovert and draws the onlooker beyond himself; one less than the human scale leads rather to introspection. The miniature bust at Hidcote expresses intimacy and the quiet thought of the recluse. The great Fame at the Villa Garzoni is the epitome of the exuberance of Baroque man.

Since sculpture is an expression of the creative spirit of man, each work, to keep its value, must retain its individuality. Its force is lost if imitations are mass-produced, however good the original may have been. The interest of a focal point is gone as soon as it is realised that it is but one more copy of the Mercury which we have seen in a dozen other gardens. It cannot be the genius of the place if it has already been met in the same role elsewhere. The same stricture does not apply to the use of a classic pattern of vase or oil jars, or of the good modern designs of plant container. For here lies the difference between craftsmanship, which is the fashioning of a shape evolved through use and the character of its material and which loses nothing by repetition, and creative art, which is an individual expression, unique to one time, place and personality. Both have a place in gardens and sculpture, in particular, is needed in the gardens of to-day to bring interest into a small space and a strong, humanized focal point into the compositions of plant form.

Walls and Steps. Since the decline in the use of sculpture, almost the only architectural features in English gardens of the last generations have been the purely functional ones of walls and steps. Lutyens used these components of his gardens to develop something akin to a sculptural composition in brick, but, apart from this, little attempt has been made to use them to fill the gap left by the banished temples and statues.

They have suffered occasionally from pointless ostentation, but more often from the recent malaise of timidity and lack of purpose which has attacked English gardens. In the terraced gardens of Italy the intention behind each wall and flight of steps is evident, and expresses a desire for some particular effect.

The steps may be broad, easy and inviting, or they may soar upwards, narrow, steep and exciting (Plate 36), or they may curve seductively out of sight forming a composition in themselves (Plate 37). A perfect example of gently rising steps is the flight in the gardens of Isola Bella, Lake Maggiore (Plate 38). These, too, show the value of the horizontal pattern of light and shade made by deeply overhanging treads. There are occasions where a solid block forming the front of the tread and the riser gives a clean line and look of solidity which fits into a particular design, but where there is to be an overhang it should be generous, to give a deep clear shadow. Generosity has been a feature of all great gardens and meanness of architectural detail has played a large part in the decline of the last century.

The worked nosing of the treads and the graceful curl of the lowest step give the civilized character to the steps at Bramham (Plate 39), while the

37. Steps curving seductively out of sight form a composition in themselves—Villa
D'Este, Tivoli.

38. Steps at Isola Bella, Lake Maggiore.

39. Steps at Bramham Hall, Yorkshire.

40. Solid blocks of stone give masculinity to the steps at Villa Lante.

solid blocks give a strong masculinity to those at Villa Lante (Plate 40).

An easy proportion for steps in a leisurely ascent is a riser of $4\frac{1}{2}$ inches and tread of 17 inches. A useful guide is that twice the riser plus the tread should equal 26 inches. Shallow steps should always be broad in relation to their surroundings whereas steep ones may on occasion be narrow and dramatic.

Plinths and balustrades were the vehicle for some of the most enchanting detailing in renaissance flights of steps, and the lumpy, ill-proportioned wing-walls and piers of the English York stone period were a sad parody of them. Where economy does not allow a well-proportioned plinth, it is better to reduce it to a narrow string course backed by planting, which can be clipped into a living plinth of the right proportion.

Similarly, if generous stone work is too expensive, it is better to devise well-proportioned steps in concrete, or with brick riser and gravel treads, or, as is often done in Scandinavia, with wooden baulks and blocks. The possibilities of free-soaring flights of curved steps in prestressed concrete have scarcely yet been exploited and open up endless possibilities of grace and movement (Plate 41).

There are delightful Georgian examples of wrought iron steps leading down from the doors of town houses to their gardens and there are simpler modern ones expressing the same idea in light metal. Steps will again become an enrichment of our gardens when we use our modern techniques with imagination instead of producing heavy-handed copies of renaissance models with all the enrichment and grace omitted.

The terrace walls may have drama and majesty like the great walls of the Villa D'Este or the flanking wall of the Villa Gamberaia (Plate 42) or they may have the quiet repose of a low horizontal line. In each case their proportion is a necessary part of the composition of the garden as a whole. In both walls and steps, the detailing of balustrades, treads and coping should form in itself a sculptured composition.

The York stone walling, which became fashionable in the first half of this century, missed all these qualities. Worked stone became so costly that balustrades or wrought treads and copings were rarely used, and the proportion which would have given the structures, however plain, some meaning in the composition were also lacking. The terraces tended to be neither high and dramatic, nor broad, low and dignified, but mean and nondescript.

The same horrors of dullness were perpetrated in piers, 3 feet 6 inches high, with a 1 foot 6 inches by 1 foot 6 inches section, which conveyed no sensation except one of boredom. They were not low and broad enough to pin the composition to the earth, not solid enough to give a feeling of strength and solidity, not high enough to draw the eyes and the imagination upward.

Terraces. House terraces are an extension of the building into the landscape, serving to unite the two, and to do this they should partake either of the character of the house or of the landscape or in some way blend the two.

In most of the great formal gardens of Italy, France and England the walls of the terraces were as finely finished as the house itself, except that sometimes at the far side of the garden they merged into the natural rock of surrounding hills. At the Villa Lante, the carved Neptune leaning from the rock at the upper end of the garden marks the transition between man and nature. At Wilton, and in many other English gardens, the wrought balustrade of the terrace carries forward the house, while the smooth green of the lawn sweeping up to it unites it with the surrounding landscape.

Frank Lloyd Wright and many architects in South America and Sweden have shown how the rock and vegetation of the surrounding land can be brought up to the base of the house itself, and this again relies for success on perfect relationship between building and site (Plate 43). They are buildings sprung from the earth, as opposed to buildings imposing themselves on nature. In these cases, rough undressed walling can make the transition from ground to building, provided the stone is of the nature of the surrounding ground. In the same way, in the eighteenth-century English parks, the grass sweeping up to the walls, and becoming smoother and more cared-for as it reaches the house, enables the house to spring naturally from the true landscape of lowland Britain, just as their ancestors, the Palladian villas of the Italian Veneto, made the finest of all transitions from house to landscape in the very different conditions of their terrain. The feet of their great terrace walls are planted in the landscape of terraced vineyards and olive groves against the backcloth of mountains and belong equally to the landscape and to the sculptured architecture of the villas.

But to interpose a terrace wall of rough stone or rock between a rockless, pasture landscape and a house of brick or concrete is to divide the house from its setting instead of uniting it. Lutyens understood this well when he built his terrace walls of brick and dressed stone in the same style as his houses. Thus in the Lutyens/Jekyll gardens the interlocking between house and landscape is achieved by his architecture thrusting outwards and her planting drifting inwards.

Dry walls are in their appropriate setting in the Cotswolds and other stone counties, where they partake of the character of the stone walls of the countryside and the stone-built houses. In stoneless country they are seldom successful unless they are given a congruous setting of their own, cut off alike from the house and the landscape. They are sometimes used because they are looked upon as natural, but in parts of the country where stone does not occur nothing could be less natural than rough hewn stone carted at great expense from Yorkshire to make an imitation dry wall in a London garden. The effort required to bring it calls for more deliberate and creative use. There is no incongruity in bringing stone hundreds of miles to carve it lovingly into a work of art, but there is incongruity if the only purpose is to build it up roughly into a wall of no particular significance.

The merits of a dry wall lie in its evident strength, its ability to endure by the weight and careful placing of its stones, by its carefully calculated batter and in its particular quality of texture and light and shade, made by the dry joints of its coursing. Part of the attraction of any plant growth on it is the way in which the plants penetrate along the lines of the courses, thickening at the T-shaped joints, and emphasizing the pattern of the wall. All these qualities are lost in the mock dry wall with cement joints and holes left for plants.

Seats. Seats have always been a traditional garden feature and must remain so, for the invitation to pause, rest and look is the essence of a garden.

The essentials for every garden seat are that it be placed where one wishes to sit, that it be comfortable and that it takes its part in the view. It may beckon at the end of a long vista or be come upon suddenly as a pleasant surprise. It may command a wide view or be secluded in its own glorietta.

In appearance, if it is to be a terminal point, it must have an air of permanence, such as was always given by the seats in classical gardens. Many modern designs lack this static quality and have a casual look. This is in keeping with the garden of movement or the open-air room, in which the seat is a movable piece of furniture, but even in modern gardens there are positions where a note of finality is needed to pin the design down and for this the seat which looks as if it were about to take flight is not suitable.

Topiary. Topiary is an ancient form of sculpture, well suited to this country, where the massive forms of clipped yew show to the best advantage in the misty atmosphere and against the soft background of deciduous trees. Its natural quality is a quiet solidity, not cut into fine details, but rotund and flowing in outline. We have seen its value as a focal point and steadying foil to exuberant plant-form in the garden of Hidcote Manor.

In all gardens of the past, architecture and ornaments have played their part. There have been the classic statues, the Japanese tea-houses and lanterns, the Tudor banqueting halls on top of the mounts and the temples of the eighteenth-century parks. Each was individual to the particular style of garden.

That architecture is apt to play so small a part in our gardens to-day is largely due to its cost, but it also reflects the prevailing uncertainty of taste. Where a garden house is built, it is often in a pseudo-rustic or traditional form. But the light and airy look of some modern construction in metal, pre-stressed concrete and Perspex is particularly well suited to gardens, and the free shapes which it is now possible to build open up opportunities of composition both with naturalistic landscapes and with the abstract shapes of modern gardens and carved land-form.

The interpenetration of trees and buildings and the floating shapes of roofs in the Tiefenbrunnen gardens at Zurich shows the possibilities of carrying the movement of design into the architecture of the garden. In the same way bridges, which have always provided some of the happiest opportunities of garden composition, can now be translated into clean graceful lines which leap across the water.

The creative response to the costliness of traditional materials and workmanship is not to cling to them in an emaciated form, but to explore the possibilities of new techniques.

CHAPTER THIRTEEN

GARDEN BOUNDARIES

B ETWEEN the stockade of the Dark Ages and the ha-ha of the eighteenth century lies the difference between the man who still feels insecure and the man who believes himself master of the world. Between them too lie all shades of those competing ideals—security and freedom. We have seen how the first tentative opening up began even in the Middle Ages; with trellis replacing the castle wall, pleached lime instead of thorn thickets and the look-out from the mount showing the desire to see, if not to venture, into the outer world. This was a desire which culminated in Bridgeman's use of the invisible barrier, the ha-ha which allowed the whole countryside to be seen as an extension of the garden. From that vanishing point, the history of the garden fence travels backwards into the need for security and forward into a renewed need for seclusion.

Only a minority of houses to-day are fortunate enough to open onto a countryside which one would wish to consider as an extension of one's domain. More often our present needs have swung back to something approaching the early cloistered gardens, a place of peace.

It is fundamental to a design whether the boundary is to be apparent and defined or whether it is to be concealed. If it is to be defined, then it must be part of the design and contribute to it. Examples of this are the hedges at Hidcote and the walls at Montacute. Here the boundaries are part of the essence of the gardens. Beautiful in themselves, they make a plain statement of the size and shape of the enclosure and relate directly in design to the space within. For success, this type of boundary must be right both in proportion and position and pleasant in texture, colour and form. Its height and shape determines the character of the space enclosed. For instance, tall hedges splayed out at the top can give a feeling of elation; incurving tops suggest mystery and seclusion; a stoutly buttressed wall is static; a ribbon wall is full of movement. Solid yew is sombre and digni-fied, treillage light and playful. A flat surfaced boundary exaggerates length and minimises the width of an enclosure, while one with recesses and side openings will have the opposite effect.

In colouring, the same principles apply as in the walls of a room, dark surfaces tending to close in, light ones to recede. The extreme example of treating the surface of a wall to increase the apparent size of an enclosure is in the use of the *trompe-l'oeil* and perspective treillage, a device much used in France during the eighteenth century.

The first departure from the plain statement of complete enclosure is the introduction of windows, framing glimpses of the outer world. They may be in the form of grilles, which the Spaniards know so well how to use, giving added delight not only to the enclosed patio, but also to the passer-by who sees the sun-splashed wall and cool fountain through the dark scrolls of iron work (Plate 45). Or they may be in the form of openings cut in yew hedges or pleached limes. All these devices are suitable where a firm line of enclosure is to be combined with views from selected points out into the world beyond.

A stage further is the use of trellis or iron-work, still giving a firmly defined line, but with a partial transparency throughout its length. Finally, there is the entirely revealing boundary which defines the enclosure visually and protects it physically, without obstructing the surrounding view. Such is the hedge or wall below eye level. These mark the boundary without defining the height of the enclosure, and unless all sense of space division is to be lost there must be a higher boundary beyond, such as tall trees or hills, making the surroundings themselves part of the garden composition, or allowing the garden merely to form a foreground to the landscape. The gardens at Powerscourt, Co. Wicklow, leading to the mountains beyond, are a fine example of this (Plate 44). On a smaller scale it is equally suitable to any farm or country cottage, whose garden looks onto a pleasant view of fields and woods. In these cases, if the boundary marks the transition from garden to farm, a wall or hedge is better than an open fence because it marks the line more firmly and hides from view the ragged line of transition between the well-groomed garden and the rough fields.

But in those rare cases when a garden can be allowed to merge visually with another garden, or with a town park or square, a light, decorative fence may be better, for this will allow the landscape to flow freely through it. A case for this type of boundary is the small private garden opening on to the communal garden. It is also used with great success in Scandinavia when space division is wanted without breaking the continuity of the landscape.

There are occasions when a visual barrier is wanted without the necessity for a physical one. The typical answer to this is the colonnade, often translated in a garden into spaced tree-trunks. The natural prototype of the colonnade enclosure is the forest glade, and in the garden of the Villa

Lante can be seen an example of the tree-trunk colonnade gradually merging into the formality of the spaced stone columns (Plate 46). These, beautiful in themselves, are strong enough to mark the enclosure, yet they do not arrest the eye from travelling on into the shadows of the wood beyond, giving depth and mystery to the main enclosure.

A variation of the colonnade is the urban use of bollards. For although they serve the physical purpose of preventing vehicle access, from a pedestrian's point of view they mark a visual space division, less emphatically than a colonnade, but more so than a change in ground pattern, which is the slightest of all space divisions, and yet in its contribution to garden pattern immensely effective. It is seen equally in the change of pavings in towns and in the change from smooth to rough-mown grass in the garden.

All these methods, to a greater or less degree, give definition to the boundaries of a space. But sometimes sharp definition is not wanted, as for instance where it is intended to conceal the true boundary of a garden and merge it with the countryside. The finest examples of these melting barriers are the tree-belts of Capability Brown. Here the shadowed outline conceals the true boundary, which may be formed by a brick wall on the outer perimeter of the park, while the eye is carried on to the wider landscape beyond. Yet melting and amorphous as its boundary may be, the trees, whether in belts or clumps, still form a definition of space enclosure and are as carefully placed for this purpose as are the more rigid boundaries of wall and hedge.

In a small garden the same principle can be applied, by planting trees and shrubs to sufficient depth in front of the boundary fence to allow the eye to lose itself in shadow, a method which is defeated if the shrubs are planted in a continuous barrier, which itself forms the boundary. This planting in shadowed depth, rather than in a hard line, particularly applies if the boundary of the garden is to be hidden because it is ugly or at an unpleasant angle. This may often happen in the obliquely shaped plots given to corner houses on closely developed estates, and with tennis courts, which, correctly orientated, may make an ugly angle with the view from the house.

There are two types of boundary which give physical protection with complete visual freedom. They are the ha-ha and water. The ha-ha correctly used gives no visual break whatever. The sunken ditch is imperceptible and the view sweeps on unbroken to the parkland beyond. It was a brilliant method of including the whole eighteenth century landscape within the garden and it still has its uses to-day. To meet the difficulties of upkeep modern owners of country houses must often reduce the pleasure garden and increase farmland. Yet at the same time they may wish to keep the feeling of space and freedom which the view from a country house can give. Provided the outlook is pleasant, the ha-ha answers the need perfectly. Since the modern ha-ha is likely to be nearer to the house than in the spacious eighteenth century, care must be taken that the angle of vision does in fact carry the eye across into the fields beyond and not down into the ditch. It is also necessary to make sure that

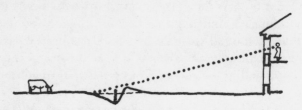

Fig. 23. A combined bank and ha-ha carries the eye across the shallow ditch and sunk fence.

the ditch is deep enough to stop cattle, without the addition of a fence protruding over the top. One method of overcoming both these difficulties is to slope the ground up gently towards the ha-ha from the direction of the house, which will both increase the effective depth of the ha-ha and carry the eye across it (See Fig. 23). Sometimes the planting of a very low, wide hedge such as box between the ha-ha and the lawn will give all the visual freedom required and at the same time hide a protective fence in a too shallow ha-ha. It also overcomes the difficulty of cutting grass close to the edge of the bank.

Water, in the form of moats, was one of the earliest boundaries of all and is still unsurpassed in giving a complete physical boundary with an unfettered view. It is seldom a practical possibility in a private garden, unless the water is already there in a form which can be used for the purpose. There was a lavish use of even the smallest streams to form ornamental water in the seventeenth and eighteenth centuries. To-day it is not only the cost which usually rules it out, but also the falling water table has resulted in many of the old lakes disappearing, while streams are often polluted. The possibilities of water should, however, never be neglected and it might well be used more often in planning the landscape of public buildings and parks. The Stratford Memorial Theatre and the Town Hall at Stockholm are two well known examples of the dignity which water gives to large buildings and the advantage of the unbroken ground line which is possible when water forms the barrier. It could also be used as a boundary for those industrial plants where cooling requirements make water easily available.

41. Free-soaring steps offer opportunity of grace, lightness and movement (Ammann).

42. The drama of high walls—Villa Gamberaia

43. In a rocky land-scape ground-form, vegetation and rock can be brought up to form the base of the building. Flats near Stockholm.

All classic schools of garden design have accepted the challenge of boundaries to produce an added delight to their enclosures, and while we may not care for Bacon's description of his trellis-work hedge set with bird-cages and coloured glass (see *On Gardens,*) at least his fancy was painting something in which he took a delight. It has been left to us in this age to surround our gardens with monstrosities which can only fill us with a desire to hide them.

Apart from hedges, scarcely any garden boundary in common use in England to-day makes a contribution to the garden it encloses. This is partly due to economic reasons, but if there were a greater realization of the part which a boundary should play the necessary cost would surely be found, as it is found for decent facing bricks and interior decoration in the case of the house. The commonest fence for small gardens, and perhaps the worst, is concrete post and wire mesh. Ugly in itself, it does not even serve the purpose of giving seclusion or provide a good support for climbing plants. Close board at least gives seclusion, but it is almost equally ugly. Chestnut paling quickly becomes untidy and can be considered only as a temporary protection for hedges or other planting.

Wattle, if securely framed, is better in appearance, particularly for a country garden, but it is not durable and soon becomes untidy. A better fence for informal boundaries where seclusion is not needed is that used by the L.C.C. for its park woodlands, made of chestnut slats fastened to oak posts and rails.

Whether fences are to contribute to the design as a dominant feature, as Japanese fences often did, or whether they are required to be recessive, they should express some definite character. For a background fence, simplicity is the best foil for the intricacies of plant growth, and a strong vertical pattern is particularly helpful. This can be executed in various forms of slatted wood, vertical bars, bamboos, corrugated asbestos or ribbed concrete. Framed panels of wood can give a simple rectangular pattern, dividing the fence into any desired scale and proportion. A simple town fence can be made of panels of wire mesh framed in metal tubing. Neat wooden picket fences are an old cottage garden tradition and have reappeared in some of the new towns. A sound and imaginative range of fencing has been developed by Thomas Church in California (see *Gardens are for People*).

Some pleasant slatted fences have been produced to screen washing greens and the spaces between housing terraces. They give seclusion and rely for their effect on severe simplicity and the interest of strong vertical lines.

A strong, simple fence with panels of trellis or wire mesh can be planted with climbers chosen to give some particular character to the garden.

Small-leafed ivy or *Euonymus radicans* will make a quiet, closely-patterned background, akin in value to an evergreen hedge. If the boundary is to play a more active part in the design than that of background, endless variations can be made. There may be a formal recurring pattern of alternate panels of winter jasmine and ivy, or a free composition of purple vine and various shades of clematis, or regular buttresses of clipped pyracantha.

In the case of many small gardens in towns a wall of not less than 6 feet is by far the best boundary and should be given priority over any other garden expenditure, for within it a garden can be gradually developed, but without its seclusion and protection whatever else is done will be largely wasted. Whether it should be of brick, flint, stucco or concrete depends entirely on the surroundings and the local sources of supply. But whatever the material it should be honest, sure its own character, and gracious in its proportion and detail.

Honesty does not preclude richness of invention, as may be seen in such delightful examples as the walls and balustrades at Montacute. But a brick wall is not improved by the insertion of a random piece of stone nor by a hollow trough left along the top for alpines. The alpines seldom thrive and, if they do, will look messy and ill-placed. Another unhappy finish is a row of bricks placed on end instead of on their sides. Lutyens, like many great men, was followed by a host of incapable imitators. He played tricks with bricks and tiles in his garden walling, and he succeeded. But it was an individual style of his own and not one to be safely copied. Moreover, his gardens were an extension of the Lutyens house and, without it, have a strange incongruity. A more fruitful source of inspiration is the character given to old brick walls by their sturdy shaped buttresses, far more expressive than the emaciated piers so often used to-day.

The cost of stone boundary walls makes it rare for one to be built now, even in the stone counties. How lovely they may be and the diversity of ways in which they may be built can be seen by looking at the walls surrounding the Oxford college gardens. Some are of dressed stone with worked coping, some of rubble built in the vernacular. Each has its own particular character and all have dignity. Pattern and proportion can be given to a stone wall by the arrangement of coursing. The small scale of narrow courses, the dignity of large blocks, true-cut and close-jointed; the rhythm of courses carefully graded in diminishing widths—each expresses a particular character.

Coping can also define the character of the wall. One with a wide over-hang will emphasize the ceiling height of the enclosure and affect the proportions of the space within, while a high coping flush with the wall or receding from its face carries the space up into the sky.

The possibility of using a local material for walls should always be considered. The flint walls framed in brick, typical of Kent, are as pleasant in their way as the better known stone walls of the Cotswolds. Where no local material is available, concrete and stucco walls are often preferable to imported stone.

Concrete, to-day a material of universal use, has many possibilities in the garden, if its own potentialities are explored, instead of using it as imitation stone. It can be rendered to overcome the cold grey of natural concrete, and the Generaliffe shows how good a background is made by a plain stucco wall, in white or pale wash. Even though concrete is not as kind to plants as the more porous stone and brick, climbers will grow against it if it is wired, or if panels of trellis are fastened to the face. Alternatively a variety of finishes are possible, either by the use of special shuttering or mixes, or by external application. Corrugated shuttering will give an interesting effect of rippling light and shade (see Plate 47), and there are many similar devices to give the depth of texture and the play of light and shade which is lacking in a plain concrete wall. It also lends itself to the ribbon wall, a device with delightful possibilities, giving a great sense of length and movement to a garden. There is one in the garden of Cliveden. Wrought iron fences are now rare because of the cost, but they make a contribution which no other material can replace. They, too, can be studied in infinite variety in the Oxford college gardens. They are used on the top of walls to prevent undergraduates climbing over, and such examples as the one crowning the wall between Merton and Christ Church meadows shows how even this restrictive practice can result in delight, with the little arrow-heads piercing up gaily into the sky.

In other places iron railings are used to fence off the Fellows' gardens without impeding the general view. Transparency and the framing of views are the great virtues of wrought iron and are best served when the pattern is simple, graceful, and more open than closed. The happiest results naturally come when the design is based on the potentialities of iron work, particularly its readiness to change direction and form while keeping the same volume of section. The old English patterns of wrought iron expressed this character to perfection and some modern German work has given it a new form and vitality. The thin iron strips, bent and welded together which are seen in cheap modern ironwork, do not express this quality and are correspondingly impoverished. Ironwork is perhaps seen at its best in sunny climates. The clear cut deep blue pattern of shadow cast by the fence in the Boboli Gardens in Florence is something we cannot equal in this country (Plate 48).

Although extensive wrought iron fencing may be rarely possible, more use might be made of wrought iron grilles, for these are particularly suited to small gardens and town courtyards, as may be seen in nearly every Spanish town. The elaborate pattern of some of these Spanish grilles shows up well against the plain walls of a patio. But in England wrought iron gates are often used as an introduction to a flower garden, where the eye has quite enough complication to deal with in unravelling a typical herbaceous border without seeing it through a pattern of floral scrolls. What is needed here is a strong, simple pattern whose firm lines will help to clarify the riot of form and colour within. A plain opening through a good archway, or through the windows of pleached trees, has the same steadying effect.

Wooden trellis should equally reflect its own particular qualities of straightness and simplicity, relying for effect on good proportion between the section of members, and their relation to the openings and the sizes of panels into which the trellis is divided. The usual defect of garden trellis is a look of impermanence and improvisation, failings which are particularly evident in rustic and criss-cross patterns, but also appear in the more sober squared trellis if it is in too light section and lacks solid framing and capping.

Hedges are the most flexible of all boundaries and are capable of infinite variation. They may be little more than a thickening of informal planting, like a free-growing hedge of roses, or they may be a living wall as strongly architectural as brick or stone. It is important to decide which role a hedge is to play and to choose the species accordingly. Flowering hedges can be delightful in the right place, but the idea that one can have the architectural value of a wall, and a riot of blossom too, is pandering to the modern weakness of thinking that one can have all the good things all the time and results only in insipid compromise. The architectural hedge and the flowering hedge are two separate conceptions, not to be confused.

There is the same lack of decision in the shape of hedges. Most hedges are neither low nor high, thick nor thin, but dully average. Hidcote shows the dramatic possibilities of the really high hedge. Owlpen is the classic example of the massive sculptural hedge, but there are also many examples of it along cottage gardens in the village streets. At the other extreme, the very tall thin hedge, which can easily be achieved in beech or hornbeam, is an excellent solution for the boundary of narrow gardens where every foot of space is of value and yet where complete screening is essential.

The shaping of the hedge can be full of character. It can be straight, the sides sheering up into the sky, or it can have a free-growing top to give the corniced effect of the French trees; or it may taper, or be cut back to an angle of 45 degrees. Each shape has its individual character and can be made to contribute to the pattern of the garden.

Pleached trees are also of value where a high screen is needed in a small space. It is a strictly architectural use of trees which can take a variety of forms. The most usual is a solid wall of growth held aloft on a colonnade of stems exemplified in the hornbeam walk at Hidcote. It is equally suitable as a boundary, which defines space and yet permits a view through, or as an extension in height to a lower boundary, such as a wall. It is used in the first way round the sunk garden at Kensington Palace, and in the second is valuable in new housing estates to heighten the screening afforded by 5 feet brick walls (a height which otherwise allows a full view of the washing hanging in back gardens).

Over-riding all the considerations of different types of fencing are the two questions: Is a fence really necessary and, if so, what purpose is it to serve? The answer to the first question depends primarily on whether the space enclosed is to have the seclusion of a private garden or whether it is to be part of the general landscape. In the latter case the boundary should be used only where it is needed visually for a space division. Nothing could make a greater contribution to our urban and suburban landscape than a general opening up to permit the free flow of landscape which alone can unite our sprawling building. On the other hand, the private gardens need the absolute privacy which was theirs in medieval times. At present we have an amorphous compromise which puts up around public and private land alike half-hearted barriers to disrupt the view without giving seclusion or beauty in themselves.

CHAPTER FOURTEEN

GROUND PATTERN

THE groundwork of a garden has two functions. It is the horizontal plane on which the composition is built up and it provides access to the different parts of the garden.

Visually it may be passive, of quiet tone and texture, forming a background on which the design is imposed, or it may play an active part, contributing pattern or direction to the design or uniting the component parts into one composition. On the practical side, it may have to stand considerable wear or only an occasional footprint.

In England, grass is the most widely used ground cover. As we have seen, it is an essential part of the English landscape garden and one of the reasons why that particular style evolved in this country rather than in any other.

It is the perfect material where the ground is required as a quiet, harmonious background, revealing with equal emphasis the true level of a bowling green or the subtle contouring of modelled land-form. In colour and texture it is the most restful of all surfaces, sympathetic to soft shadows, to the gleam of dew, and to evening mist, pleasant to walk on, and conveying a sense of spaciousness. Where these qualities are wanted, grass is the finest of all ground coverings, provided the soil and climate are suitable and provided it has not to withstand too much wear. It may be used in many ways. Only a perfect sward of fine grasses closely mown could make the impeccable floor of the Oxford quads. But coarser grass allowed to grow longer will still give the broad green sweep of the great valley and hills of Stowe, while the grass slopes which William Robinson made at Gravetye were like an alpine meadow full of flowers. Sometimes the pattern of the garden will depend on this contrast between rough grass and closely mown paths and glades.

The colour and texture depends not only on the cutting, but also on the species of grass used and on the soil which supports it. The fine festucas will make a close, intensely green carpet if grown on well-fed soil, but will have a paler, silvery hue on poor, thin soils. Rye-grass, however grown, will always be coarse and is only suitable for large stretches of green, where the coarser texture is lost in the scale of the surroundings.

But while grass is so admirable a surface in many places, it has its limitations. It will stand only a certain amount of wear. Just how much depends partly on soil and climatic conditions and partly on the type of grass. Once the sward is worn through to expose the bare earth, its particular virtues no longer exist; for the colour, the texture, the unbroken sweep and the tranquillity are all destroyed.

It is, therefore, important to realize in advance when over-wear is likely to make grass impracticable. Its wearing capacity can be increased by a process of stabilization, which allows the grass to grow through a strengthening layer of bitumen, and on playing fields and public open spaces this process has great possibilities, which have not yet been fully tested. But it appears that it requires periodic renewal and, ideally, some more permanent solution to the problem should be found.

The first step in avoiding over-wear in grass is to ensure that it is in the right place and that paths are provided where they are needed. As a further protection, it may be slightly raised and treated rather as a decorative panel than as a surface to be walked on. In a private garden or in any community where there is respect for the garden, the problem is far easier than in public open spaces. The Oxford quads are a perfect example of protection by social sanction. Only Fellows, whose numbers are not sufficient to damage the grass, are allowed to walk on the lawns, others using the paths even if it means going round two sides of a triangle.

But this happy solution is possible only in a highly developed society, ruled by tradition. In less well-ordered milieus, some more physical barrier is needed. Sometimes a low kerb or ankle rail is sufficient deterrent even in a public park, but whatever means are used they must not destroy the essential virtues of a sward. There must still be tranquillity and the eye must be able to glide without hindrance over the smooth surface. Any barrier which prevents this nullifies the advantages of grass, and for the same reason isolated beds cut in the grass destroy its character. Trunks of trees on the other hand still allow the grass to flow between and beyond them, as long as they are not cumbered round with rings of planting and seats. On the same principle, a drift of bulbs between the trees may enhance a lawn, while a tight ring around the trunk is tiresome, unless it is part of a deliberate formalized pattern.

Grass is essentially a ground covering which acts as a foil and background emphasizing everything which rises from it and the shape of the ground beneath it. Also because of its smoothness and lack of pattern, it reveals the shape of the space which it covers with great clarity, and for this reason a grassed area becomes a clear-cut unit of composition, whose outline and proportions must be designed with care.

But sometimes the groundwork has to play a more positive role in the design, perhaps by imparting a sense of direction, or by contributing a strong pattern of texture and tone, or by dividing the space into pleasant proportions. In these cases, and also where grass will not flourish, other materials must be found.

No other plant forms as good a wearing surface as grass, but some are suitable for positions of light wear, and among these the medieval lawns of chamomile must have been very attractive, although from the experience of those who have tried to grow them, they need considerable care. Close-cut heaths can form a good covering on hungry, acid sands and white clover is useful where nothing else will grow, giving an intense green even in drought.

But for a purely visual cover, there is a great range of suitable plants (See p. 113). They may be used to form a patterned carpet of tone and texture; for instance, in a damp, shady place the round discs of creeping Jenny on a background of *Arenaria caespitosa* or, on thin chalk, *Achillea* 'King Edward VII' interwoven with *Thymus serpyllum coccineus*.

The Danes, in their public parks and private gardens, use a carpet of creeping plants which completely covers the ground in front and between the larger plants. The effect is infinitely better than the practice of showing carefully dug and hoed bare earth as we do and it is much nearer to nature's method of maintaining ground cover as part of the complete plant colony.

The best effects are obtained when two or at the most three species are used at a time and chosen for their contrast of colour and texture. The bronze-grey *Acaena buchananii* is an excellent foil for other plants and so is *Cotula squalida*, which will grow in difficult and shady positions. *Cotoneaster dammeri* and *Vinca minor* introduce a slightly larger scale and a tougher texture of foliage, while the ivies give a still larger and more definite pattern.

When the cover is to mould itself closely to the ground, the qualities to look for are a dense, low mat of foliage, spread by stolons and rooted runners rather than a large head spreading from a central root. For example, *Thymus serpyllum* will spread, rooting and establishing itself as it goes, while nepeta, springing from its central clump, will become straggly unless constantly cut back.

Under trees where the shade is too dense for grass to thrive, a covering of plants is often needed to form the equivalent of the natural forest floor. Here plants of comparatively loose texture are sometimes more in keeping

44. The hills beyond the terrace at Powerscourt are a visual extension of the garden. No intervening boundary is needed.

45. The cool fountain and sun-splashed wall of a Spanish patio are even more seductive seen through the dark grille of ironwork in the high wall. Duke of Alba's garden, Seville.

46. The boundary between wood and garden. The tree trunks merge into the formal colonnade. Villa Lante.

47. Corrugated shuttering gives interesting effects of light and shade (Sylvia Crowe).

48. The clear-cut shadows of wrought iron in the strong Italian sun-light. Boboli gardens.

than a dense, close carpet, especially if one of their functions is to form a background to naturalized bulbs, whose dying grass will be hidden by such low plants as vaccinium, trillium or ferns. There is an excellent example of this type of ground planting near the Temple of Aeolus at Kew. But for a covering which will reveal every nuance of the contoured ground, ribbed by the roots of trees, nothing can surpass the covering of moss, used in the Japanese garden of Matsuo Kyoto.

The Scandinavians often use permanent materials in conjunction with grass. In the right place, this can be very pleasant. The setts let into the Garden of Resistance at Copenhagen are a delightful example of the use of ground pattern to formalize and humanize an otherwise natural scene (Plate 14). In the small garden designed by Langkilde in the Copenhagen exhibition of 1955, an abstract pattern let into the grass formed the main theme of the design (Plate 49). Scandinavians are also adept at placing stones in grass, to give that light, carefree type of design which is their speciality. Leading to a building of domestic character in informal surroundings, the use of stepping stones is very appropriate. It suggests casual use by occasional callers. But it is seldom suitable for public buildings or for those which are subject to much coming and going, nor is it in keeping with formal surroundings where the path should approach its destination, fearlessly and definitely, as part of the design and not seek to mitigate itself by disappearing into the surrounding grass.

The technique of stepping stones and setts, and even of isolated plants placed in the grass, is perhaps less suitable here than in Scandinavia, because the growth of the grass here is more luxuriant and extends over a longer season, making hand-cutting round obstructions a tiresome problem. Where stepping stones are used in the grass they should be large enough to retain their usefulness even if the grass grows over their edges, and they should be sunk just below grass level to allow the mower to pass over them without damage.

Alternatively the stones may be set in ground planting instead of in grass. In dry positions *Thymus serpyllum* can be used and in moist ones *Mentha requienii* or *Arenaria caespitosa*. But where the object of using stepping stones is to give the appearance of unbroken lawn flowing through the path, this method will defeat its purpose by breaking the continuity of texture.

The intermingling of stone and herbage as a floor surface is a peculiar contribution of Northern Europe, perhaps an echo of the stone-strewn forests, where the pattern of moss and fern and grey stone must have been an inspiration to the German and Scandinavian landscape architects.

For a parallel reason it is not surprising that the most highly developed use of purely dry surfacing is found in Spain with its tradition of desert influence. The country is rich in inventive and sensitive solutions to the problem of giving character and pattern to wearing surfaces, from the the intricate pebbled designs of the old piazzas of Granada to the modern paths of exposed aggregate concrete at the Madrid airport. But just as the Scandinavian practice cannot always be transplanted here without adaptation, neither can the Spanish; for many of their pavings, particularly those with small, closely set, protruding pebbles, would disintegrate here under the influence of damp and frost.

We must, therefore, as usual, examine and learn from their principles, without necessarily copying their methods. In the Patio di Aranjes at Seville, the irrigation channels are used to pattern the courtyard and tie the orange trees into the design (Plate 50). In principle the pattern is applicable to urban open spaces in any country.

At the Alcazar in Seville the strong diagonal pattern in the courtyard has a steadying influence on the exuberant planting (Plate 51). A simple, easily-grasped pattern running right through an area where plants and other features are placed asymmetrically gives the eye a welcome grid of reference. The honeycomb of setts in the little Swedish flat garden shows the same principle of using the floor pattern as a unifying background (Plate 59). But at other times a directional pattern may be needed; a path leading with certainty to one point can be emphasized by the direction of the coursing or by a change of material, such as a flagged path leading across an area of setts or cobbles.

In other cases the paved area may be neither a background nor a path, but rather a pattern, sufficient in itself, or at least which plays the role of a beautiful carpet to the surrounding walls of buildings or hedges. In the Granada piazzas endless interest and variety is given by such patterns, sometimes heraldic, sometimes free or floral, worked out in black pebbles set in a background of grey. Even drainage runnels become things of delight, by the pattern formed by the setting of the stones at different angles.

Scandinavia is also rich in paved spaces within the towns where the interest is created more simply than by the use of the Spanish mosaics. Such necessities as tree grids and bicycle stands are made to contribute to the pattern (Plate 52). In the few places in England where setts and cobbles have not given way entirely to concrete and asphalt, there may still be found delightful patterns of texture and direction.

Recently there have been isolated but welcome signs that the art of ground pattern is being brought back. At Roe Green in Hatfield New

Town, the old combination of paving and cobbles is used in a straight-forward and modern manner. The concrete paving makes no pretence to be other than it is and gets its effect by the strong pattern of its jointing. The cobbles, a contrast in colour and texture, are used to take advantage of what is usually considered one of their drawbacks; they are exceptionally large and protruding, and the discomfort which they would cause to anyone walking on them is used to keep people away from the top of a high retaining wall.

In the small quad in front of the library at University College, Oxford, setts are used in the traditional shell pattern, the design being given emphasis by the cambered panels falling to radiating channels. This part of the design is essentially space-filling, the directional design being supplied by the flagged paths (Plate 53).

The use of intricate patterns or of too many different materials can be tiresome and the conscious imitation of the picturesque is as dangerous in this as in any other medium. The picturesque effect of paving in old towns and villages is the result of using different materials for specific purposes, such as the use of flags to make smooth wheel tracks through an area of cobble, or the use of setts to form a drainage channel. This careful choice of the right material for each purpose can be made the basis of interesting patterns. Every paving material has its special character and scale. Rect-angular York paving is one of the best known for garden work and deserves its high reputation. It has a good colour, pleasantly varied, and is of good texture. It can be cut to pattern when required or used in rect-tangular slabs of random sizes. To appreciate the quality of its grain, it should be laid dry or, if there is jointing, it should be raked back from the surface to show the clear cut edge. In scale it is not suited to very small details nor, used by itself, to very large areas.

Crazy paving should be used only in special circumstances. The sharp-cornered pattern in which it is usually laid is fussy and unattractive. There are, however, examples of carefully selected shapes, particularly of Hornton or ripple-faced Sussex stone, where the acute angles are replaced by more rounded or hexagonal forms, which can be laid to an attractive pattern by using large island stones as the backbone of the path, with smaller pieces forming a mosaic between them. It is also helpful if the sides of the path are held in with a border of rectangular stone.

Setts are a traditional paving for old streets. They are good in colour, texture and proportion and lend themselves to simple patterns, either in bands or runnels in other types of paving or, by themselves, in the traditional shell or some other pattern.

Cobbles form a complete contrast in scale and texture to both York paving and concrete. They are valuable for forming a pattern in conjunction with other materials or in surfacing an area where foot traffic is to be discouraged. For the latter purpose they are sometimes used at the corners of road verges or as a protective area round a tree. They can be used in a variety of sizes, shapes and colours. Flat stones laid on edge parallel to each other give a directional pattern. Small rounded stones set close together give an all over texture, which can if necessary be used on large areas, whereas more definite patterning can be achieved by large stones. The usual fault in laying them is to allow the concrete in which they are bedded to show between the stones. Unless this is required as a deliberate effect, the stones should be set touching each other, with no jointing showing.

Brick is one of the traditional materials for cottage garden paths and its most valuable use is in this scale of garden. It is true that in Holland it is used on roads, but although the areas themselves are large the surroundings are usually on a small domestic scale, and the brick here serves to bring down the scale of traffic roads to that of small housing, a disparity of scale which is very evident in our own modern housing.

On those rare occasions when very narrow paths are wanted in a garden, brick is often the most suitable material because of its small unit of subdivision. As the background to a parterre it combines small scale subdivision with a restful and regular all-over pattern, in the same way that it does on the elevation of a large building.

An interesting pattern can be made by sinking logs into the ground, the rounded shape of their cut sections forming wooden stepping stones. This is a device used in Scandinavia and is very suitable for woodland gardens.

Because of the cost and scarcity of other materials, concrete has become one of the commonest paving materials. As its natural colour is cold and its texture dull, it is not surprising that there have been many efforts to improve it. The most unfortunate treatment is the scoring of the surface in imitation of crazy paving, a bad imitation of a poor pattern. Its more successful uses take full advantage of its chief virtue, which is its adaptability to any straightforward pattern and any reasonable size. It can be used in conjunction with some other material, provided there is a definite contrast. A mixture of stone and concrete is not usually suitable because they are too alike, but cobble, brick, slates and setts can all be used, in the form of panels or intersecting bands. It can also be used as pattern on a background of gravel or tar macadam. Used by itself, the design is formed either by the expansion joints alone or in addition by the use of different coloured or textured concrete. The expansion joints contribute to the pattern by

49. Setts sunk into the grass to form an abstract are the main theme of a small garden by Eywin Langkilde.

50. A unifying pattern in a public patio in Seville.

51. A diagonal pattern steadies the exuberant planting. Alcazar, Seville.

dividing the concrete into panels, and their definition varies from the almost imperceptible, where no visual break is desired, through normal jointing, which merely defines the proportion of the concrete slabs, to the strong patterning of joints marked by strips of black slate or wide strips of wood.

There are many ways in which the appearance of the concrete itself may be varied. Different exposed aggregates will vary the texture and, within a narrow range, the colour. More definite colour can be obtained with coloured cements. Almost any colour may be used on occasion for formal and frankly artificial effects, but in the more natural parts of the garden the various stone colours are the most suitable; not because they imitate stone, but because they are the kindest and quietest foil for grass and plants.

It is possible that much more than has yet been done could be achieved in giving interesting surfaces to the concrete. In some positions a slight ripple in the trowelling is enough to give the desired character, while in others pebble aggregate exposed by hard brushing may give the effect. At times the very smoothness, which is often one of the drawbacks, may be precisely what is wanted, particularly when concrete is used in the free and abstract forms of certain types of modern gardens, a use to which it is well adapted.

There are many places where gravel remains the best of all path surfaces. It is recessive, forming a background and not a pattern in its own right, quiet in colour and in texture. Where a completely uniform background is wanted, Bredon gravel is even better. It is a crushed limestone which when watered rolls down into a hard-setting surface of a warm honey colour. These recessive paths are needed in gardens of the French tradition, where they serve simply as shapes in the design.

Tar macadam and bitumen surfaces are used extensively for the sake of ease of upkeep and economy. Untreated, they are not pleasant either in texture or colour, but surfacing with stone chips of good colour or pea gravel can effect great improvement. It can also help if the surface is divided into panels with other materials. A car park has recently been constructed in one of the Oxford colleges where the tar macadam space has been divided into car-bays by sett runnels, with direction arrows laid in cobbles (Fig. 24).

Whatever may be used as surfacing, the most important point is the pattern which each path and space contributes to the garden as a whole, its effect on space division and its quality as an element of movement or as a static area of rest.

The surface may serve as the background on which the design is built

up, like the grass in the landscape park, or it may be directional, like the
central path at Tintinhull, or it may itself draw the lines which form the

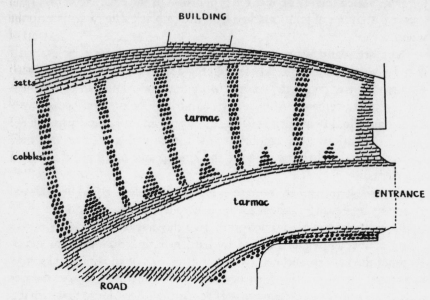

*Fig. 24. A functional pattern of setts, cobbles and tarmac for a car park, University
College, Oxford (Sylvia Crowe).*

pattern of the garden, as the long walks do at Vaux, or it may make a
patterned grid uniting the other elements of the design, like the honeycombed garden at Gröndal near Stockholm. Each of these purposes needs a
different material, chosen and used specifically for the effect required.

PART FOUR

SPECIALISED GARDENS

THE PRIVATE GARDEN

PARKS

ALLOTMENTS

COMMUNAL AND FLAT GARDENS

WILD GARDENS

ROCK GARDENS

FACTORY GARDENS

SCHOOL GARDENS

CHAPTER FIFTEEN

THE PRIVATE GARDEN

MEN in every age and every country have made gardens to suit their own conditions. Each age has borrowed and adapted from the past and styles evolved in one country have travelled, often in a changed form, to another.

In making our own gardens to-day, how far are those of other times and other lands applicable? The same climate which favoured the old English cottage garden and the landscape park is still with us. But while the cottage garden persists as it has always done, a changeless native growth, the true landscape style is only rarely valid in the private gardens of to-day both for lack of space and for lack of the surrounding landscape.

The enclosed medieval garden gave seclusion, which we need as sorely as our ancestors did, and they had a simplicity which strikes a chord in this over-complicated age. Yet theirs is the simplicity of a newly evolving design, a stage in progress to which it is difficult to return without affectation. In this it differs from the ageless cottage garden, which is at the same primitive and fully developed.

In the Spanish patio we find an analogy to the small town courtyard, but here the difference in climate makes some adaptation necessary. Nevertheless, by the economy with which a few plants and pots give the effect, its livableness and fluid asymmetric arrangement, it answers many problems of the outdoor room. But it does not cater for the slightly larger area, nor for the owner who wants some scope for playing with his garden. The love of gardening as an active occupation also rules out the Japanese garden, which in some ways has much to offer. For to many people of the present day the idealization of an informal landscape is more sympathetic than a frankly artificial garden; because the outer world is over-regulated and man-ridden, we seek the counter-balance of nature. But in the Japanese garden nature is in reality more rigidly restrained than in any formal garden. It is, moreover, a purely static garden for contemplation only. The Englishman is seldom contemplative, but needs a garden in which he can be active; and while it is true that the Japanese garden requires the most meticulous upkeep, from the raking of the sand to the shaping of the plants, it is set on pre-determined lines which do not allow for the changes and improvisation which are part of the joys of an English gardener.

Perhaps the most helpful models are some of the gardens of Scandinavia. Informal, they rely for their composition on contouring, the grouping of plants with strongly contrasted pattern and texture, and the humanizing touch of sculpture or the strong bulk of an evocative stone to give a focal point to the composition. Closely related to the house, they are simple, small, free in treatment, yet, in the best examples, with a strong feeling of design.

But even though ideas and inspiration may come from these various sources, we should not slavishly copy them, for their strength is that they have sprung from the character of their countries and people. Instead, we should try to assess our own needs and the characteristics of each individual site and let these two factors form the basis of the design. Whether or not a work of art will result depends on the skill of the designer.

It may seem pretentious to consider the classic masterpieces of the world, when confronted by the small and uninspiring plot of ground which is often the starting point of the modern garden. But if the principles behind these masterpieces are followed, the result will have the simplicity and air of inevitability which results from finding the right answer to any problem, while pretentiousness comes from the imitation of ready-made answers. For this reason, stock plans of gardens are useless. Even preconceived ideas are better banished, allowing the picture of the final product to evolve naturally from the site and from the personality of owner and designer. A general idea may well spring to the mind's eye at first sight, but before working it out there must be a survey to note not only the size, shape and levels of the site, but all the details of its surroundings and any special features it may possess, such as trees, or water, or some unusual land-form. Soil, aspect and climate must also be taken into account.

Against the background of this survey the particular role which the garden is to play can be considered. Is it to include vegetables and fruit? Is it to cater for children? Is it to be a garden primarily to look at, to sit in, to work in, or all three? When the possible combinations of all these factors are considered it is evident that there can never be two gardens to which the same solution will apply.

But the greatest difference between one garden and another will still be caused by the vision of the designer, who will take all the prosaic facts and transmute them into an individual answer.

Let us examine the effect on the design of these two sets of facts—those inherent in the site and those imposed upon it by the use to which it is to be put.

We have traced the influence which climate has had on the development of national styles, but even within the British Isles there is enough variation in climate to influence individual gardens. Most important is the need for wind shelter on exposed sites. In extreme cases this will dictate the main lines of the design. For instance, it may mean dividing the site into a series of sheltered compartments, leaving space for a wide,

Fig. 25. A garden scooped out of encircling wind-shelter.

high shelter belt on the windward side and eschewing single specimen trees in favour of groups where the trees will protect each other. But in any part of the country some provision for shelter is needed and will add to the pleasure of the garden and the number of days on which it can be enjoyed. Instead of looking upon it as an unfortunate necessity, it should be seized upon to give some particular character. It suggests, for instance, a garden carved out of the solid, rather than one built up from the open. On a large scale this may develop into a Hidcote, but on a small scale it might suggest a pool of lawn, scooped out of encircling banks and plant-growth, (Fig. 25), or a series of related small spaces like the cells of a honeycomb, or a narrow bowling alley flanked by walls or pleached trees, having the simplicity and sense of direction of the lime walk at Sissinghurst (Plate 16).

The polluted atmosphere of towns is a man-made climatic condition, which will affect the type of plants which can be grown, encouraging a design of clear-cut shiny leaves contrasted with light, seasonal colour, and not relying wholly upon plant growth for its effect.

Aspect is a localised form of climate and will control the position where flowers should be grown, the siting of sitting places, and the position of any feature which requires the light upon it. Often, in a long narrow garden, aspect is ignored and a symmetrical arrangement of border on each side fails because one faces south and the other north. Not only does this fail in its purpose, since the south-facing border is full of flower while the other is subdued, with the flower heads tending to turn away, but an opportunity has been missed of having a more interesting arrangement with a wide flower border on one side and some quite different treatment on the other, such as trees or groups of shade-loving foliage plants with the lawn running back between them to the foot of a wall or screen.

Soil should determine the range of plants from which choice can be made, for although soil improvement is possible and usually desirable, it is more interesting, more successful and less expensive to use plants which are natural to the conditions. We have mentioned elsewhere how obedience to natural conditions in choice of plants can be one of the means of achieving unity of design. The subsoil may also affect the layout in other ways. Extensive levelling is expensive on heavy clays and almost prohibitive on rock; whereas on those rare soils several feet deep, shaping can be carried out without the need to move and replace topsoil, which is a considerable part of the cost of levelling or contouring on average soils. The possession of such deep soil might suggest a gently contoured hill-garden, a form of design with infinite possibilities of landcape composition even on the smallest site.

On those sites, rare in England, where rock formation outcrops or lies close beneath the surface, there occurs the opportunity for really effective rock gardening or for the compositional use of occasional boulders on the Swedish pattern.

The contours of the ground have influenced all the great gardens of the world; it has been the basis of the Italian terraces and of the slopes and valleys of the English parks. Even the smallest garden should recognise the land-form and use it to full advantage either by terracing or by informal contouring (See Chapter 9).

On the surroundings of a garden depends whether it is to be inlooking or outlooking, or to have merely selected glimpses of the outside world.

The majority of small modern gardens in urban and suburban surroundings will necessarily be inlooking. They must provide their own boundaries and create a world within themselves. We may, however, hope that if the landscape of our towns and suburbs improves, there will be progressively less need to block out all our surroundings. Even in a seemingly unattractive neighbourhood to-day there is often some glimpse of the outer world which is worth framing and accentuating, to suggest that, while the garden is self-contained and secluded, it is still linked with its surroundings. Sometimes a distant view of country or park, a group of trees or a good building may be pleasant in itself, but passes unnoticed because it is flanked by chimney stacks and roof tops, or has a foreground of allotment shacks. If these unwanted elements can be excluded from the view a greater depth and interest can be given to the garden.

In Mr and Mrs Lanning Roper's garden at Park House, Kensington, the spire of St Paul's, Onslow Square, is used as part of the composition, giving a focal point to views from within the garden whose lavish planting excludes the rest of the surroundings (Plate 54).

Where it is possible for neighbours to co-operate by having an inconspicuous boundary and making each garden part of the view from the other, their apparent size will be doubled. This is noticeable in Switzerland, where a feeling of space is given to the back gardens of very small plots by the omission of all boundaries except a low post to mark the corners of the plots. Privacy is still maintained by planting and arbours which screen sitting spaces.

A garden in the country will almost always have some view to lead up to and sometimes the garden's chief function is to be a foreground to the country beyond. In either case the position and character of the view should be the basis of the garden's design. The planting should frame and compose with it, while the eye is led towards it, with no impediment, either in the form of a distractingly bright bed of flowers placed across the line of vision or a harsh boundary line. Nor should the vegetable garden be placed in such a position that it will be seen as a foreground to the view.

Gardens and landscapes both gain by incorporating existing features on a site, for they are living things which should grow out of their own past, rather than spring from a vacuum in time or from a blank sheet on a drawing board.

Trees should be looked upon as a gift to any site and no felling be done without long thought and strong reasons. If there are many trees on the site, then some thinning may well be necessary, to open up views, to gain light and to give a better grouping to the remaining trees. But if there are only a few and they are healthy, the design should use them to the full, giving them precedence over other features. They give scale in both size and time, a sense of seclusion and a feeling of maturity which will not be attained by newly planted trees for a generation. A few flowers, grown in a garden which has a framework of great trees, will be far more effective than massed borders on a bare site, while there can be great beauty in a garden whose only plant materials are grass and trees. There is in it a feeling of tranquillity at all seasons of the year and it is, incidentally, the most labour-saving of all gardens.

In order to use trees to the greatest advantage, their exact position must be recorded on the plan, together with their spread, height, species and condition, and also the ground level at the foot of the trunk. This is important in deciding on any levelling which has to be done, for the level cannot satisfactorily be changed more than a few inches over the area of ground occupied by the main body of tree roots. Many devices are used to overcome this difficulty, such as leaving the tree in a well or building a retaining wall to maintain it at a higher level, but if the change of level is brought too close to the trunk, no device is wholly successful, either from the point of view of appearance or culturally. As a rough guide, the change of level should not come nearer than the spread of the main bulk of the tree branches. The device must also be so planned that the tree appears inevitable in the design, or as a happy accident, not an interloper unwillingly retained.

The compositional value of trees for framing and to give perspective may be judged by the lengths to which a photographer will go to obtain a view of a building through a framework of trees. The landscapes of Claude Lorraine, which inspired the designs of the eighteenth century English parks, always have a group of trees to give point and perspective to the view. His, too, are always beautifully shaped trees, either perfect examples of their species or grown with a picturesque irregularity. Even worse than the needless felling of trees is their mutilation by unskilled lopping. A branch cut back to a stump or a beheaded tree will at first look like a skeleton and later, if the stump does not die and cause the tree to rot, it will throw out a thicket of new shoots at the point of the cut, resulting in a mop head, having no beauty and providing the maximum obstruction to view and light. But a tree properly thinned, with its superfluous branches removed by a clean cut back to the main branch or trunk, can be improved in appearance, health and safety.

When trees are overshadowing a window, there should be very careful study of which branches are casting the shadow. It will often be found that the trouble occurs when the sun is low in the sky, either in early morning or evening, and that it is only the lower branches which need to be removed to let in the light.

If a garden is bounded by a spinney or even by an old field hedge, it gives an opportunity to lose the distance in shadow, always helpful in a small garden. No existing growth should be written off as useless scrub until it has been investigated to see if it contains small trees which, if cleaned of their dead wood and rubbish and pruned into shape, will make shapely or picturesque trees. The value of these selected and cleaned trees can be seen in relation to new housing in some of the new towns, where they have given an immediate look of maturity and composition which the areas relying on new planting will not attain for many years. In a garden, such existing growth makes a perfect place for naturalizing woodland plants, which are far happier here than in the open.

The house is usually the dominating feature of the site and its close relationship with the garden has progressively increased until to-day in some modern houses we have the garden forming an outdoor room which is almost one with the glass-fronted living room, itself so lavishly set with plants that it is hard to see where the house ends and garden begins. It is a matter of personal taste whether we prefer the almost imperceptible merging from indoors to outdoors or whether, like the British agricultural worker, we like to be snug and enclosed indoors and step into the garden as into a separate world. Probably the tendency to merge the two is strongest in indoor workers, who feel the need of more outdoor life than they are able to satisfy, and if this is so the trend is likely to increase.

The decision as to whether the garden is a place into which you go from the house or is an open-air part of the house has a considerable effect on the design of a garden. It shifts the centre of balance, for in the first conception there is a line of demarcation at the house frontage, in the second the whole area of living room and garden is one unit.

Ideally, the general lines of the garden design should be considered at the same time as the plan and siting of the house. It can then be ensured that the main living room will look onto the best aspect of the garden; that the house will be kept clear of existing trees; that the best use is made of the surrounding ground; and that the garden-maker will not be faced with narrow dark strips at the side of the house or with the problem of the house corner butting up at an awkward angle to the boundary. It will also enable proper consideration to be given to the levels. The siting of a house in relation to the contours of the ground is one of the greatest reasons why the eighteenth century houses have the air of belonging to the landscape, and the same is true on even the smallest scale.

Sometimes it is unavoidable that there shall be a heavy fall in the ground either across or away from the house. There are many ways of overcoming this in the garden design, but the problem is made much more difficult if the levels of damp proof course and facing bricks have not been related to the garden treatment. The walls cannot be exposed below the level of the facing bricks, nor can the ground be brought higher than 6 inches below the damp proof course. There is also the question of the placing and height of manholes, which can be very unsightly protruding above ground level; particularly as their angle, fixed by the direction of the drain, is usually counter to that of the house-terrace or path. The best position for them is within a paved area, where they can be covered with a movable slab or, failing this, well within an extensive area of planting where they will be concealed. An ingenious method has been devised by one of the Oxford colleges of constructing a shallow, movable tray, set with turf, which fits over the cover, a method suitable in cases where access to the manhole is rarely required, and where the grass can be watered if necessary.

Another advantage in planning the garden at the same time as the house is that the surplus excavation from the foundation can be used to good advantage in the shaping of the garden, either in forming a terrace or in contouring the ground.

An important practical point is to ensure that the top soil is taken both from the site of the house and from any area where excavations are to be spread. Failure to do this results in the garden being plastered over with a layer of clay, a condition which has broken the hearts and the spades of many suburban gardeners.

The first points of relationship between the house and the garden are the views from the windows and access from the doors. Nothing is more irritating than a formal vista placed just off centre from the main view point, or than a path which does not connect directly with the door.

The second point is the relationship of levels between house and garden. It is seldom that a site is completely flat. More often there is either a cross fall or else a fall or rise from the house to the garden. If the house has been sited with the design of the garden in mind, the best use can be made of these changes of level, but very often, particularly if the house is one of a terrace, whose position on its plot of ground is unalterable, the garden design will have to overcome the difficulties as best it can. The simplest change of level to manage is a gentle fall away from the house and parallel to it. This allows for a terrace, which will both form a transition from the house to the garden and give a convenient sitting out space.

A steep fall is more difficult to manage, but can also give more exciting results. Many town houses have steps coming down into the garden from the sitting room, and a semi-basement or garden-store on the lower level. This gives opportunites for a pleasant treatment of steps and hand-rails and is more becoming to a small house than a high-walled terrace. Where there is more space, the fall can be taken in a series of terraces or the ground can be shaped to hold the house within sympathetic land-form.

A slope upwards from the house is less satisfactory for several reasons. Unless a level terrace is excavated well back into the rising ground, the effect will be cramped. The view up the hill is fore-shortened, reducing the apparent size of the garden; and there are practical difficulties of drainage to be overcome. Nevertheless, if the condition is accepted and tackled boldly, it is possible to get some dramatic effects. The classic example is the spectacular backcloth of the Villa Aldobrandini at Frascati.

A cross fall presents a greater challenge. A fall across the line of vision needs correction to prevent the appearance of slipping sideways. Moreover, looking from the garden the horizontal lines of the house will show up any fall against them. The only case where this relationship of level succeeds without rectification is when the house is designed to grow out of the side of the hill. The traditional example is the mountain châlet of Switzerland. But here we have the whole balance of the mountain landscape to contribute to the result. The châlet is not a unit on its own, but is a small detail in the general view, and the stopper which balances the

Fig. 26. A house set on a cross fall can be put in equipoise by planting to counterbalance it on the lower side, and by land-shaping.

slide down the hillside is the mountain on the other side of the valley. To apply the same principle on a restricted site, the role of the opposing mountain side must be filled with a counterpoise either of another building or of land-form or planting.

The easier and more usual treatment is either to contour the ground to counterbalance the fall and allow the house to sit in equipoise on the site (Fig. 26) or to level out a terrace along the house frontage. In the latter case special care is needed in the treatment of the terrace ends to bring them back to natural ground level. This particular problem was solved long ago by the flanking bosquets of the Italian gardens, and in small gardens the same role can be played by lower planting masking the terrace ends.

With the freer shapes of modern design, the terrace is no longer necessarily straight nor parallel to the house, and on occasion it can come out in a sweep or angle to conform more comfortably to the land-form or to face the view or sun. The terraces of some Californian gardens take the form of wooden platforms, poised among the tree trunks, far above the lower garden. In the more traditional treatment care is also needed in dealing with the cross fall beyond the terrace. The main view must still continue balanced. This can be achieved either by informal contouring, in the same manner as the cross fall of the great avenue at Stowe is balanced out by the folds in the ground, or it may be done by means of a level walk, with different treatment at the sides which will accept the differences in level. This is a small scale version of Le Nôtre's solution of the same problem at Vaux-le-Vicomte and it provides more interesting and truthful treatment than levelling across the whole site. A typical solution in narrow town gardens is the long walk leading down from the terrace and a border at one side raised on a low retaining wall.

Whether the house will be improved by planting at its base, or whether it should rise cleanly from the ground, depends entirely on its architecture and proportion. A house, which is box-like or rather high in proportion to its length, may be greatly improved by being widened at the base with planting. But if it is low and long or needs the whole of its height to make the proportions of the façade read, it is better unplanted or with only a light climber or occasional low plant.

The house may either spring direct from the ground, as the Palladian mansion did from the landscape park, or as Frank Lloyd Wright's house does from the rock; or it may unite itself to the ground by continuing its architecture out into the garden. This may be done with a terrace or by wing walls or formal hedges tying the building into its surroundings. This is the method of the Italian and the French gardens, of Montacute and of Tintinhull. A modern conception is that of the house having alighted on the ground like a bird in flight. (See *Gardens in the Modern Landscape*, by Tunnard.)

The colouring of the house affects the tones and colours to be used in the garden, more particularly on a small site, when the house is by far the most important feature. It is unfortunate that the strong colour of new red brick is not a good foil for plants. Mellow old brick is delightful, for not only is the colour quieter, but the broken tones of weathering have given it life and softness. Some of the multi-coloured bricks are pleasant in a somewhat negative way, while the London yellow stocks are extremely good if the right range of plants is used.

With the strong red bricks, dark green and grey-green foliage is best and flowers of white or very pale yellow. The rather drab colour of the multi-coloured is improved by touches of pure dark red, such as rose Etoile d'Hollande or the clear yellow of R. Mermaid. Yellow stocks will take the yellowish greens, which are not happy with the other bricks, and the whole range of yellows and oranges, particularly tawny yellows. Purples are also very good, from the pale shades of *Clematis* Nellie Moser to the depth of *C. jackmanii*. The only colours which clash with them are the strong pinks. White or any pale colour-wash gives the widest opportunities of all. Grey foliage and white flowers can look delightful with it against a darker background, but it also gives the ideal foil for dark green and strong colours. The classic example is the white Georgian house set in evergreen oak with window boxes of scarlet geraniums.

The most delightful background of all is the subtle range of stone colour from the coolest grey to the golden warmth of Ham stone. This will not only accept any plant colouring, but can be made to intensify its own qualities by the right choice of flower. The pure red of rose Frensham brings out a glow in the stone of Montacute, which is unrealised when it is planted with the more negative colour of nepeta.

Naturally the architectural style of the house must influence the garden. But there is no necessity to lay out a garden in period with a house. A good contemporary garden can look as well with a traditional house, as good contemporary furniture can look in an old room. It does, however, need to be in sympathy with it, as, indeed, it is bound to be once the principle is recognised of considering the house and garden as one entity.

Having taken into account all the physical conditions of the site, they must be reconciled with the purpose for which the garden is required and the personal tastes of the owner.

An English garden will almost certainly be wanted as a place of seclusion. This will mean providing boundaries which will screen all or part of it from neighbours and passers-by. Also it suggests that it will be more pleasant not to see the whole garden from the house. There should be, except in the very smallest courtyard garden, some equivalent of the *giardino segreto*, an air of mystery and the pleasant expectation that there is more to see round the corner.

Then it should be decided whether it is to be a garden mainly to look at or also to garden in. For the first there should be economic use of plant material in carefully composed groups, which require little attention, but which can be relied upon to provide their effect year after year, and there should be a minimum of exposed soil, all areas being either covered with dry surface, with grass or with other plant growth.

The grass should be in a form easily mown or, in a very small garden, it can be omitted altogether. There will be a limited range of plant material designed to give a static and enduring composition.

If, on the other hand, part of the owner's pleasure is to grow plants, the design must be more fluid, capable of minor adjustments without losing the essential lines of the design. It must be possible to change or augment the plants, to experiment with new varieties. This is a factor which has played a large part in the development of the typical English plantsman's garden. Its usual weakness is that the design is not strong enough to carry the diverse and shifting population of plants, and the owner is too often carried away by the love of novelties and variety without sufficient thought for the picture as a whole.

Most successful gardens of this type are either very small and simple, falling into the cottage garden category, or they are held together in a strongly designed framework. The latter follow in the tradition of the Spanish gardens, with their beds of mixed flowers outlined in box, or the Hidcote tradition, where the same principle is carried to greater lengths and an enormous variety of plants is contained within the framework of the great hedges and woodlands. On a smaller scale, a mixed border can stand a great deal of latitude if it is backed by a high wall and punctuated with strong and solid forms.

With knowledge, restraint and constant care, a design wholly in plant forms can be maintained without being set in unchangeable groups. But it takes a Gertrude Jekyll to do this really successfully and it is certainly not a type of garden which can safely be designed for someone else to carry on. It is as fleeting as a flower arrangement, and even at its best is more successful when used in conjunction with a lasting composition of more solid form, whether architectural, sculptural or of land-form and trees.

If, as well as growing flowers, the owner wishes to grow vegetables, the usual course is to screen them off or to devote the far end of the garden to them, regardless of appearance. The latter is nearly always an unfortunate position, for it means either that the effective length of the garden is curtailed by screening or that the whole of the vegetable garden is open to view. It also prevents the exploitation of any view there may be beyond the end of the garden.

If the garden is not wide enough to site the vegetables at one side, the main view can be narrowed down to a way through at the far end of the garden, bordered with fruit trees or cordons and cutting-flowers with the vegetables kept back on each side. If the land-form permits it, the vegetable garden may be dropped out of sight at a lower level, or the ground may be contoured to form a gentle mound to conceal it. But although vegetables are not a suitable termination for the main view, one has only to look at some of the old walled kitchen gardens to realise that they may still be a creditable feature of the garden. This is particularly so if mass production of potatoes is given up in favour of smaller quantities of the more interesting vegetables. Herbs, salads, carrots and curly kale are all attractive plants, while salsify and artichokes are as handsome as many flowers grown for ornament. The great attractions of the old kitchen gardens were the neat paths edged with box, the carefully trained espalier fruit and the occasional flowers for cutting. All these can still be used; box, lavender and herbs can

52. Tree grids form part of the paving pattern at Gothenburg.

53. A space-filling pattern of setts with flagged directional paths. University College, Oxford (Sylvia Crowe).

54. Seclusion is given by the luxuriant planting, distance by the framed chu steeple. Garden in Onslow Square, London—Mr and Mrs Lanning Roper.

border the paths; espalier or cordon trees are the best way to produce fruit for the small garden; and cutting borders are well worth having, especially if the remainder of the garden is kept on restrained lines. There is one necessary feature of the garden which needs complete screening—the compost heap.

Children's play is often one of the most necessary uses of a garden and requires careful planning if it is not to spoil the appearance. For the very small child a sand pit in a sunny corner will provide endless delight and can be designed as an attractive feature. In the garden designed by Kenneth Booth for himself, the terrace is divided into large squares, some being paved, some planted, some cobbled, one a sand pit and one a splash pool. In this way the children's needs are met within the overall pattern, and when the sand pit is outgrown it can be given a new treatment. It is one more example of the principle of sub-division as a means of combining detailed use with a uniting pattern.

Older children will want more space for active games. An open lawn, set in trees or groups of shrubs, is more suitable than one surrounded with flower borders which will be easily damaged by balls. A sunken or gently dished lawn will help to prevent balls going out of bounds. Children prefer an informal garden to a formal one and will appreciate hidden reserves. A small woodland dell is one of the best places for them, for there they will both find what they like and be reasonably screened from the rest of the garden. In a suburban garden an arrangement of artificial hillocks can serve the same purpose.

Occasionally there are very special requirements in a garden. A sculptor may need it as a studio or a writer as a study. In both cases it would take on the attributes of an open-air room. It can be sheltered, of easy access from the house, set with rather massive planting to make a quiet and solid background, and containing trees whose leaves and shadows are a help to thought and whose height gives the necessary sense of seclusion from the world. Nor should flowers be omitted, particularly those with scent, for there is no more evocative setting than the scent and sight of luxuriant summer flowers.

The open-air room is the most common use for a small garden. If this is realised, it will be seen how uncomfortable as a room are the narrow, constricted passages which comprise many small suburban gardens, or the series of restless features, the small sunk garden, the rockery, the rustic pergola, none of them inviting to sit in and making neither one comfortably furnished room of the complete garden nor the series of small rooms, united into one design, which is the alternative. Equally unsuitable is the hard bare rectangle, as attractive to sit in as a railway waiting room.

The garden must, above all, have a sense of containment and offer an invitation to enter, and to linger.

The series of small gardens designed by Danish architects for an exhibition in 1955 (Figs. 27 and 28) show the variety which can be brought into the single-room garden and by the simplest means. One theme, of light and shadow, of texture, of the reflection of water, of a harmonized colour scheme, is enough to give character to each. Of the

Fig. 27. The Chaussee Garden by Eywin Langkilde.

slightly larger garden, sub-divided into rooms, there can be few better examples than Tintinhull (See p. 181).

Besides use and personality, there is another imposed factor—economics. Before beginning to design it must be known what sum is available for the construction of the garden, and by what means it is to be maintained.

The capital cost will be greatly increased by heavy movement of soil and by stone work. The least expensive gardens are those where surface modelling only of the ground is employed and which rely for their effect on planting. It is better to confine the garden-making to these simple elements rather than to introduce shoddy work and poor substitutes in an effort to get an effect with walling and sunk gardens. It is, however, well worth while striving to have one really good humanizing touch; a piece of sculpture, a well-proportioned flight of steps, a well-designed seat or, if it accords with the garden, a striking piece of topiary. In a small garden any one of these is enough to give a focal point.

Upkeep is usually an even more limiting factor than initial cost and one which can be greatly affected by design. The elements requiring most upkeep are bedding out plants, annuals, small beds cut in lawns which

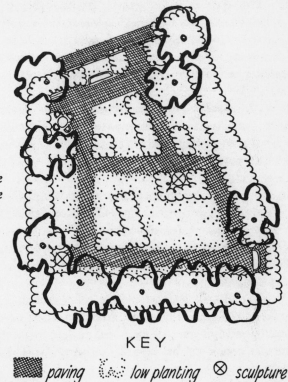

Fig. 28. The Little Garden by Jorn Palle Schmidt.

KEY

paving   low planting   ⊗ sculpture

require edging, and extensive flower borders planted with the types of plants which need staking.

The easiest to maintain are woodland, rough grass which needs scything only twice a year, paved surfaces, shrubs and those sub-shrubs and sturdy herbaceous plants which need neither staking nor frequent division. Flags laid flush with the grass, as an edging to borders, make grass cutting easier and allow the low-growing plants such as dianthus and nepeta to grow forward without getting entangled with the grass.

In larger gardens upkeep becomes an even greater factor. It is considered reasonable for one man to look after some three acres of average garden, and in these days the design of any greater area must usually be governed by the problems of maintenance. This need not apply where the garden is part of a wealthy estate, or where it is open to the public at a charge, but in general the owner of a larger garden will seek means to reduce or recoup upkeep costs. There are several possible approaches. The garden may be simplified to consist mainly of rough grass and woodland, with naturalized plants, which will almost entirely look after themselves; the woodland may be used for timber production and only partially civilized. Or if a farm or parkland is attached, grazing land may be brought close to the house by use of a ha-ha and incorporated in the view.

One of the most fruitful methods is to devote at least half the acreage to production, growing whatever is best suited to the soil and local markets, whether it be fruit, vegetables, cut flowers, plants or a combination of all of them. The essentials for success are that it shall be run as a serious business, under a first-class grower, and that it shall be given a suitable site with good soil and aspect and not relegated to an unwanted corner of the garden. An old walled garden is most suitable for it. It has been found possible to make the proceeds cover the cost, plus the upkeep of an equal area of pleasure garden.

In any garden, except the smallest, the design should take into account the possibility of using machinery for upkeep, ensuring that areas where it can be used are kept accessible and that lawns, for instance, are of a shape which is easy to cut. Open lawns and clipped hedges are no longer difficult to keep now that there are mowers and electric clippers suitable for all conditions.

All the collected facts of the site, of its use, and of the user, present together a problem to be solved in the terms of garden design, and if the answer is satisfying it will be found to have observed not only its own particular problems, but also the universal laws which run through all designs.

Unity will ensure a common theme and a common vernacular of treatment. It will preclude the bringing together in one small garden of a formal lily pool and rock garden, of dressed stone walls cheek by jowl with rustic work. It will leave in the mind a clear impression of the garden as a whole, of something with an individual character, and not as a collection of unrelated incidents. This sense of unity can create something memorable from the most unlikely materials.

A few years ago in a garden competition in North Kensington many remarkable displays of flowers and ingenuity were shown in minute spaces, but the most memorable, because it had the stamp of a genuine creation, was a small strip of garden in a poor quarter, which had been laid out by an old seaman. A border of flowers was protected by white bollards and white painted rope. The sweet peas on the wall were supported by a square-meshed rope net, the woodwork of the fence and gate was painted in nautical black and white. Not exactly a work of art, perhaps rather folklore, but it expressed completely the personality of the owner and it was a congruous whole.

Good proportion is the basis of all design, and no amount of after treatment and planting can compensate the lack of it. The proportion of breadth to length, of open space to planted area, of horizontal to vertical and, finally, the relation to the scale of the surroundings on one hand and the human body on the other makes the real foundation of the garden.

On a small site the mistake is often made of scaling down too much. For although the site is small, the garden's inhabitants remain the same size; they still need a path wide enough for two to stroll down together and a sitting-out space large enough for freedom of movement. It is not even invariably true that smaller plants are better suited to small gardens. One great oak in a courtyard may give a far better effect and sense of scale than a small almond. On the other hand, it is quite correct to choose compact growers rather than invasive subjects like the polygonums.

The most fruitful scaling down for small gardens is simplicity of design and the omission of features for which there is not sufficient room. A sunk garden, for instance, is a dangerous feature in a small space and may easily degenerate into the appearance of a bath. The sunk garden at Kensington Palace is 183 feet × 107 feet × 3 feet deep. In roughly the same proportion, a sunk garden of 35 feet × 20 feet would be 8 inches deep.

The relationship of closed and open spaces, which runs through all the classic gardens, can still be translated on to the smallest site. Because one should be dominant over the other, grass walks and borders should not divide the space equally between them. Because there should be clarity of design, the open space of lawn should not be cut up or dotted with planting.

Whether the garden is a descendant of classic formal gardens or whether it is the open-air room, set with the forms of plants and sculpture, it must have the simplicity which comes from the carrying through of one idea and the restfulness which comes from good proportion.

TINTINHULL HOUSE

On first visiting Tintinhull, Somerset, it is hard to believe that the flower garden is barely an acre in extent, for the skill of its space-division gives an impression of far greater size.

Even so, a garden of one acre is larger than the average to-day, but the principles followed in the design of Tintinhull are applicable to far smaller areas. For instance, existing trees have been used as essential points in the design. The great cedar of Lebanon dominates the north garden and sets the pattern for its open, asymmetric character (Plate 55); an asymmetry which echoes the older north elevation of the house, in contrast with the strict classicism of the west façade; an openness which allows a window to the sky and to the country beyond, in contrast to the *Quercus ilex* which forms a massive full stop to the south-west and a solid background to the pool garden.

The yews, smaller either than the ilex or the cedar and intermediate in weight and texture, serve as a colonnade, dividing yet linking the three main divisions of the garden (Plate 56).

Although it is a country garden, it is almost wholly inlooking and owes little to the surrounding country, and in this again it has something in common with many of the newer gardens of to-day. It is also applicable because it is divided into several parts each complete and satisfying in itself, although combining together into a united whole.

The garden leading westward from the house illustrates a sound, traditional method of treating a long, narrow space. The terrace and grass forecourt is purely an extension of the house, whose architecture is extended round it by the wrought coping and stone eagles on the walls and piers. The height of the surrounding walls is sufficient to give the courtyard its true dimensions as a room. The planting against the walls is subsidiary to them and does not detract from the character of an enclosed open space. In colour the flowers pick up the tone of the wall, the roses Peace and Easlea's Golden Rambler echoing the rose-coloured old bricks and golden Ham stone. The view beyond the courtyard is canalized straight ahead, between the eagle-topped piers, down a long straight vista to the fountain and terminal seat. But it is evident even from the house that the long walk holds surprises. Across the courtyard it marches between solid domes of box and from there on it is bounded, not by a continuous hedge, but by a series of baffles at right angles, suggesting, by the shadows between one plane and the next, that there is penetration to the sides. The small gardens which are revealed by walking down the strongly marked central vista are progressive. First comes the architectural, walled courtyard, then the freer apse-shaped lawn dominated by the *Quercus ilex*, then through a thickly planted narrow neck to the fountain garden, small and enclosed, but with an opening beyond to shadowed recesses and the terminal seat. Having reached this, there is the satisfaction of looking back to the classic perfection of the west façade, framed and concentrated in the receding planes of yew and box (Plate 57).

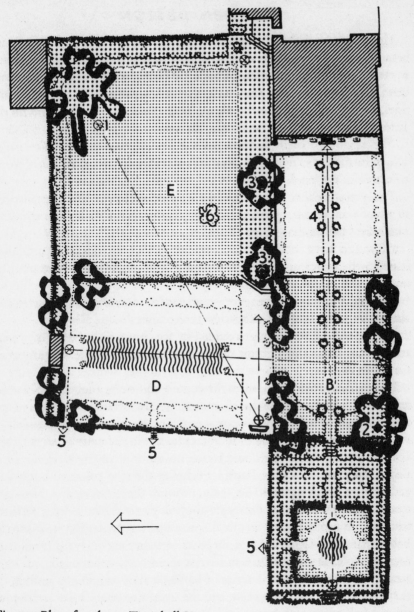

Fig. 29. Plan of garden at Tintinhull House.

A. *Architectural open air room, extension of house.*

B. *Progressive vista.*

C. *Dark diminishing view.*

D. *Open. Reflecting sky.*

E. *Static asymmetric room, mosaic light and shade.*

1. *View through cedar to open sky.*

2. *Quercus ilex.*

3. *Connecting colonnade of yews.*

4. *Box domes.*

5. *Narrow glimpses to fruit and flowers.*

6. *Magnolia.*

The character of the long walk is formal, axial and enclosed. It succeeds because it is well proportioned, and it has a satisfying and different terminal point at each end. Its component parts are contrasted without taking away from the strength of the main axis, and it has glimpses of interest to the sides, which never compete with the main view. It combines the merits of unity and variety, of clarity and mystery.

The other two main divisions of the garden are a complete contrast. The pool garden is light and open, the expanse of sky accentuated by its reflection in the pool. The flower colours are light, with borders of white and grey, pale yellow and sky blue; it is a gay, sunny garden. The pool and its paved surround stretches the whole length, with a wide grass panel on each side. Had the grass been carried right round, the serenity of the long canal would have been broken, and the garden would no longer have linked with the cross axis from the long walk, but would have become separate and disconnected (Fig. 29).

The third main division, the cedar garden, forms an asymmetrically arranged room, with the colonnade of the yews on one side, the cedar on the other, and the furnishing provided by the strong-charactered magnolia and *Cornus kousa* and the soft contrast of rose Celeste above a carpet of *Geranium ibericum*.

The garden as a whole is in the Hidcote tradition because it consists of a series of carefully proportioned spaces, firmly defined with hedges or walls, within which are free-growing plants. Its particular success lies in the contrast and proportion of its spaces, in the use of existing trees to pin down and unite the design, and in the beautifully contrived views, each with a character of its own, each revealed at a special point in the garden and never competing with each other. Pots and architectural features are used to give emphasis, but they are used with restraint. It is a garden in which to wander and to sit, to be seen and experienced from within, rather than to be looked at from without. Its planting is probably unique, because it combines a use of very varied species grown naturally, and yet used strictly as elements of design. No plant, however lovely in itself, is grown unless it contributes to the picture, and those whose form and colour are needed again and again, such as *Senecio grayii* and bergenia, are constantly repeated. In spite of restraint it is anything but austere. Its scent and profusion give it the same enveloping sense of the joy of creation as the Generaliffe, thereby showing that certain qualities of the greatest gardens can reappear in quite other circumstances if the instincts behind their creation are allowed full play.

CHAPTER SIXTEEN

PARKS

᭦᭦᭦᭦᭦᭦᭦᭦᭦᭦᭦᭦᭦᭦᭦᭦

THE history of public parks goes back to ancient Greece, where the city of Athens set aside certain open spaces for the enjoyment of the populace, the philosophers argued and meditated in their gardens and the hippodromes became the ancestors of our playing fields. It is typical of the balanced outlook of the Greek mind compared with our narrow specialization that they considered beautiful surroundings an essential part of physical recreation.

In Northern Europe the industrial revolution made municipal parks a pressing need for the over-crowded townspeople during the nineteenth century. At first public parks were adapted from Royal or private gardens, from common land, hunting parks and, on the continent, from the open spaces along the lines of the old fortifications. In London, Hyde Park had been open to the public since James I's reign. But the widespread making over of parks to the public came much later.

Many of the most crowded manufacturing towns had no historic open spaces, and in 1845 Joseph Paxton, at Birkenhead, laid out the first specifically municipal park on an expanse of waste land. This had a great influence, proving as it did that it was possible to provide a park for the townspeople, financed by the town. The idea soon spread and in 1858 Olmstead and Vaux were entrusted with the development of Central Park in New York. The principles which they followed are set out in *Forty Years of Landscape Architecture*, which throws an interesting light on the nineteenth-century approach to park design.

Olmstead's views were those of a great lover of natural scenery and a practical farmer. The result might have been very different if his background had instead been architectural and classical.

In the working out of his design Olmstead showed a masterly control of space division and his plan is a clear pattern of open spaces contained within a background of massed trees—a type of lay-out well suited to the accommodation of the diverse uses which must go into a big town park. One of his happiest ideas was to sink the necessary through traffic roads, so that the landscape and walks flowed uninterruptedly above them. The two strong principles behind the design were a respect for the configuration of the site and the creation of a natural landscape within which every class of citizen should find refreshment from the city and from buildings. In particular, he wished it to be a place where the poorer people could get the equivalent of a country holiday. Such buildings as were necessary were to be kept subsidiary to the landscape. In this it went much further than the eighteenth-century English park, which, while idealizing nature, still welcomed buildings as humanizing focal points. This was a natural historic development, for the English park was part of the wider landscape of the English countryside, while Olmstead's park was set in a sea of building, which he sought to shut out and forget. It marked perhaps a decadent stage in city civilization when the need for a park became escapist and ceased to be the extension of an acceptable urban life.

Whether the escapist park or the genuinely urban park is the better depends on the size of the park itself and the city which it serves. While the public garden, designed as an adjunct of the city buildings, must always have its place, in a large city the escapist park fills a very real need, for precisely the reasons set out by Olmstead. Man needs nature and if the genuine country is beyond his reach, he must be given a substitute; particularly as the country, even when reached, becomes more fully cultivated and occupied by uses which do not allow the free roaming which is possible over less intensively cultivated lands. Some of the north midland cities such as Sheffield are more fortunate in this respect than London and Coventry, for they are within easy reach of open moors and hills, which provide an outlet for at least weekend recreation.

The extent to which lack of natural recreation areas increases the need for urban parks is reflected in the enormous demand for playing fields in England compared to the demand in countries where the normal weekend recreations are mountaineering and winter sports. In the constant pressing of the city out into the country, the distinction between urban parks and rural common-land becomes blurred, to the detriment of both. For while an area, where nature and agriculture have been destroyed by too much recreational use, should be treated as a public open space, this does not mean that it should necessarily be designed in the same manner as an urban park. It should rather conserve the greatest possible degree of its original landscape value, or be designed as idealized country, or as a completely new type of landscape, broader in scale and less urban in character. Good examples of such extra-mural parks are Wimbledon Common, where the original character has been conserved, and Virginia Water, where an idealized landscape has been created.

To a diminishing degree, open spaces even further afield may be considered as parks, the signs of park maintenance becoming ever less obtrusive, until in the National Parks it should be entirely effaced (See *To-morrow's Landscape*).

But here we are concerned only with parks at the other end of the scale, whose urban character is not in doubt. Town parks serve a two-fold purpose—physical recreation and visual pleasure—and the success of a park system depends on how far these two ideals can be combined. To a well-balanced mind they should be inseparable. The squalor of our surroundings is due to the habit of separating beauty from the other aspects of life and looking upon it as an ornament to be indulged in on special occasions, instead of as a necessary and all-pervading quality.

The physical activities for which the parks must cater include games, children's playgrounds, open-air entertainments, boating, walking and, not least important, just sitting. It becomes more and more necessary to escape from the noise and rush of the city and to have somewhere in which to draw apart in peace and quietness. In this connection, the part which trees and shrubs can play in deadening noise is now one of their most important roles.

Visually the parks supply the trees which are needed as a foil to the city's architecture, the peaceful contrast of open space between massed buildings, and the refreshment and pleasure of green grass and flowers. A connected park system is undoubtedly a help in achieving these parallel uses of appearance and physical exercise. For instance, an isolated football pitch, over-worn and devoid of trees, is a dismal sight. Yet the necessary additional land to give it a setting of trees, and the possibility of changing the pitch to reduce wear, means an extravagant use of land unless the other park uses of walking and relaxation can be combined on the same area. Thus, if the different open spaces are linked together, it is possible to give a landscape setting to walks, which can connect schools, playing fields, parks and finally the open country, into a continuous park-way. Each space contributes something to the other; the trees beside the walk frame the playing fields, while the playing fields give the feeling of space and a green expanse to the paths. The valley of a stream is particularly suited to be the line on which such a park system is developed.

The most famous example of this arrangement is the Kensington Gardens, Hyde Park, Green Park, St James's Park complex, where the original stream widens out into the Serpentine and the St James's Park lake. But there are less ambitious versions of the same idea running through many towns, including Bournemouth, Bournville and Louth. In each case the effect of the combined spaces is far greater than it would be if they were separated.

In all design there should be one dominant element and in each view either architecture or green landscape should predominate, unless they form together one unified composition. One of the weaknesses of the garden city style of layout is the even, overall distribution of the open space among the buildings, so that no view is either wholly closed or wholly open, dominantly green or dominantly architectural.

In a true city there is none of this duality. In London, Parliament Square is dominated by buildings, to which the grass and trees make a foil and foreground. In Hyde Park, on the other hand, the grass and trees are dominant. In St James's Park the landscape foreground culminates in the architectural climax of the Horse Guards.

In following this principle the open spaces divide into two types—those subordinate to the architecture and those capable of being themselves dominant. The first type includes all those areas which serve the purpose of rest gardens in busy parts of the city, the squares and spaces for sitting and strolling, and for visual refreshment. Even a single tree may qualify in this category so long as it is treated as part of the surrounding urban scene and not as a separate garden. The little rustic and rock gardens which have sprung up on vacant sites in London during the 1950's fail entirely to relate to their surroundings. They are out of key in scale, design and material and only bring ridicule on the streets they are meant to adorn.

The second type of open space must be larger and serves for active recreation and for finding seclusion from the city's crowds. If it is to be a park of the escapist type, the space must be large enough, both in actual area and in relation to the population using it, to make a self-contained landscape, dominant over its surroundings, and capable of providing seclusion and escape from crowds.

The Buttes Chaumont, a park of fantastic mountain scenery, constructed on the site of an old quarry in Paris, is an escapist park, which fails partly through poor detailing, but mainly because it lacks the space to shut off the incongruity of surrounding buildings. As it is, it compares poorly with the gardens of the Tuilleries, which show how well the formal tradition can be adapted to a public park, provided the surrounding city is sufficiently civilized to be united with it.

Unity between open spaces and their surroundings is an essential quality of civic design. It can be seen in Nash's conception in Regent's Park, where the landscape flows up to his terraces, an effect which still reads from a distance although at close quarters it is somewhat disrupted by the traffic. St James's Park shows an even more marked relationship to the Horse Guards.

The present habit of shutting off landscape into separate compartments is part of the tendency to reduce all landscape to terms of a private garden, to be fenced off and protected, rather than as a normal part of everyday surroundings. The vandalism which gives the excuse for so much fencing is perpetuated by this attitude, which treats plants as aliens going in perpetual fear of their lives.

It is unfortunate that the majority of municipal parks date from a poor period of design. The hand of debased *jardin anglais* lies heavily on them, and it still seems to be generally accepted that the town park must consist of an amorphous background of trees and grass cut up by paths and incongruously shaped beds of brilliant flowers.

Most of the London parks suffer from the prevalent disease of wanting everything all the time. The basic design of Regents Park is an exceptionally fine idealized landscape, but it has been spoilt by the intrusion of too many features and by the tightly packed beds of garish colours which throw the landscape of the lake out of key. It is right for the parks to have these flowers, but they should be given quarters designed for them and not be thrust into a picture which their brilliant colour and formlessness is bound to disrupt.

The Long Walk in Kensington Gardens is better designed for the display of flowers; it is separated from the park landscape by the trees which form a background to the borders and the flowers are seen in perspective instead of head-on; always a happier arrangement.

In their very different ways the Tuilleries, Holland Park, South Bank, the Tivoli Gardens of Copenhagen and the few parts of Kensington Gardens which have been spared flower beds show how an urban park can have quality of design and distinct character. An interesting experiment, which has not yet appeared in this country, would be to make the brilliant flowers so beloved of the public into the major part of the park, using them after the manner of Burle Marx, as a painter's palette of dynamic abstract forms.

For very large parks the landscape tradition has proved a success provided it is carried out with consistency. The perfect composition of the lake in Regents Park and the landscape quality of the grouped trees framing the views at the Round Pond, Kensington Gardens, show the same clear-cut contrast of massed trees and open space which was a feature of Olmstead's plan.

In a country town or in a quiet city the free landscape can drift in to form a setting for the cathedral or public buildings, as the Backs at Cambridge form a landscape setting for the colleges. But on smaller areas there can be little doubt that the traditional landscape garden is not suitable for large crowds. The reason is that the basis of the landscape park is perfect and unworn grass. To ensure this under urban conditions, one must either have a very large area indeed, well insulated from crowded thoroughfares, or there must be provision for ample paths and some method of preventing people from straying over the grass, conditions which can easily destroy the special character of a landscape park.

In a formal garden, on the other hand, the paths can be increased to any extent necessary to take the crowds and still remain part of the design. Designing for crowds is a problem to which the French school and the

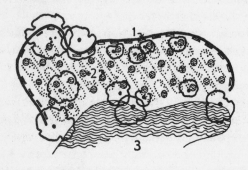

Fig. 30. Tivoli Gardens, Copenhagen.
1. *Brick retaining wall.*
2. *Fountains.*
3. *Lake.*
Rhythmic yet informal.

Baroque age found most of the answers. There should never be the feeling that the crowds are overflowing the design, they must not only be contained easily within it, but should themselves be part of it. Life and movement is an essential quality of the genuinely urban park (as opposed to the escapist park), something to be used as an addition to the design and not admitted grudgingly and with safeguards. This is one of the reasons for the success of the Tuilleries in Paris and the Belvedere gardens in Vienna, which welcome the crowds as part of their composition.

Departure from the landscape tradition, however, does not necessarily mean a return to axial design. One of the most delightful small city parks is the Tivoli garden in Copenhagen. Here the brick-paved flower garden invites the crowds to wander among rhythmically placed but informally planted beds, each with its bubbling fountain. The large trees are asymmetrically placed and the whole design is informal but not naturalistic (Fig. 30). The Liseberg gardens at Gothenburg and the London South Bank gardens are in the same tradition, though less compact in composition, and the Paul Klee type of design developed at Tiefenbrunnen (Plate 17) is a variation of the same idea. It is one well suited to the interlocking of diverse activities within one space. The play of light and almost transparent structures, floating across the ground pattern at different levels, gives movement and gaiety to the whole design and adds both to its apparent size and to the number of people who can enjoy it at one time.

t is also well adapted to the new school of civic design, which raises
ome of the buildings on pilotis, leaving the ground surface free for
pedestrians. The necessary stairs and galleries to give access to the buildings
and across traffic routes become a natural part of the design. The ground
cover is pavement, the trees and flowers and foliage plants are precious
furnishings, and the grass a cherished panel. Perhaps the closest parallel
in historic gardens is the Alhambra, with its mingling of plant and
architecture, of stairs and galleries, allowing the ladies of the harem endless
variety and a sense of space, needed now by the no less confined city
workers.

This interpenetrating quality gives an equally good answer where a
space is required to interlock with the surrounding buildings or where it is
too small for the use of the Olmstead method of cutting a series of cells out
of a uniting background of trees.

This problem of fitting a great many activities into a cramped space
often arises, for even if the large playing fields are sited elsewhere,
perhaps outside the town, one park may have to contain tennis courts,
bowling green, children's playground and paddling pool and a display of
flowers. It will also have to accommodate the necessary buildings for tool-
sheds and offices. The welding of all these together into a garden is no easy
matter, particularly as they are not all pleasant features in themselves.

It is unfortunate that the quest for efficiency in games is leading to the
use of new materials which make good playing surfaces, but which
compare badly in appearance with the turf of the old bowling alley and
tourney ground. To hard tennis courts are now added concrete cricket
pitches, cinder running tracks and asphalt cycle circuits. The running and
cycle tracks are usually contained within a stadium, and there have been
exciting solutions to this problem in German designs, where the needs for
shelter and embankment have been met by surrounding the stadium with
a saucer of rhythmically carved land-form, thus making it part of a larger
landscape composition.

Tennis courts are particularly hard to deal with. Their orientation must
be correct, while both for economy of space and surrounds, and for ease
of supervision, they should be placed side by side in one block. Hard
courts, which are almost universally favoured for public parks, are far
from beautiful, surrounded as they are with 10 feet high netting. They
must not be overhung or unduly shaded by trees and they should have
ample space at the side for spectators and those waiting their turn to play,
and these seating spaces should if possible be on west the side so that the
spectators will not be looking into the setting sun during evening play.

In the interlocking type of design, their angle can be accepted as part of the pattern and ways may be found to make their surrounds an acceptable part of the garden. They might, for instance, be held within the framework of one of those airy structures which the Swiss school handles so well. But if the park is to be of the type which holds its component parts within an enveloping background, screening will be needed to harmonize the tennis courts with the rest of the design. In this case the mistake is often made of attempting to do this by means of a hedge, row of trees or trellis which follows the line of the court boundaries, and merely serves to accentuate them. This may be satisfactory if it has been possible to accept the direction of the courts as a line in the design; but more often particularly if the design is on free landscape lines, the screen should be used to create a new shape.

The bowling green is a far easier element to deal with. There are not strict laws of orientation and no need for a high surround. The lawn itself is a beautiful thing, with the dead level green of its perfect turf sunk slightly below the surrounding ground. An important point to remember is that there must be no temptation for those not playing to step on the green, therefore it is better kept off the main routes of access.

Children's playgrounds need careful siting. Adventure playgrounds should be completely screened, for the essence of their success lies in encouraging the children to build and do what they like with old bricks and cans and drainpipes, and although the results may be a delight to those who are interested in children, they are bound to be untidy.

But other types of playground require only partial screening, to give the children some feeling of being secluded and to break but not hide the view of the playground from the outside. Stockholm is full of delightful examples of how these playgrounds can be worked into the general picture of the park with the happiest results. The design of everything concerned with the children's playgrounds should be of the highest standard, for their effect on the children's appreciation of good surroundings is incalculable (Plate 61).

The remainder of the park uses are more flexible. The buildings, whether potting sheds, bandstands or shelters, should never need to be hidden away, but should be seized upon as opportunities to give added delight and supply focal points to the design. This can only happen if they are in complete accord with the spirit of the landscape composition. One of the worst features of our town parks are the heavy handed hipped-roofed Georgian or municipal rustic of the buildings.

Pools, putting greens, walks and flower garden are all elements which can be welded into an harmonious whole, which should contain within it the more intransigent uses. Even in a small park the design should flow, so that one passes inevitably from cne part to the next. There must be ample path surface for crowds to walk on, for perambulators, for children on their tricycles and for wheel chairs. There must also be plenty of places to sit, both in sun and shade, but more in the sun and out of the wind, and each seating place should have something of interest to look at—a distant view, if there is one, flowers, trees, or other people playing games. Old people particularly will spend hours sitting in the sun, and they should be catered for just as much as the young people (Fig. 31).

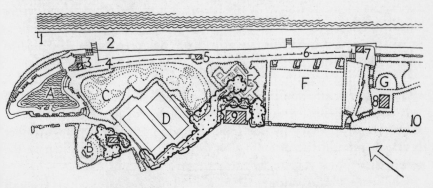

Fig. 31. An interlocking design for a small public garden containing many uses. Sutton-on-Sea. A. Children's boating and paddling pool; B. Children's theatre; C. Putting green; D. Hard tennis courts; E. Flower gardens; F. Bowling green; G. Tea lawn. 1. Sea wall; 2. Promenade; 3. Ice cream kiosk; 4. New colonnade; 5. Attendant's office; 6. Old colonnade; 7. Pavilion; 8. Existing café; 9. Existing public conveniences; 10. Sand dunes.

The scale in parks is that of the crowd, and this breadth of treatment should be carried through the design, with large-scale planting compositions, well-defined divisions of closed and open areas, wide paths and steps and long views. A place can be found for more intimate design, within the framework of the park as a whole, just as the *giardino segreto* was held within the grand sweep of the classic gardens.

In large cities there is room for parks having a specialised character, but often one with multiple use can contribute most, both in appearance and physical enjoyment, without in any way losing its individual character.

The L.C.C. park at Holland House is an interesting example of how this can be done. Its character is quite distinct from that of any other park in London and it succeeds in combining various recreational needs with a high standard of design (Fig. 32).

The playing fields are surrounded on all sides by large trees, a better method than attempting to grow trees within the playing area, as it allows complete flexibility for moving pitches, a necessary precaution to minimize

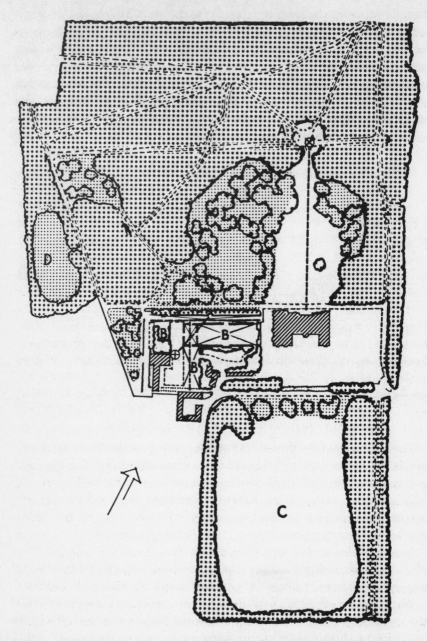

Fig. 32. Holland Park. Woodlands for walks (A) contrast with open space for games (C). Formal flower beds are concentrated in a walled garden near the house (B). (L.C.C. Parks Department). A. Woodland. B. Formal gardens. Defined rooms carpeted with beds and furnished. C. Playing fields. D. Children's playground.

wear. The proportion here between the open space and the 80 feet high trees is good, giving to the field the quiet beauty of a village cricket green. Yet the trees do not isolate the playing fields from the rest of the park. The games can be watched from seats under the trees or seen as a lively, distant activity framed between the tree-trunks from the walks bordering the ground. The cool sight of cricket whites, seen under the heavy green foliage on a hot summer day, or the bright colours of football shirts against the grey background of winter, are sights which can add to the delight of our parks as much as the bright-clothed courtiers added to that of Versailles. Compare the pleasure to be derived from this setting to the bleak aspect of the isolated fields to be found at Acton, for instance.

The woodlands on the north side of this park show how much greater an expanse appears when wooded than when left as open ground. There are secluded walks and places for sitting and even painting, which are denied in the bare open fields which sometimes pass for parks. Moreover, the woodland makes it possible to site unobtrusively a reserve for the children, where they can play with log huts and bridges and be completely untidy without spoiling the appearance of the rest of the park.

Near Holland House is the formal garden. Well planted with broad effects, it is full of interest at all times of the year, sheltered, yet with good views and well supplied with dry paths, which are not thrust in from sheer necessity but form the groundwork of the design. For the display of flowers, as opposed to trees and shrubs, there can be little doubt of the superiority of a formal garden, such as this, over the grass parks, where beds are cut in the lawns to meet the demand for flowers and colour, although they are alien to the design, interposing harsh blocks of bright colour into a landscape of grass and trees. The space division in Holland Park makes a clear pattern, a contrast of open lawn and closed wood; of unbroken turf and the intricate pattern of the formal garden. The result is a desire to proceed from one part to another, a sense of purpose and direction, which is lacking from those parks where vague shrub beds and single trees are scattered evenly over the area.

Parks are particularly suitable sites for sculpture and in Holland Park imagination has been used in siting. Ideally they should be off the main circulation routes, so that they may be seen without the confusion of moving crowds, but at the same time there should be dry access to them to allow their study at close quarters.

It sometimes happens in old industrial towns that spoil-heaps or quarries are the only land available for a park. Where these derelict sites are used they are most often levelled to form playing fields. This is often necessary because of the extreme shortage of sports areas. But where they can be spared from this use, or where a combined use is possible, their particular features should be seized upon to make a park of some special character whether a landscape of hills and dales among the spoil-heaps or a formalized composition of amphitheatres, pyramids and cones. With the use of bulldozers as carving machines, there is no limit to the possibilities of landscape compositions. Old quarries can be made to show the particular character of their bared rock, chalk-loving plants showing against the white cliffs and reflected in the blue-green chalk water, or heaths and cistus on the warm, well-drained banks of an old sand or gravel pit. Whatever is done should accentuate the unique character of the site, not blur it into one more lawn and rose-bed.

There are already many interesting examples of parks on old quarries. The Buttes Chaumont in Paris accepts and accentuates the towering pinnacles of limestone and fails only through lack of a congruous setting and because it contradicts its character in such details as the mock rustic of fencing and steps.

At Dudley, Worcestershire, playing fields, surrounded most pleasantly by trees, are set in the saucered summit of the rock outcrop from which quarrying was carried on for centuries. In the Black Country vast areas of old tips could be converted to parks, but drive and imagination are needed to make the best use of this exciting, if exacting, terrain.

Adjuncts of public parks, which are likely to gain in favour with the growing interest in horticulture, are Botanic Gardens and trial plots. Among the latter are the examples of trained fruit trees at Wisley Gardens, and this type of display would be a great help in raising the standard of small private gardens.

Two well-known examples of botanic gardens, very different both in size and treatment, are the Botanic Gardens at Oxford and the Royal Botanic Gardens at Kew.

Kew shows how well the landscape tradition can be adapted to an arboretum, given the space and good initial design. In the older part of the garden, originally laid out by Capability Brown, the botanic arrangement of tree species is raised from a mere collection to a landscape composition by being planted as woodland with open glades, and by the brilliant use of ground contouring, which gives reason to the groupings and a sense of rhythm to the design. On a smaller scale the collection of peat-loving plants near King William's temple makes the same use of land-form and combines careful composition with an arrangement of botanic interest.

Oxford achieves its success by serene simplicity, the superimposition of informal tree planting above a formal ground plan and the interest of

55. The Cedar in the asymmetric garden seen across the pool garden.

56. Yews form a linking colonnade. Both these pictures are of Tintinhull.

57. From the pool the classic façade of Tintinhull House is framed in the receding wings of yews.

uperlatively good architectural detail and sculpture. For a small botanic garden it is probably a better solution than an informal layout.

The London squares represent the most distinctive contribution made by English landscape to civic design. The earliest, in Bloomsbury, date back to the seventeenth century and it was a form of development which continued throughout Georgian times. The landscape tradition flowed into them in the shape of freely grouped plane trees, giving them a character unique to this country. Originally most of them were private gardens and attempts to convert them to public use have led to some difficulties. Most have failed either through half-hearted measures or because the chief visual value of the squares has not been understood.

They are among those smaller urban spaces which are subordinate to the surrounding architecture, and their role is to unite rather than separate the buildings on each side of the square. They do this on three planes. The over-arching branches make a light canopy, connecting, yet not concealing the buildings; the trunks fill the space of the square with a uniting vertical pattern; and the ground line runs through from side to side, flowing between the pillars of the trunks and beneath the canopy.

If the trees are removed, or reduced to a few isolated specimens, or replaced by smaller species, the effect of the canopy supported on the columns will be gone. If the square is surrounded by a solid barrier near or above eye level, the flow of the ground plane will be lost, as it will be if the interior of the square is blocked with lumps of planting or any form of construction.

The visual ideal is undoubtedly a smooth green lawn beneath the trees, but unfortunately in most cases this is not practical, for without protection the grass will become worn, and the squares are needed for use and transit as well as for appearance.

To find the best solution, it must first be decided what role each particular square is to play. Almost all London squares open to the public are wanted both for transit and as places of relaxation, and these are not easy requirements to meet in one small space in a busy area. The balance of one need over the other will depend on the size and position of the square. Those sited in a backwater may be devoted almost entirely to relaxation, while those lying directly across well-used routes of access must make provision for people to walk across them. Some of the larger squares have still other uses to cater for. Bloomsbury Square, for instance, is used by the L.C.C. as a place of open-air entertainment.

A square used almost wholly for transit is Sloane Square. It is small and wisely there is no attempt to introduce grass, so that the difficulty of determining the direction of transit does not arise. Flower stalls and a few

flower containers and seats give it sufficient colour, life and use, withou
blocking the clear view from side to side. It is a type of town square see
more often on the continent than in England, except that the free-growing
informally placed planes are typically English. There are many of thes
dry surfaced squares in Scandinavian towns, particularly in Copenhagen
where far more use is made of patterned floor surface and plant containers
and the street furniture is well designed. Small spaces where there is no
room for the traditional English planting of large free growing trees coul
well be laid out on these lines, which are so much more in keeping wit
civic architecture than the scraps of garden thrust into odd corners of th
London streets and then fenced in.

Leicester Square presents a different problem. As small a space a
Sloane Square, it is in a far more congested area. It is used for transit an
also fills a great need in supplying somewhere to sit for the shopping an
theatre crowds. Its present form caters for both these wants, but fails on th
count of appearance. The design is still obsessed by the ghost of the land
scape garden, one of whose essential characteristics is that it is a landscap
background on which access routes are kept subordinate or, if possible
ignored. This is not a logical outlook where there is to be heavy traffic
The reverse process is needed—a background of circulation space o
which a garden is superimposed. There are small town squares in Stock
holm where this is achieved by flower boxes or beds designed solely t
form sitting places, arranged to make a pleasant pattern on the backgroun
of floorspace.

Bloomsbury Square, spacious and set in less busy surroundings, demand
a different treatment again. Here there is no need for all-over access
but there are certain well-defined directions in which people wish to go
for which broad and direct paths must be provided. It is so large that it
relationship with the surrounding buildings will be helped by some sub
division of the ground space rather than an unbroken stretch of grass
it is, therefore, quite possible to use shrubs to give seclusion for sitting
areas and even to include provision for open-air entertainment; but it i
not, or should not be, possible to include such incongruities as roc
gardens, nor to cut it up in such a way that its cohesion is lost.

Grosvenor Square has shown a way of providing both for transit an
rest without destroying the unity of the square; but there is danger o
losing the clear uniting sweep of floor space, unless the surrounding yev
hedge is kept cut very low, so that the eye will pass easily over it in th
same way as it passes over a kerb or low retaining wall.

This principle of the boundary which prevents access without obstruc
ting view is one which can be applied in a variety of ways. Provided ther

are adequate paths and points of access, a comparatively slight deterrent is enough to prevent trespass on the grass, especially in the well-policed central areas of a city.

One method is to raise the grass by the provision of a low retaining wall with a runnel between the wall and the pavement (Fig. 33). Another is to plant a very low, wide band of compact planting, either parallel to the boundary or in certain cases irregularly shaped. Iron railings, if light and of good design, can be a delight in themselves and little check to the free flow of landscape through them.

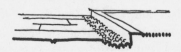

Fig. 33. Grass protected from casual trespass by curb and runnel in a town square.

Where informal shrub or ground planting is used, it should be so disposed that it represents pleasantly grouped islands in a sea, not impeding the flow of water between them but rather guiding it. Very slight contouring of the ground will help this treatment.

If the ground is flat and not contoured, the paths should take a direct line in the direction in which they are needed rather than follow some arbitrary curve. There need be no conflict between the straight path and the informally placed trees, because they operate at different levels.

The direct path can be seen in many of the Oxford quads. But the success of any path system laid across a grass square is dependent on the grass area being large enough to remain indisputably dominant. In small spaces the grass becomes disconnected by paths, and when this point is reached the dry surface should be allowed to become the dominant background of the square. The same trouble arises where roads cut across greens in new housing development, which are intended to have the effect of squares. But the width of the road with its pavements completely disrupts the continuity of the grass on each side. The grass-floored square is suitable as a precinct, not as the setting of a traffic artery. Indeed where it is necessary for vehicles and pedestrians to occupy the same level, a new factor of landscape design is involved. The vehicles nullify the ground pattern and can be contained only in some framework higher than themselves. They are mobile counterparts of the bungalow and call for the same setting of large-scale trees.

CHAPTER SEVENTEEN

ALLOTMENTS

ALLOTMENTS have been discouraged from many quarters and, as far as appearance is concerned, for very obvious reasons. But there seems little doubt that they are a genuine need in an urban civilization. There is a steady demand for them in England, Scandinavia and Switzerland, and they fill a fundamental human desire which should be encouraged, as well as contributing to the nation's food supply.

In England they have earned a bad reputation because they are often untidy, covered with shacks and scarcely ever laid out with thought for their general appearance. That they can be made attractive may be seen in Switzerland, but it must be accepted that this is only possible at increased cost and by using a proportion of the land for flowers and fruit trees which might otherwise be devoted to vegetables.

The concession will be thought worth while once the public has come to regard their environment as a thing of importance and to look upon the whole landscape as an extension of their own home.

The most satisfactory way to get better allotments would be for every allotment society to treat their area as a whole and see that each plot, while remaining the responsibility of the individual, would fit within a framework which would make the whole an acceptable part of the landscape.

Small areas are undoubtedly easier to make attractive than large ones, but an area of less than about four acres is not economic for an association to run. Water must be laid on and an access road provided. A central store is wanted for the storage of fertilizers and seed potatoes bought in bulk. The better solution is, therefore, as in many other problems to-day, to subdivide the large area into more intimate units.

The first step is to substitute well designed store-sheds grouped together for the ramshackle sheds, and to lay neat and attractive paths. The simplest unifying treatment is to hedge the area and to divide it into units of not more than about one acre, separated from each other by internal hedging or fruit trees. A communal orchard, grouped near the store-sheds, is convenient for the proper care of the trees and gives a focal point and a setting for the sheds. This simple treatment, combined with an encouragement to grow flowers beside the intersecting paths, and an insistence on all plots being kept tidy and well cultivated, would be enough to make the areas at least seemly.

A scheme in Denmark makes use of the cell treatment, which is a favourite theme in many aspects of their landscape design. Here the individual plots are held within a background of common planting. This would convert them from being merely seemly to something actively pleasant. But it would occupy more land and raises the problem of the maintenance of the planting. These difficulties might be overcome if the background planting were of fruit. Given sufficient co-operation among the allotment holders, a delightful scheme incorporating flowers, fruit and herbs could be devised, somewhat on the lines of the old walled kitchen gardens.

CHAPTER EIGHTEEN

COMMUNAL AND FLAT GARDENS

THE landscape which the Scandinavians have evolved round the flats and housing in Denmark and Sweden must rank as a distinct form of garden art. It has an ancestry in other times and lands, for it derives in general conception from the English landscape park and in detail from the principles of planting design first propounded by William Robinson and Gertrude Jekyll and later developed throughout Northern Europe. But it has caught the spirit and conditions peculiar to its place and time, and has made a distinctive contribution to the problems of creating a landscape for an urban democracy.

The style presupposes a high standard of living, a strong public spirit and a recognition that pleasant surroundings to everyday life are as important as the dwelling house itself. In Denmark the living space within a dwelling is on an average less than in comparable housing in England, but the standard of the surroundings is far higher.

The particular virtue of the Scandinavian flat gardens is that they combine a scale in keeping with the buildings and an intimacy in tune with the individual. The large scale is given by the broad masses of the planting and the use of a few species only, preventing the worried appearance which results from too great a mixture. Allied to this there is a creative use of both natural and artificial land-form. The intimacy is given by the space division made possible by lavish planting, changes of level and the use, where necessary, of light fencing sufficiently attractive in design to take its place as part of the composition.

The gardens designed by Sven Hermelin round the Star Flats at Gröndal show how all these features contribute to a reconciliation of the human scale with the building (Plate 58). Land-form and trees are used to give both a setting for the flat blocks and secluded intimacy behind their shelter. Between the arms of the flats, the ground is honeycombed with an octagonal pattern of brick let into the grass. Within the honeycomb there are small individual features—an oil jar, a seat, a group of flowering shrubs—all brought down to the human, individual scale of a room, yet held together within the bigger framework of the binding webs of the pattern (Plate 59).

Throughout this scheme, full use is made of the landscape for the enjoyment of the tenants. For instance, a long narrow strip of ground, which in most English layouts would have been left as a rather pointless piece of grass, becomes here an extension of the life of the flats by placing seats within a simple all-over diagonal pattern of planting (Plate 60).

In these ways the gardens are made not only part of the general landscape, but succeed in meeting the quiet, contemplative needs which a garden should fill, providing somewhere to sit, to stroll and to admire the flowers.

For the children, there are small sand pits, climbing logs and paddling pools, sometimes gathered together into a large playground, but also scattered among the landscape all round the flats. Their very number prevents the over-wear of the ground and the concentration of noise which accompany the sparse playgrounds of our own urban areas, while the single sand-pit or climbing frame can be absorbed into the landscape in a way impossible for a large asphalted area (Plate 61).

Even in Sweden, however, there are certain human wants which the flat garden does not supply. There is little scope for adult activity, the people cannot garden, chop wood, pull their motor bike to pieces, or in fact mess about without disturbing the beautifully laid-out grounds. At present these needs are met, if at all, away from the dwelling in creative playgrounds for children and in week-end and summer allotments for the family. There are obvious advantages to this arrangement. Plenty of space can be given to these activities without making the density of the town too low or creating untidy areas in it, which is likely to happen if the allotment areas are attached to the dwellings. But it does not allow of that pleasant strolling out for the odd hour to do a little jobbing, nor does it allow the children to let off steam at any hour of the day. In a densely populated country it can also be difficult to find the room for the play reserves and the allotments even at some distance from the flats. In Scandinavia the allotments usually include week-end bungalows, which are sometimes inhabited for the whole summer. This means in effect that the people have both a town and a country dwelling, a pleasant solution, as the wealthy in England have long appreciated, but not one to help solve the problem of land shortage to which the building of flats is supposed to contribute.

It is probable that England, as usual, will find a compromise and adapt the practice of other countries, using their principles of dividing space with planting and land-form to accommodate as many as possible of the home activities which the average English family enjoys. There have already been experiments in London of using part of the ground as private plots available for those of the tenants who particularly want them and who are prepared to keep them in a high standard of cultivation. This is a good plan provided that the individual plots are fitted within a framework which will form the setting of the building and of the communal garden. Children's playgrounds should similarly be fitted into the general design.

These principles are diametrically opposed to those which have been followed here in the past. The practice has been to surround the flats with grass or asphalt, with only the scantiest of tree and shrub planting. Usually the site is too restricted for this treatment to result in a good visual setting, especially when the surroundings are not particularly pleasant. It also depends for success on an unbroken stretch of grass, which means that in high-density flats the grass must not be used at all, nor, if it is to serve its visual purpose, must it be broken into with intrusions such as playgrounds and drying greens. These conditions are obviously quite unrealistic in relation to flats in towns.

The needs and possibilities for flat gardens depend on their area in relation to the number of people using them, and also on the kind of life which the inhabitants live. The most difficult problem is naturally that of a small area catering for people who have no country cottage, no car, who seldom go away for week-ends, and whose children do not go away to school. For these the flat gardens must somehow provide for their everyday open-air life.

If the area is not big enough to cater for all needs, precedence should be given to old people and small children, for other members of the population can, if necessary, go further afield for their recreation. The old people need a choice of sitting places in sun and shade in a variety of positions; some secluded, but some also where they can see life, perhaps overlooking the road and within hailing distance of passers-by, filling the same need as the seat by the village pub.

For the small children, the playground should be sunny, secluded, sheltered from the wind, and within sight of as many mothers' windows as possible. These are exacting conditions, and it is evident that they are unlikely to be fulfilled unless they are taken into account in the siting and architecture of the flats in the first place and given precedence in the design of the grounds.

Trees and groups of flowers and shrubs, growing, where necessary, from a hard surface, will give a framework to the composition and combine a measure of seclusion and space-division with a dapple of shade.

58. Land-form and trees give setting to flats from without and seclusion within. Gröndal (Sven Hermelin).

59. Honey-comb pattern of brick paving introduces intimate scale within breadth of landscape. Gröndal (Sven Hermelin).

60. Pattern and texture used to fill a narrow space with quiet interest. Gröndal (Sven Hermelin).

61. Small children's playground within the larger landscape.

Within this setting, the seats and sand pits can be placed without the appearance of litter which they give to a bare, open space. Wherever there is room, large trees should be grown to give scale and setting to the buildings, but even small trees, if planted in groups or, more formally, on the lines of an orchard, will have a unifying effect on the whole design.

In most new towns it has been found that, in spite of providing indoor drying rooms, there is a demand for drying greens. Where these have to be worked into the flat gardens they present a very difficult problem. Once again it can be solved only by consideration when the flats themselves are being designed. At Harlow the drying yards have been surrounded by open-slatted fences, which screen the washing without preventing circulation of air. These enclosures are absorbed into the garden by a light planting of small trees, such as silver birch, or groups of shrubs which will make a transition between the hard lines of the fences and the informal treatment of the rest of the garden. In a more formal design, their line could be accepted as part of the composition.

The more use to which a flat garden is subjected, the more carefully it must be designed. Where there is a high density of use, grass will become worn unless it is protected. There are various methods and degrees of protection. The first and most important step in protection is to provide adequate dry surface and ample paths going in the direction in which they are wanted. A beaten track across a lawn is a sign that an access need has been overlooked and must be provided for. Given the correct paths, grass in a well-kept garden, used by reasonable tenants, can be protected simply by moral persuasion and tradition. But in some cases more stringent methods are necessary. The object of whatever steps are taken should be to prevent wear without appearing to impose restraint, and without breaking the smooth flow of the grass. To do this the grass may be raised on a low retaining wall, or the ground may be contoured so that the path runs through a valley with the ground gently rising on either hand. A more emphatic prevention is a raised kerb or a low fence, either inconspicuous, like the ankle rails in some of the London parks, or light and decorative, like some of those in Stockholm parks. An area of rough cobbles between grass and path can discourage casual straying and planting can form a deterrent at vulnerable points.

The final deterrent, and one to be avoided at all costs, is a high and forbidding fence. If this extreme measure is necessary then the grass should not be there and should be replaced by a hard wearing surface combined with planting.

Grass, however, should still have a place in these high density gardens, because it is the most restful and refreshing to the eye of all surfaces and the most delightful to the feet of small children.

Where it is for the eye only, it may be raised as a panel and treated more as a flower bed than a lawn. The grass then becomes a defined shape on a background of other material, as opposed to its more usual role of serving as background. Where it is for the small children, it should be kept solely for their use if this is possible, and if it becomes over-worn it must be renewed as necessary. Stabilized grass may be used to increase its wearing life.

The backbone of planting in flat gardens should be trees and shrubs, both to give solidity and permanence to the design and to ensure that it holds together at all times of the year. But how far bedding and herbaceous plants can also be used depends almost entirely on provision for maintenance. Where it can be afforded, the bright splash of colour, provided it is the right colour in the right place, can be very welcome, especially in a town. And there is no doubt that the average flat dweller finds more interest in flowers such as delphiniums and wallflowers than in the majority of trees and shrubs. But a very few flowers rightly placed can give this interest without disrupting the framework of the garden. Small beds near the buildings can be left for tenants to fill with flowers and will have the same value in the design as window boxes, strictly subsidiary splashes of colour.

Where colour with the minimum of maintenance is needed, the hybrid polyantha roses are invaluable, but they and all roses should be associated with other plants or be in hedged beds if they are not to produce a thin and prickly wilderness in winter.

The cost of maintenance is one of the difficulties in providing communal gardens for flats and houses at low rents. The yearly cost is considerable if the garden is to be well kept and if it is not, it soon becomes sordid under the conditions of heavy wear which it endures. Experiments have been tried in communal upkeep, but although they may succeed for a time, they usually break down because the work is left to one or two enthusiasts, who eventually tire of doing all the work or perhaps leave and are not replaced.

These communal gardens have special needs which should develop a distinctive character. Visually, the first essential is that they shall have a unity with their surroundings and with the buildings which they serve. But within this unity they need considerable diversity, space division and a series of compositions. Their object should be not to bring the eye to one focal point, still less to lead the feet along one main axis, but rather to lure each individual to some separate place, forming a complex of pleasant spots each with some special attraction, a secluded backwater rather than a bead on a chain. For each of the many owners of the garden will seek to find their own glorietta and will not want others constantly passing through it.

The most sociable inhabitants will be the children, who appreciate an open lawn for their ball games, as well as plenty of tough shrubberies and groves of trees and paths for their other ploys.

The garden which these needs conjures up has something in common with the Victorian garden, which for family use had much to commend it. The tea lawn, the summer house, the shrubberies for hide and seek, the long winding gravel paths for wet days and toy carts, compare favourably to a child with the neatly squared gardens of the twenties and thirties, and for our communal gardens they may form a useful starting point. Should we, for this purpose, go back to the beginning of the *jardin anglais*, take its good points and see where it went wrong? This was chiefly perhaps in the heavy rigidity of the shrubberies, in the lack of composition and in the introduction of crude and misplaced flower beds. Imagine the shrubberies in some places lightened and opened up so that the ground-line of lawn or close ground planting flows through them while in other places they are consolidated into a satisfying background, making a pattern of contrasted shadows and streaks of sunlight, combining mystery with solid form. Imagine composition of form and texture in the shrub grouping, and the paths, instead of curling like a snake on flat ground, swinging gently with the contours of the ground. Then, instead of the round beds of harsh colours, let the herbaceous plants complete the composition of the shrub groups and ground planting. Or grow them in a separate border or flower garden away from the grass and trees.

The result can be a quiet garden, good at all seasons of the year, easy to keep up, giving opportunities for all the separate nooks that can be devised, fun for the children and not too vulnerable to their games.

This type of garden is, however, suitable only for a relatively low density of use, probably not exceeding 200 persons per acre of garden.

On the smaller sites a more compactly designed garden is needed, with a greater area of hard-wearing surface. Really good results will be achieved only if the surrounding landscape is considered as a whole. On the L.C.C. estate at Putney it is possible to see how the trees and landscape of one part of the site can be made to contribute to all the rest. Here is a satisfying, unified landscape, within which it is possible to develop gardens for the individual needs of the tenants. In this case the complete landscape is composed of a mixture of two-storey houses and tall blocks, private gardens, flat gardens and public landscape, combining into a landscape which contains within itself the varying shapes and sizes of the different buildings. It is another example of the cellular principle so successful at Gröndal: land-form, buildings and plants composed into a framework within which the cells are developed as separate rooms, the age-old pattern of a garden for outdoor living.

CHAPTER NINETEEN

WILD GARDENS

A 'Wild Garden' would have been a contradiction of terms in the first dawn of gardens when men fashioned an enclosure of order and safety out of the surrounding savagery, and it is natural that the first mention we have of them comes from an age when the renaissance had begun the long process of imposing man's order on nature, and when already the first nostalgic pangs for primeval wildness were being felt.

Bacon's heath, with its thyme-covered mole hills and thickets of eglantine, conjures up a pleasant contrast to the formal alleys, trellis and clipped hedges of his main garden, while Milton's description of the garden of Eden shows an even greater appreciation of the beauties of natural growth, only partly tamed by the pruning and tying which kept Adam and Eve so fully occupied. For those who believe that a wild garden ends all maintenance problems, it is salutary to remember that, according to Milton, it was the pressure of this work which caused Adam and Eve to work in different parts of the garden and so gave the serpent his opportunity.

A wilderness was a common adjunct of seventeenth-century gardens, and by the eighteenth century Uvedale Price and Richard Payne Knight were doing more than applying a little gentle civilization to existing nature—they were going to great lengths to reproduce her rugged accidents, bringing rough thickets and rooted banks into the garden, rather than removing them.

The natural craving for an occasional return to nature as a contrast to urban life is stronger than ever to-day, when man's background has changed from a matrix of jungle to a backcloth of brick, steel and concrete. But there are certain inconsistencies in the conception of a wild garden which need to be clarified.

What is one trying to obtain? A slice of nature with no obvious sign of man's hand can be a pleasant part of the pleasure grounds, but it scarcely comes into the category of garden, and it is only a substitute for one if it is on a sufficiently large scale and a good enough natural composition to make a self-contained landscape. More often, in this circumscribed age, the piece of land chosen for a wild garden must be deliberately composed within comparatively narrow boundaries, for the average natural composition is of far greater extent than the normal garden. A Swiss chalet set on a mountain side has little need for a garden, but eight plots on an acre of woodland will not each retain the spirit of the wood as a whole.

There are two lines of approach to the design. One is the deliberate humanizing of a wild scene, the desire to show that although this may appear to be just a wood, it is nevertheless under man's influence. This method of approach is exemplified by the statues and temples, placed both in the hunting forests surrounding the French chateaux and in the woodlands of the English landscape parks. It is an attitude still showing the desire to impress man's intellect on nature.

The other method is to idealize nature herself, to introduce only those things that can be made to appear subservient to her. In some ways it is a less honest approach. A woodland can be ennobled by a fine statue and cheapened by poor rustic work. In either approach the trees and natural spirit of the place must remain dominant; the statue is a complement to them, subsidiary and not challenging their supremacy, as it would be challenged by extensive man-made intrusions such as over-emphatic paths or incompatible planting.

Most wild gardens are based on some existing natural feature. It may be a woodland, a stream, a pond or an old chalk pit, and success depends on conserving and accentuating the natural characteristics. In a chalk pit plants may be introduced which are not indigenous, but they must, both in appearance and in their ecological needs, be appropriate to chalk.

The stream may be dammed into a pool or into a series of waterfalls, but no suggestion of concrete construction should be allowed to appear. A bridge, on the other hand, is a fitting incident and can be equally acceptable in wood, stone or slender concrete.

Wild gardens as they are usually treated to-day derive from the natural gardening phase of the late nineteenth century, and the principles of planting a large woodland on these lines set out by Gertrude Jekyll in *Wood and Garden* is as valid to-day as when it was written. Her injunction to follow the natural grouping of plants, allowing one species to predominate and then to change gradually to another (See p. 120), is sound advice which needs to be even more carefully observed now that the increased variety of plants available adds to the temptation to put too much in too small a space.

Sometimes a woodland is used simply as a habitat for a collection of a particular species, as Battlesdon Hill is used at Wisley for rhododendrons.

But this limited range of planting can be organized into an idealized landscape by grouping the plants in relation to ground form and by giving the essential contrast of strong mass and open glade. Where there is not this strict limitation, the choice of plants should still be selective, the plants being chosen equally for their ecological suitability to the site and for their relationship to each other, the contrast of their foliage, their colour and their pattern.

The first principle in their grouping is the need for some open space. The most lovely woodland pictures are nearly always in a glade where the pool of light contrasts with the surrounding darkness of the wood, and where the full beauty of the tree-trunks springing from the ground can be appreciated. The second principle is the need for congruity of treatment. If it is to be a natural woodland, then the paths should be woodland paths, dying away naturally each side into the forest floor.

The Savill Gardens in Windsor Great Park and the woodland garden at Wisley are interesting examples of the wild garden. A wide range of plants is grown, but they are well chosen and well grouped. Each colony follows the lines of a natural plant community. Compatible plants mingle together, but one species is dominant at each time of the year. They are strongly, but not too solidly, grouped and thin out into scattered out-riders at the edges. There is no suggestion of a made-up bed, nor of one effect competing with another, each being allowed to fill the whole picture and to drift into a neutral background of woodland before a different species holds the field. In both these gardens, woodland gives the setting and natural environment for the introduced plants. In the Savill Gardens particularly, there is a clear distinction between the closed and open parts of the composition, the long expanse of water giving form and clarity to the design. Any necessary construction is subordinated to the natural surroundings.

The paths are woodland paths, and where there are steps, or supports for a bank, they are made with branches of trees, not in the usual style of rustic work, but as naturally as a fallen bough or exposed root terraces a steep fall in the wild woodland.

Although it is a lengthy process to create a woodland garden where there is not already a wood, there are many places where one can be developed. Even a small spinney or old hedgerow can be converted into one and, if a house is set on a wooded site, it is possible to have the interest and humanization of a garden without sacrificing the trees. If it were realized that these gardens could be as satisfying and as full of interest as any other, and with far less labour, they would become increasingly popular and there would be less demand for treeless open plots.

The value of a woodland setting for the modern type of small housing can scarcely be exaggerated. The monotonous pattern of small houses on plots of land varying from 1/12 to one acre is enormously helped by the recurring pattern of the vertical tree-trunks and by the background of tree-tops. At the same time they provide some privacy between one house and another. The woodland garden is labour-saving because the trees keep down the growth of rank weeds and coarse grass, and the selected plants can easily be kept clean, growing either straight out of the leaf-mould of the forest floor or from a carpet of easily managed woodland grass or low woodland plants.

In Scandinavia the use of woods as a setting for the house is common, partly because the houses were built while the main forest background of the country was still intact, instead of there having been, as in England, an intermediate stage when the land was cleared for agriculture. Among the features which give their woodland gardens an interest and sense of composition, often lacking in ours, are the boulders and great rocks protruding through the ground. These provide solidity and focal points which give meaning to the design. There are parts of England, particularly in the north and west and in the Sussex woodlands, where the same conditions occur, and even elsewhere such boulders could be used on the principle of *objets trouvés* (See p. 216).

The most discouraging woodlands are on hungry soil or those from which the leaves have been removed and burnt for generations, leaving a dry and impoverished soil. Under these conditions the available plants are very limited. But in a woodland under which the leaf mould has collected in a deep moist layer, the range is enormous and by good fortune includes a sufficient proportion of striking foliage and interesting form to enable compositions in plant form to be the mainstay of the design. It is easier to obtain the sculptural group of plants rising from a clear base in woodland than in any other type of garden, because of the naturally maintained forest floor.

A specialized form of wild garden is the heath garden, whose possibilities are worth exploring because heaths will thrive on the hungry Bagshot and Hampshire sands, which are discouraging to the majority of plants and yet which constitute the soils of a big residential area.

Their chief asset as design material is that they cover the ground with a textured and moulded carpet, which looks well all the year round and has a pleasant range of quiet colours both in flower and foliage. Their disadvantage is a sameness of scale both in flower, foliage and stature, particularly in districts where the tree heaths are not hardy. This weakness is evident in their wild state where an unbroken stretch of calluna on the flatter parts of Surrey and Hampshire can be extremely dull. But on hilly ground, contrasted with Scots pine, rowan and great grey boulders, it takes on a new quality. Equally in the garden the problem of making a composition with heaths on flat ground is almost insoluble, but on a contoured landscape, against a background of trees and with the help of other plants to give a change of scale, it is possible to make the most of their good points.

The floors of the valleys should be planted with low growing plants, such as thymus and fescue, while on the higher land groups of other plants give contrast in scale, form and tone. The choice of plants, which have these contrasting qualities and which are compatible with heaths, is limited. For instance, berberis, although compatible, does not give enough contrast. Juniper, on the other hand, by its greater solidity and scale can be valuable, so for the same reason can gorse. Arbutus, *Cistus ladaniferus* and stranvaesia are all useful for the scale and texture of their leaves.

Scots pine with its rugged strength of trunk is perhaps the perfect tree to give the vertical accent. The hybrid rhododendrons are too large in scale of flower and foliage to associate well, but some of the small-leaved species such as *hippophoides* and *praecox* are excellent. The wild rose is a common incident on heaths and it, too, can be used in the heath garden, as well as such small scale species as *farreri* and *hugonis*. The choice among the heaths themselves is much wider in sheltered parts of the south of England, where the tall-growing *australis* and *arborea* can be used.

The moist peat areas give far wider possibilities of compositions and on them the true American garden can be developed with its great range of fine charactered plants, such as arbutus, zenobia, *Cornus kousa* and kalmia.

The basis of any wild garden must be the idealisation of some natural habitat. It matters little what the habitat may be, so long as its typical pattern is accentuated, organised into a composition and given its appropriate setting.

CHAPTER TWENTY

ROCK GARDENS

So many monstrous and misplaced rock gardens have been produced during this century that one's first instinct is to reject them out of hand as a contribution to garden art. But to do this is to deny the possibility of adapting one of the finest of natural formations to garden use.

As in so many other garden elements, the rock garden has suffered from a general haziness of intention as to what part it is intended to play in the garden.

There are at least three distinct and legitimate types of rock garden. It may be intended purely to supply the best growing conditions for a collection of alpines. To those who take pleasure in a collection of these entrancing plants, there could be no better justification. But in this case it is better to give it a background which will create for it a small world of its own rather than to make it part of the general garden picture. The rock garden at Kew is an example of this. It is fascinating to wander through it and enjoy the small gems, which are often conveniently at eye level. In this particular garden there are in addition some very pleasant compositions of rock and background trees. But it is too varied, too full of detail, to make a good composition as a whole, and it cannot be otherwise if the full range of alpine plants is to be grown in a reasonable area. But here it is effectively cut off from the rest of the gardens and winds through a valley, screened on each side with thick planting.

The second method is applicable where the rock is either natural to the site or can be made to appear so. This method cannot be combined with the first, because, to appear natural and to achieve the dramatic composition which is its special virtue, the planting must be as restrained as it would be in nature, where one species is usually dominant and it is rare to find more than half a dozen in a few square yards. Also for success it must have extremely bold bluffs of rock, which does not allow for the multitude of small pockets found in a plantsman's rock garden. This style was developed during the 1930's by Colonel Gavin Jones and B. H. B. Symons-Jeune.

For success the surroundings must be in keeping with this treatment. It could, for instance, be the culminating feature of a garden planted mainly with heaths on contoured ground, or it could rise from the side of an informal pool set in a gently contoured lawn, or it could be in a woodland garden. It cannot look at home between a rose garden and a tennis court, nor in a formal garden. The rockwork at the falls from Virginia Water shows the legitimate use of rocks in this way; well arranged in themselves, they are in keeping with the waterfall and surrounding wood.

Figs. 34 & 35. The rock, the bamboo and the mounded azalea of a Japanese garden is basically the same composition as the temple, the tree and the shrub of the English landscape park.

On a site which is naturally rocky, the strata can be revealed and a natural landscape created by careful planting and management of the land-form. Frank Lloyd Wright showed how successfully this type of rock could form the base of a house, uniting building to ground, in the most dramatic way, and there are many modern South American and Swedish examples of the same kind. These are utterly different from the rock banks which intrude between a lowland garden and a house built on a level site, which only serve to disrupt the union of house and land (See p. 142).

In both the rock garden for the culture of alpines and the rock landscape, the correct geological bedding of the stones must be observed and care taken to make it appear that the rock is protruding from the underlying strata and not lying loosely on the surface, except in a scree formation or where the effect is desired of odd boulders having rolled from the main formation. Equally important in the scenic type of rock garden is to show the same sense of design and composition which would be accorded to any other form of garden art; a bluff of rock need not be beautiful because it is natural, nor will a replica of part of a scene of natural beauty necessarily retain its beauty when taken out of its context and reproduced in other surroundings. In its natural setting it will be part of a picture whose boundaries are the horizons; the tilt of a foreground rock may make its appeal by being seen in relation to some far distant peak. A study of the

Japanese garden shows that the translation of the spirit of a mountain scene lies not in copying one part of it, but in re-creating its essence in a reduced scale and simplified form.

The third method of using rocks bears no relation to nature. They are used here not as natural outcrops, nor as homes for alpines, but simply for their solidity and sculptural form. They are *objets trouvés*, given significance by their selection and placing, as opposed to that given to sculpture by an effort of creation. They have something in common with the Japanese method, where each stone has a special connotation, such as the standing stone, the waiting stone, and the moon stone.

For this purpose the stones must be carefully chosen and, as a rule, those which are weathered or water-worn are the most suitable. It is a method with great possibilities for small gardens and even courtyards. Delightful compositions are possible with flat stones, rounded pebbles, gnarled, scooped or upright stones grouped with the carefully chosen plant. Because it is a frankly artificial composition there is no incongruity in having it near the house or in close relation to any man-made object, just as the Japanese compositions are so often completed with a stone lantern and surrounded by a bamboo fence. In Japan even the narrow passage beside the house is made interesting by the economic placing of the rock, the bamboo and the fence.

The rock-strewn stream-bed designed by Peter Shepheard for the London South Bank Exhibition was an excellent example of this type of composition in stone and plants, and Western expressions of it appear in many Californian gardens. It is also akin to the Scandinavian use of rock. For although the rock there is usually found on the site, its place in the composition is often as individual and selective as if it had been placed there deliberately; the only difference being that the composition is brought to the rock instead of the rock to the composition.

The single rock can give the same significance to a group of plants as the temple gives to the groves of trees in a landscape park. It clarifies the design by providing solidity, focal point, contrast of texture and reason for the tall form on one side and the low grouping on the other. The same underlying composition can be seen in the temple of the English landscape park and the Japanese group of the rock, the bamboo and the mounded azalea (Figs. 34 and 35).

CHAPTER TWENTY-ONE

FACTORY GARDENS

THE idea that a factory should have a garden at all is comparatively recent. Bournville and Port Sunlight were two of the pioneers in the attempt to give garden surroundings to places of work as well as to the workers' homes. Since then it has become common practice in newly built light industry to have some garden treatment, if only in the form of a window box.

There are several points of view in determining the kind of garden which a factory is to have. It may be designed as part of the surrounding landscape or townscape, or it may be an advertisement for the factory, or it may be for the pleasure and recreation of the work people. Ideally all three objects should be served, but in practice one is usually stressed at the expense of the others and, perhaps naturally, the advertising angle is the one which most often receives attention. There are unfortunate examples of this on some of our main roads, where the blatant displays of bedding out and the misplaced rockeries bear no relationship either to the factory building or to its neighbours and contribute nothing to the recreation of the worker. Even if advertising is accepted as the main motive, the best value is obtained by making the factory both attractive to the employees and a credit to its surroundings.

Industrialists could get a far better result by co-operating with each other in the same way that the traders of Bond Street and Regent Street achieve results by a unified scheme of decoration on special occasions.

This over-all effect has to some extent been achieved in the industrial estates in some of the new towns. Here, while the landscape of each individual factory is agreed with the industrialist to accord with its architecture and special requirements, there is a unified plan for the estate as a whole and for the treatment of roads which ensures that all will fit into one general picture. Groups of trees are placed to make a good composition in the view down the street, in some cases a low broad hedge is carried along the frontages of the sites, and certain species of trees and shrubs are used throughout a road to give it a homogeneous character.

The requirements of factories on an industrial estate are likely to be quite different from those of an individual factory sited among other types of development, or in the country.

On an estate the recreational needs of the employees can best be met on areas sited in convenient places to serve a large number of factories. This has many advantages. The recreational areas can be more spacious and cater for different tastes and they provide a more complete break from work with the opportunity to meet a wider circle of people. There is also a considerable saving of land-space, which must be a matter of increasing importance in this country. On the valuable sites usually occupied by industry it is seldom that much space on an individual site can be spared for recreation, and any provision made is likely to be cramped. Temporarily vacant land is often held in reserve for expansion, which naturally makes the industrialist unwilling to spend money on laying it out as a garden or planting trees which may have to be felled before they have reached maturity.

The industrial area of the new town of Basildon is an example of shared recreation areas as well as of an overall landscape plan for the estate. The recreation area forms a strip of open land dividing industry from the Southend road. A stream runs down the centre, along part of which are some fine trees. The space has been laid out with football and smaller kick-about pitches, tennis courts and a walk and picnicking area beside the stream. The trees have been kept and others planted to give a framing to the frontages of the factories beyond. Big drifts of *Salix vitellina*, *Cornus siberica* and lythrum are planted beside the stream. Within the estate the majority of the trees have been preserved, each road is designed as a whole, and the services so placed that groups of large trees can be planted at certain points where they form a background and framing for the buildings. Between each factory site the boundary is planted with a thorn hedge and standards, which are intended to grow into a solid band of planting which will screen the untidy back yards of the factories and give homogeneity to the whole area.

Factories which must rely on their own resources should, however, make the best possible use of whatever space is available and the provision of outdoor facilities should be considered as of equal importance to that of indoor canteens and rest rooms. The chief needs will naturally depend on the type of labour employed. In heavy industry and all works employing youths, the greatest need will be for a kick-about space. If the use of this will not be too heavy, it should be of grass or stabilised grass; but in cases where the grass will obviously be reduced to a mud patch, it is better to accept the fact and give it a hard surface. But even so every effort should be made to prevent it having a bleak and sordid appearance. It is useless to plant beds of flowers where the ball will constantly wreck them, but space should be found for trees which, if necessary, can be protected by tree guards in their early years. Some relief of simple green, either of grass or tough growing shrubs, can also usually be provided by growing them in beds raised above ground level or on the surrounding banks. The use of tall close hedges or pleached trees for screeening yards and storage places can add both to the tidiness and greenness of the surroundings. In light industry, where women are employed, the favourite recreational facility will be tennis courts or a netball court, but even more important will be the provision of a pleasant place to sit and eat sandwiches. It will be more truly the factory garden and less the playing field. The design should be simple and easily maintained, but it should give seclusion and have enough interest to hold the attention and make a stroll in the garden a thing of pleasure and variety. The provision of intimacy within a unifying framework is a problem which recurs throughout landscape design and is especially acute to-day, when the aggregate of our development is on so great a scale, yet the individual feels as never before the need for the human scale. There are many ways of attaining this. One of the simplest is the hedged garden, in which the green walls of the hedges form an architectural extension of the building, while the garden within the hedges may be as intimate as the interior of a room. Or the enclosure may be less formally achieved by the use of land-form and shrub planting, which can also serve the purpose of uniting the building with its surroundings. One of the best methods of all is by means of a woodland garden, preferably of some light trees such as birch or Scots pine.

Here the trees will form a setting uniting the factory building with its surrounding country or with other buildings (especially if they can receive the same treatment), for the trees provide a simplifying framework to the buildings and to their often tiresome ancillaries of sheds and storage yards. Some of the new factories in Basildon are sited in an old orchard, and the landscape treatment has consisted simply of retaining all the trees possible and supplementing them with new trees of *Malus spectabilis* to maintain the character of an orchard.

Opportunities are often missed of providing an open-air extension to the canteen. There are few things which add more to the health and happiness of indoor workers than the opportunity to spend their midday break out of doors. To make full use of such an arrangement, the garden should open straight off the canteen and be both sunny and sheltered. In a single-storey building where the sun will not be cut off, even a small courtyard can be very suitable and can be made attractive with tubs of flowers and a few climbers on the walls.

There are examples of factory gardens which go beyond the immediate needs of the people while at work and provide clubs for leisure hours and playgrounds for the children. One of the finest examples of these is the Marabou Works in Sweden, whose grounds were laid out by the Swedish landscape architect, Sven Hermelin. They combine a good overall landscape with sensitive detailing, which makes them a place of real recreation designed for the workers and their families and include a delightful children's pool set about with grey foliaged plants and weeping willows.

There are also good examples in Switzerland of factory gardens, which reach a high standard of design. In one at Zurich, designed by Walter Leder, the principle has been followed that the first things a worker should see on leaving his machine-shop are growing plants; accordingly, facing the stairway up from the workshops, is a glass panel behind which can be seen an arrangement of growing foliage plants. In both Sweden and Switzerland great importance is attached to the psychological effect of good landscape surroundings on the workers, and there is little doubt that the general standard of education could be immensely improved if more attention were paid to this point in England. From the business angle it would pay in productivity and eventually would be a far better advertisement than the display fronts, which are often all that a factory supplies at present.

Switzerland and Sweden have the great advantage of clean electrified railways and factories, which removes the difficulty of dirt and smoke. Most light industries in England are now clean and offer few difficulties of pollution, while heavy industry requires in any case a different type of landscape, partly because of the different needs of the workers and partly because of the scale and type of building.

Any garden treatment will look out of place in relation to the great buildings, yards and fuel-stands of heavy industry and, consequently, the requirements of both workers and landscape are best met by a broad simplicity. Massive tree planting, where this can be arranged, and a general tidying up of the surroundings can achieve far more than the odd variegated shrub and trivial flower bed. There may often be an opportunity to use water in the landscape setting, either in the form of an old flooded working or if it is used in quantity for cooling purposes in the works. If some more humanized garden is wanted, it should be related to the administrative block with whose scale it will probably be more in keeping and it can be brought into scale with the wider surroundings by one of the methods already advocated.

Sometimes the land available for a factory landscape is on an old spoil-heap. Unless the ground is required for a playing field, it is better not to level it, but to take the opportunity to make a more interesting landscape either by accepting the existing contours or by some slight modification.

One of the problems in this case will be the provision of soil and care must be taken to ensure that there is no substance poisonous to plants in the waste. The amount of soil needed will depend on the nature of the waste. Iron slag or ashes, for instance, requires only a thin layer of soil to produce grass and still less to get a cover of white clover. Experiments have been carried out in various types of waste and almost all are found capable of supporting some species of tree, alder being one of the easiest. In such conditions, it is much more satisfactory to create a landscape out of the plants which will most easily grow than to attempt some more orthodox garden, which can only be established at great cost and even then may not thrive.

In dealing with all types of factory gardens, there are certain practical problems. First it must be accepted that the main object of a factory is to get the work done. If a certain place is needed for unloading or stacking crates, it must be left clear for that purpose and the workers must not be expected to make a diversion round a lawn or flower bed.

Secondly, the garden will be used by a great number of people and must be designed accordingly, with ample circulating space and seats. Because of the number of users and the generally difficult conditions, the maintenance standard must be high and the labour available for this should be ascertained before the ground is laid out. In the case of dirty industry or clean industry in a dirty area, plants must be chosen which will stand the conditions. For the dirtiest conditions of all some of the most reliable among the trees are *Acer platanoides*, ailanthus, crataegus, robinia and sorbus, and among shrubs the deciduous cotoneasters, *Cornus alba*, *Ligustrum lucidum* and *sinensis*, rhus and philadelphus.

In moderate conditions there is an enormous choice, but those plants should be selected which look good for the longest possible period of the year and which are not likely to be ruined by the unskilled pruning which they may receive. Cotoneasters are among the best shrubs for this purpose and for banks *C. horizontalis* and *C. conspicua decora* are invaluable.

The hybrid polyantha roses are excellent as a permanent substitute for bedding-out, provided certain precautions are taken; they should be combined with some other plant, either as an edging or inter-planted, which will clothe the bed in winter, and colours should be avoided which will clash with the building. Most of the strong pinks are likely to do this, since they look equally wrong with red brick, yellow stocks and the strong primary colours which are now fashionable for doors and panels.

Although a proportion of evergreens are needed, there should be due emphasis on seasonal change, for the rhythm of the seasons is one of the fundamental joys of life, which industrial workers are in danger of losing.

CHAPTER TWENTY-TWO

SCHOOL GARDENS

Nowhere is the need for broad overall scale, combined with intimate detail, more evident than in school gardens. The buildings—particularly the alighted-bird type of the new Hertfordshire schools—call for simplicity and broad effects in their setting. The gardens must cater for large numbers and by far the greatest area will be taken up by open playing fields.

The school and its grounds will very likely form the major feature of its neighbourhood and, wherever possible, they should serve visually as an extension of the local open space system. This means that they should not be tightly closed in and shrouded with planting, but should have at least some visual openings linking with the outside world and divided from it only with light, well-designed fencing. Well placed groups of boundary planting will ensure both the necessary scale and setting, provided the trees are limited to two or three species, carefully chosen to accord with the surroundings and planted in broad drifts.

Yet within this broad framework the child must be able to feel at home. Its individuality must be respected and not lost in something big and impersonal. There is in most modern schools a deliberate scaling down of detail to achieve this end—little chairs, little fences and little gates. Whether this is really an advantage is not certain. It perhaps smacks of talking down and the child may prefer to show its ability to deal with things of grown-up size.

But however this may be, there is certainly a desire to find their own corner, to cultivate their own garden, to divide into their own chosen small groups. There is also in some schools the excellent idea of having open-air class-rooms into which the class can move on a fine day. All this calls for the most careful and sensitive space division within the framework of the building and its wider setting. This division can be achieved by smaller planting of a more intimate and varied type than that of the boundaries, by fences of the imaginative type used in Sweden, and by land-form. Contouring of the ground is not only a great help in space division, but provides the grass banks and knolls beloved by children.

Since so much of the grounds must be open to provide the playing fields, the remainder can afford to be closely designed and in small compartments. Grass should be used as the surface wherever it is practical, for it is a surface kind to bare feet and nice to roll on. But there will have to be a proportion of hard surfaces, both to withstand wear and to provide a dry space after rain. Ingenuity, sensitivity and the necessary allocation of funds are required to prevent this degenerating into the concrete and asphalt deserts which have been so depressing a part (or often the whole) of school grounds in the past.

The first care should be in the siting and shape of the hard surface as a whole, the second in the possibilities of making the surface itself more pleasant, in texture and colouring and in sub-division and patterning where this can be done, without interfering with its use for games. Swiss schools show excellent and simple ways of doing this with setts let into the asphalt and patterns formed by bands of different colours.

The provision of small garden plots should be part of every school garden, and they should be so worked into the general design that their individual treatment will not disrupt it but add interest. A simple and satisfactory way is to arrange them in a parterre edged with a low hedge. The parterre itself can be of any shape to accord with the design—traditional, abstract or in the popular Scandinavian hexagonals.

Casting one's mind back to childhood, what garden memories remain? Not, at least in early chldhood, any general picture, but an intense love of certain flowers, mostly those with clear colours, or strange forms or, most of all, sweet scents. Canterbury bells, snapdragons, mock orange, wallflowers, and the fascination of those pleasant to the touch, lamb's ear, the bark of silver birch, rosemary to pinch. For the rest, an enjoyment of ponds, banks, weeping trees and disappearing paths. These predilections can be taken as a basis for the school garden. But in addition to these simple and facile appreciations, there is the unrealised influence which will surely affect their future tastes and outlook. It is because of this that nothing shoddy or meretricious should ever be allowed in a school garden, and one hopes that it is through this that the Hertfordshire County Council's work in providing good sculpture will bear fruit.

The same end can be followed in the garden by selecting plants of good foliage and form, by careful grouping, and the best design of which one is capable, even though the children may not consciously realise the difference between that and something second-rate.

CONCLUSION

B OTH the opportunities for making gardens and the materials used in
them have changed since the last century.

In the use of materials we must hope that we shall never lose the
craftsmanship which made the beauty of the old stone work, but such
craftsmen will be rare in comparison with the amount of work to be done,
and for the bulk of the work we must learn to look to the possibilities of
new materials and techniques, just as architecture has done. Not attempting
to imitate the old with substitutes, but using to the full the grace and lightness of metal and the springing curves of pre-stressed concrete.

Our loss of the lavish man-power, which was once available, is recom-
pensed by the possibilities of machinery. The great earth-moving
machines allow us to carve the ground on a scale never before possible,
electric clippers bring back the opportunities to use high-clipped hedges
and topiary, electric pumps can give us fountains, and our vocabulary of
plants is so great that all we need is selection and restraint in their use.

If we can apply to these resources even the good taste which comes
from sincerity and a sense of proportion, we shall produce reasonably
pleasant surroundings, and if we can add the creative skill, which other
ages have produced, we can revolutionize the country, for although the
day of the large private garden is over, at least for the present, we have more
small private gardens than ever before and more opportunities for making
public ones. If these opportunities are taken, we can have the grand overall
landscape on a scale never seen before, contributed to by our parks and
playing fields, school grounds and industrial landscape, no longer designed
as isolated and incongruous gardens, but in sympathy with each other, as
were the neighbouring great parks of the eighteenth century. And within
this encircling landscape will be the small private gardens, the gloriettas of
the individual man.

A SHORT BIBLIOGRAPHY

A History of Garden Art, Gothein
Capability Brown, Dorothy Stroud
Chinese Gardens, Siren
Colour in the Garden, Gertrude Jekyll
English Gardens, Avray Tipping
Forty Years of Landscape Architecture, Olmstead
Gardens are for People, Church
Garden Craft in Europe, Inigo Triggs
Gardens in the Modern Landscape, Tunnard
Gardens of the Alhambra, Prieto Moreno
Gardens and Design, Shepheard & Jellicoe
Gardens of Europe, G. A. Jellicoe
Gardens of the Great Moghuls, Villiers-Stuart
Gardener to Queen Anne, David Green
Italian Gardens of the Renaissance, Shepheard & Jellicoe
Japanese Garden Design, Tetsur Yoshida
Land and Landscape, Colvin
Landscape for Living, Eckbo
Modern Gardens, P. Shepheard
On Gardens, Francis Bacon
On the Making of Gardens, Sir George Sitwell
Planting Design, F. Robinson
Spanish Gardens, Villiers-Stuart
Successful Town Gardening, Lanning Roper
The English Flower Garden, W. Robinson
The English Garden, Eric A. T. Dutton
The English Landscape Garden, Clark
The Formal Garden in England, Blomfield

GARDEN DESIGN

Theory and Practice of Landscape Gardening, Repton
The New Small Garden, Allen & Jellicoe
The Picturesque, Christopher Hussey
The Wild Garden, W. Robinson
William Kent, Dorothy Stroud
Wood and Garden, Gertrude Jekyll

INDEX

A

Albury Park, Surrey, 48, 70
Alhambra, Spain, 24–29, 85, 93, 191
Amman, Gustav, 73
Arabian Gardens, 17
Asplund, 103
Assyria, 17, 18
Avenues, 48, 63, 90–91
Azaleas, 124–126

B

Bacon, Sir Francis, 45, 109, 124, 149, 209
Badminton, Gloucestershire, 49
Barry, Sir Charles, 64
Basildon, 218
Belvedere Gardens, Vienna, 63, 104, 132, 190
Blenheim, Oxfordshire, 49, 55, 134
Bloomsbury Square, London, 197, 198
Booth, Kenneth, 177
Bosche, 33, 37
Botanic Gardens, 196–197
Bramham Hall, Yorkshire, 48, 138, 140
Brazil, 73–77
Bridgeman, Charles, 53, 60, 145
Brown, 'Capability', 52, 53, 55, 96, 103, 147
Burlington, Lord, 53
Buttes Chaumont, Paris, 188, 196

C

Castle Howard, Yorkshire, 49, 53
Chatsworth, Derbyshire, 102, 133
Children's gardens and playgrounds, 177, 192, 203, 204, 207, 222–223
China, 20
Chiswick House, Middlesex, 53, 85, 138
Church, Thomas, 134, 149
Climbers, 130
Colonnades, 71, 146
Colour, 83, 95–96, 114, 117–119, 174–175
Conifers, 126
Cotoneasters, 127
Cottage gardens, 121, 149, 160

D

De Caux, 49
De Cerceaux, 39, 48
Duchêne, 43

E

Eden, 17
Egypt, 17
Eridu, 17
Evelyn, John, 48, 49, 70

F

Fences, 149–153
Foster, Arnold, 82

G

Games areas, 191–192, 193–194, 218
Generaliffe, Spain, 24, 28, 131, 184
Giardino segreto, 49, 86, 175

Glorietta, 17, 29
Grass, 154–157, 205
Gravetye, Sussex, 66, 92, 154
Grosvenor Square, London, 198

H

Hadrian's Villa, Tivoli, 31
Ha-Ha, 145, 147–148
Hampton Court, Middlesex, 46, 51
Heaths, 212, 213
Hedges, 68, 69, 72, 110–111, 153
Herbaceous plants, 121–124
Hermelin, Sven, 202, 220
Hidcote, Gloucestershire, 27, 67, 72, 84, 89, 93, 123, 143, 145
Hippodrome, The, 32
Holkham, Norfolk, 53
Holland Park, London, 89, 91, 129, 130, 193–195
Hyde Park, London, 93, 185, 188

I

Ida-Varsha, 17
India, 17, 19
Italian revival, 64, 65

J

Jardin Anglais, 43, 54, 189
Jardin Anglo-Chinois, 20, 22, 43
Japan, 21, 95, 104, 216
Jekyll, Gertrude, 66, 76, 121, 135, 176, 202, 210

K

Kensington Gardens, London, 50, 153, 181, 189
Kent, William, 52, 53, 57
Kew, Surrey, 126, 129, 157, 196, 214

L

Landscape Architect's Plants, 128–130
Langkilde, Eywin, 157

Leder, Walter, 220
Leicester Square, London, 198
Le Nôtre, 38, 43, 50, 81, 82, 132
Light and shade, 94
Ligorio, Pirro, 34
London and Wise, 49
Lorraine, Claude, 51, 52, 65, 170
Lutyens, Sir Edwin, 66, 83, 142, 150

M

Marabou factory, Sweden, 220
Marx, Burle, 76, 85, 97, 106, 189
Mason, William, 54
Medieval gardens, 44–46
Moghuls, 19
Monastery gardens, 44, 45
Montacute, Somerset, 46, 47, 84, 145, 150, 175
Moreno, Prieto, 24, 27
Mounts, 47

N

Nash, John, 188
Nuneham Park, Oxfordshire, 54

O

Olmstead, Frederick Law, 185, 186

P

Palladian Architecture, 52, 142
Paradise garden, 19, 25
Patio, 24, 25, 65
Patio de Los Arrayanes, 26, 27, 28
Patio di Arranjes, 158
Paving, 158–162
Paxton, Joseph, 65, 185
Payne Knight, Richard, 55, 209
Peristyle, 31
Persia, 17, 19
Picturesque, 55
Plant grouping, 111–117

Polesden Lacey, Surrey, 48
Poussin, Nicholas, 51, 52
Powerscourt, Co. Wicklow, 146
Price, Sir Uvedale, 55, 209

Q

Quarries, 196

R

Raphael, 33, 34
Regent's Park, London, 54, 189
Renaissance, 32, 39, 67
Repton, Humphry, 54, 55, 119, 135
Rhododendrons, 124-126
Robinson, William, 64, 65, 66, 76,
121, 154
Rosa, Salvator, 51
Roses, 126-127
Rousseau, Jean Jacques, 51, 65

S

St James's Park, London, 187, 188
Savill Gardens, Windsor, 211
Scale, 87-91
Schönbrunn, Vienna, 87
Sculpture, 137-140
Seats, 143
Seclusion, 108-109, 175
Shade, 109
Shepheard, Peter, 216
Shrubs, 121
Sissinghurst, Kent, 27, 67, 85, 89, 167
Sitwell, Sir George, 84, 133
Sloane Square, London, 197
Sorensen, 103
Space division, 92-94, 109-110
Spain, 24
Spoil heaps, 195, 196, 220, 221
Steps, 140-142
Stourhead, Wiltshire, 55, 57, 82, 119.
134
Stowe, Buckinghamshire, 53, 55, 64,
84, 101, 119
Styles, 96, 97

T

Taj Mahal, India, 19
Temple, Sir William, 51
Terraces, 32, 102, 142, 143
Texture, 94, 95, 112-115
Tiefenbrunnen, Zurich, 85, 144, 190
Time, 92
Tintinhull, Somerset, 66, 82, 93, 121,
162, 178, 181, 184
Tivoli Gardens, Copenhagen, 83, 132,
134, 189, 190
Tone, 83, 95, 96, 114, 115
Topiary, 143
Trees, 111-113, 116, 117, 118, 119-121
Tudor Gardens, 46, 47
Tuileries, Paris, 188, 190

U

Unity, 81-87, 206

V

Vanbrugh, Sir John, 49, 53, 55, 57, 59,
61
Vaux-le-Vicomte, 40, 43, 82, 84, 85
Versailles, 27, 60, 137
Vignola, 34, 35
Villa Aldobrandini, 34, 172
Villa d'Este, 28, 33, 34, 40, 63, 81, 93,
132
Villa Lante, 35-37, 85, 132, 133
Villa Madama, 33
Villa Rotunda, 50
Villiers-Stuart, Mrs, 19

W

Walls, 140-142
Wilderness, 49, 51
Wild Gardens, 209-213
Wilton, Wiltshire, 134, 142
Wind Shelter, 107, 108
Wisley, Surrey, 210, 211
Wright, Frank Lloyd, 142, 174, 215